MW01252832

A Dynamic Systems Approach to Adolescent Development

The dynamic systems approach is a rapidly expanding advancement in the study of developmental research and especially in the domain of adolescent development. It examines the processes of adolescent development and of how adolescents change, and provides knowledge that cannot be gained by the common ways of studying development. However, new techniques are required for this innovative study of developmental processes and there is a great need for a handbook that helps social scientists to translate dynamic systems conceptualizations into empirical research.

This edited book provides both theoretical and technical knowledge about the application of dynamic systems theory in such a way that the readers will be able to implement this approach themselves. The first part discusses descriptive techniques that describe and assess specific process characteristics such as variability, sudden jumps and attractor states. The second part explores the different techniques for building a dynamic systems model, which can simulate the behaviour of a system to investigate the mechanisms behind the processes. Each chapter describes one technique and is based on a specific practical example of its application in adolescent development. Step-by-step instructions for model building and examples of ready-made models are provided on the website that belongs to the book.

This book is ideal for researchers who study development who are not statistical or methodological specialists. It provides a clear step-by-step description of theories and techniques that are designed for the study of developmental processes.

Saskia Kunnen is Associate Professor of Developmental Psychology at the University of Groningen where she researches and teaches dynamic systems modelling and the application of dynamic systems theory in the field of identity development in adolescence and emerging adulthood.

Studies in Adolescent Development
Series Editors: Professors Leo B. Hendry, Marion Kloep and Inge Seiffge-Krenke

The *Studies in Adolescent Development* series is published in conjunction with the *European Association for Research on Adolescence* and is committed to publishing and promoting the highest quality of writing in the field of adolescent development.

The series aims to respond to the recent shifts in the social and ecological environment of adolescents and in the new theoretical perspectives within the social sciences by providing a range of books, each of which deals in depth with an aspect of current interest within the field of adolescent development.

Each book focuses on a specific aspect of adolescence and provides either a clear picture of the research endeavours, which are currently serving to extend the boundaries of our knowledge and understanding of the field, or an insightful theoretical perspective of adolescent development. The editors encourage publications that represent original contributions to the field.

Also available in this series:

Adolescence, Affect and Health
Donna Spruijt-Metz

The Transition to Adulthood and Family Relations
Eugenia Scabini, Elena Marta and Margherita Lanz

Deception
Rachel Taylor and Lynsey Gozna

A Dynamic Systems Approach to Adolescent Development
Edited by Saskia Kunnen

A Dynamic Systems Approach to Adolescent Development

Edited by Saskia Kunnen

LONDON AND NEW YORK

First published 2012
by Psychology Press
27 Church Road, Hove, East Sussex BN3 2FA

Simultaneously published in the USA and Canada
by Psychology Press
711 Third Avenue, New York NY 10017
www.psypress.com

Psychology Press is an imprint of the Taylor & Francis Group, an informa business

British Library Cataloguing in Publication Data
A catalogue record for this book is available from the British Library

Library of Congress Cataloging in Publication Data
A dynamic systems approach to adolescent development/edited by Saskia Kunnen.
p. cm.
ISBN 978-1-84872-037-4 (hbk.)
1. Adolescent psychology—Methodology. 2. Adolescence—Research—Methodology. I. Kunnen, Saskia.
BF724.D96 2011
155.5—dc23

2011024192

ISBN: 978-1-84872-037-4 (hbk)
ISBN: 978-0-203-14764-1 (ebk)

Typeset in Times by RefineCatch Ltd, Bungay, Suffolk
Cover design by Jim Wilkie
Printed by TJ International Ltd, Padstow, Cornwall

Contents

Figures

Tables

Contributors

Harke Bosma Schapenweg 16, 9312 VG Nietap, The Netherlands. h.a.bosma@rug.nl

Tom Hollenstein 220 Craine, Department of Psychology, Queen's University, 62 Arch Street, Kingston, Ontario K7L 3N6, Canada. tom.hollenstein@queensu.ca

Saskia Kunnen Department of Psychology, University of Groningen, Grote Kruisstraat 2/1, 9712 TS Groningen, The Netherlands. e.s.kunnen@rug.nl

Anna Lichtwarck-Aschoff Radboud University, Orthopedagogiek, G&G. Postbus 9104, 6500 HE Nijmegen, The Netherlands. a.lichtwarck-aschoff@pwo.ru.nl

Henderien Steenbeek Department of Psychology, University of Groningen, Grote Kruisstraat 2/1, 9712 TS Groningen, The Netherlands. h.w.steenbeek@rug.nl

Marijn van Dijk Department of Psychology, University of Groningen, Grote Kruisstraat 2/1, 9712 TS Groningen, The Netherlands. m.w.g.van.dijk@rug.nl

Paul van Geert Department of Psychology, University of Groningen, Grote Kruisstraat 2/1, 9712 TS Groningen, The Netherlands. paul@vangeert.nl

Marieke Visser Oost Indiestraat 30, 2013 RP Haarlem, The Netherlands. marieke.visser@inholland.nl

Series preface

In the eyes of the mass media and in the minds of many adults, adolescents are often portrayed in largely negative terms, focusing on features such as their noisy and exuberant social behaviour, teenage gangs and their often violent, anti-social activities, teenage pregnancy, drinking, smoking drug-taking, anti-school attitudes and disagreements with parents.

Such portrayals are painted as if they were typical of what most, if not all, adolescents do, and, accordingly, regarded as a justification for adult society to consider the teenage years as a problem period in human development and adolescents as a problem for society.

For much of the 20th century, this popular, stereotypic picture was supported by what was written by social scientists in books and other publications, which presented adolescence as a period of "storm and stress". Adolescence was seen as a period of turbulence, inner turmoil and confusion, characterised by conflicts with parents, teachers and other authority figures.

Over the last three decades of the 20th century important theoretical changes began to emerge. Psychologists began to question the "storm and stress" perspective and to provide evidence that this developmental pattern was neither a typical nor a necessary part of adolescence. In parallel with this, a less problem-centred approach to thinking about adolescence began to emerge: an approach that emphasized processes of change and adjustment which young people undergo in responding to the varied tasks and transitions they face. An increasing number of books and articles on adolescence began to appear which differed markedly from earlier publications in emphasis and orientation. In contrast to the clinical perspective, this new work was based on a more empirical approach and focused upon a variety of different aspects of adolescent development. Further, longitudinal assessments over large time spans basically support the idea of a more gradual change leading to an overall positive outcome. Such publications stimulated further interest in adolescence as an area of study and in doing so started a process which led on to the emergence of research on adolescence as one of the most active fields in developmental psychological research. As a result, discussion of many aspects of adolescence has become a prominent feature of developmental conferences and scientific journals in Europe and elsewhere.

However, times change. The early years of the new millennium have seen technological innovations, global risks from terrorism and demographic shifts occurring in most countries of the world. For example, there are now as many people over the age of sixty-five years as there are teenagers in most of the world's societies. Macrosocial changes such as growing up in a context of ethnic diversity and living in single-parent families are increasingly experienced by adolescents in Western industrialized countries.

Further, as the new millennium advances psychology now takes a more positive view of human development, seeing changes and transitions as challenges within the developmental progress of young people, in society generally, *vis-à-vis* cultural and technological innovations and in relation to other generations.

The European Association for Research on Adolescence (EARA) is an organization which aims to promote and conduct high quality fundamental and applied research on all aspects of adolescent development. Its founder and then President, the late Sandy Jackson, devoted much of his professional life to advancing these aims. Before his death in 2003, he initiated a co-operation with Psychology Press to start this series, "Studies in Adolescent Development", and commissioned and published two books during his editorship. We, the current editors, are grateful for Sandy's vision and trust that we can progress the academic and practitioner interest in adolescence as an area of scholarly study which he initiated.

The present series aims to respond to the recent shifts in the social and ecological environment of adolescents and in the new theoretical perspectives within the social sciences, by providing a range of books, each of which deals in depth with an aspect of current interest within the field of adolescent development.

The co-editors delineate a number of broad topics that require significant attention and invite academics, researchers and practitioners to submit book proposals. Each proposal is carefully evaluated by the co-editors for selection in the series. Hence, each book is written by a chosen expert (or experts) in a specific aspect of adolescence and sets out to provide either a clear picture of the research endeavours which are currently serving to extend the boundaries of our knowledge and understanding of the field, or an insightful theoretical perspective of adolescent development.

Each book in the series represents a step towards the fulfilment of this aim. The European Association for Research on Adolescence is grateful to Psychology Press for all that it has done in developing and promoting the series and for assisting EARA in extending knowledge and understanding of the many aspects of adolescent development in a rapidly changing and challenging world.

Professors Leo B. Hendry, Marion Kloep and Inge Seiffge-Krenke
Series Editors

Introduction

Saskia Kunnen

This book is part of the *Studies on Adolescent Development* series. Probably the most salient characteristic of adolescence is development and change. Adolescence is a period of change, and often it is a period of rapid, sudden and unpredictable change. In general it is not easy to study a phenomenon that is changing while you study it. It is even more difficult to grasp change in a subject who is not always cooperative, talks back, reacts to the research tools in unintended ways, drops out from the study, and so on. Nevertheless, that is the task of everyone who studies adolescent development.

This book aims to help with this task, especially when it comes to the method of studying change. It is not easy to study change, in particular because most change is irregular, non-linear and fluctuating. Standard statistical procedures often do not offer the tools needed to study change and to answer questions such as: What does the developmental trajectory of this characteristic look like? Does it develop continuously or with a sudden jump? What makes this person change in this way at this moment? What underlies this sudden change? Is this really change or just fluctuations?

Such questions are often those that concern the development of one individual, which is not coincidental. As we will demonstrate, to study the process of change one has to start with a study of the individual change. Thus, we need methods to study individual change processes. Since the 1980s, the Department of Developmental Psychology at the University in Groningen, headed by Professor Paul van Geert, has specialized in the development of new methods that aim to assess developmental processes. Although the first author is the main responsible author, the book is actually a product of the work of several members and former members of the department. One contributor, Tom Hollenstein, is not from the University of Groningen (although he visited Groningen several times).

So the aim of this book is to offer scientists who study adolescent development the tools to help them grasp the characteristics of that development. This book does not pretend to cover all the techniques and methods that are available, which would require a handbook in 12 volumes! The techniques presented are techniques that were developed, applied or refined in research in our institute, and they have several characteristics in common. First, the techniques are accessible for a broad range of researchers, that is, they do not demand specific knowledge of statistics of methodology. All techniques discussed here can be understood by everyone who did a Master's degree in the social sciences and learned some mathematics in high school. Moreover, no specific equipment is needed. Most of the techniques described in this book became available for the common scientist only recently, because they require computer power that we did not have on our desk-top computers 15 years ago. Thus, nowadays an average computer suffices. In addition, the techniques require either easily available software, namely the spreadsheet program Excel, or software that can be downloaded for free.

Second, the techniques are especially relevant for developmentalists in the social sciences, which means that they can be applied in data sets that are common in social sciences. The study of development requires longitudinal data sets. However, compared to fields such as physics, astronomy, chemistry, etc., researchers in the social sciences often have data sets that are irregular, have missing values and have a limited number of measurement points. As already mentioned, adolescent subjects do sometimes drop out or stop being cooperative. Many of the available mathematical techniques to analyze processes are developed for the physical sciences and they require smooth data sets with thousands of measurements.

Third and most importantly, the techniques described here help to gain insight into processes, individual changes and stability over time (this point will be elaborated in the first chapter). The techniques focus either on describing individual developmental trajectories or on understanding the mechanisms behind the development under study, instead of aiming to fit data sets as with many common statistical techniques.

This book focuses on adolescent development but this does not mean that the techniques are specific for adolescent development. We selected those techniques that fit in well with salient types of research questions in this domain, and most of the examples (though not all) concern studies into adolescent development. However, developmental processes in living systems are not qualitatively different between ages or species. Thus, with a little creativity all techniques can be applied in studies of other age groups, and with a little more creativity they can even be applied to other "units of change" – for example, to animals instead of humans or in the development of institutions or groups of people.

In several chapters of the book we demonstrate the application of techniques with a step by step description. For extra help a website is available with the ready-made models (www.psypress.com/dynamic-systems-approach/appendices). In these descriptions and models we used the spreadsheet program Excel. Other software will do the job as well, but the reader will have to translate the specific notation system to the system of the other spreadsheet program. However, computer programs and spreadsheet programs tend to change and it is for this reason that we have chosen to provide the appendices via the internet on a website. This website will be updated when necessary.

With this book we hope to contribute to the growth of research into processes and individual development. For research in the domain of adolescent development, and indeed development over the whole life span, this is the direction we have to go in order to develop our knowledge of and insight into this domain.

1 A dynamic systems approach to adolescent development

Saskia Kunnen and Paul van Geert

Introduction

Early research began when I (S.K.) wrote my PhD dissertation about the development of task attitudes in children with a physical handicap. The theoretical model was clear: high perceived competence and high motivation predict better performance and, in turn, good performance increases perceived competence and motivation. To my disappointment, that model was only partly confirmed, with hardly significant correlations of around .25. The finding that a strong theoretical model describes only about 10% of the variance was challenging. What has happened? Were those generally accepted theories wrong? Were there other, more important, variables, and if so which variables? To get an answer to these questions I decided to observe what happened in the classroom, and these observations clarified a lot.

A first observation was that many children did not show stable levels of motivation; motivation was highly variable, often dependent on small micro events such as the good outcome of one calculation, a positive remark by a teacher, etc. Such fluctuation was important. Some children achieved motivating successes in short periods of good performance following a stimulating remark, whereas on average they seemed unmotivated. On the other hand, children who showed stable levels of motivated behavior for a long time expected success, and some (but not all) became very frustrated following one unexpected failure. Second, it was clear that many relations between variables were non-linear. The highly motivated little boy who became even more motivated by his successes also frustrated his own performances because in his excitement he became clumsy. The motivated girl with a high fear of failure started to perform better once she became less interested and motivated, and thus cared less about failure. Third, some children seemed to be stuck in a kind of inescapable situation. Regardless of how easy and how stimulating the tasks were, they were in a self-defeating mood. They said "I am stupid", they did not really show effort and thus they failed, using that failure as a confirmation of their statements. Finally, the teacher told me about a girl in her group who had failed for over a year to make calculations over 100. The girl was certain that she was unable to learn them and she refused even to look at them. The teacher tried with simple examples, with compliments, etc.

then suddenly, while the teacher did exactly the same as before, the girl took her pen and started to make the calculations.

So, what do these observations tell us? Several things. One variable may affect another, but only under certain conditions. It may be that the variable has only positive effects on another variable if the values of the influencing and/or affected variable are within a given range. In another case, the positive value of one variable (the ongoing stimulation of the teacher) had an effect only after a prolonged time period. All these observations are examples of non-linear relations between different variables. Second, we observed that abstract concepts such as motivation are not stable in real time interactions and that fluctuations such as peaks can have a relevant influence on other variables. Finally, we observed that sometimes different variables may mutually hold each other in a very rigid state in which attempts to change have no effect.

Several of these observations are not new. For example the U-shaped relation between task difficulty and motivation is well documented, as is the mediating role of fear of failure in this relation (Kunnen, 1992). This means that children with high fear of failure tend to avoid the tasks that are well suited to their competence, whereas for other children these tasks are most motivating. However, in empirical designs such knowledge is often neglected. What these observations taught me was that in order to grasp what really happens – which was my aim in the dissertation project – it is necessary to study the interaction between the variables in much more detail and, most importantly, look at how it works in the individual children. The differential effects of the non-linear relations are lost once we study the children as a group and calculate correlations and averages. What happened in the classroom was far more dynamic than could be grasped as long as I focused on (changes in) the average scores of the group.

In the 1980s the first publications about dynamic systems theory emerged in developmental psychology. I (S. K.) was lucky to work in the department of Paul van Geert, one of the pioneers in this field. Reading more about this approach, I became convinced that if we as developmentalists want to get a better understanding of what really happens in development, of how development works, the dynamic systems approach offered tools to gain insights into the mechanisms of development that could not be achieved in other ways. I am still convinced of that, and I am not the only one. In the field of developmental research there is a growing interest (slow at first, but escalating now) in dynamic systems theory and techniques. In the early 1990s several books appeared that made the dynamic systems approach available to a broader scientific public in the social sciences (Gottman, 1995; Nowak and Vallacher, 1998; Thelen and Smith, 1994; van Geert, 1994). Over the last 25 years the approach has demonstrated its value especially for the study of processes and mechanisms, for the study of how development works. In the last decade several publications have applied a dynamic systems perspective on adolescent development (e.g. Bosma and Kunnen, 2001; Granic, Dishion and Hollenstein, 2003; Lichtwarck-Aschoff and van Geert, 2004; Vleioras, van Geert and Bosma, 2008). We observe, for example at conferences, that many researchers are interested in this approach. However, Bosma and Kunnen (2008) conclude, in a special issue of *Journal of*

Adolescence on identity development, that there is a lot of attention paid to developmental processes and dynamic systems concepts in the introduction and discussion sections of the papers, but that the actual research designs do not address developmental processes. Thus, researchers ask questions from a developmental perspective – they interpret their findings in terms of dynamic systems theory – but they do not seem to know how to apply this perspective in their actual research design. For most researchers in the field of adolescent development the actual application of a dynamic systems approach is an unknown territory and there are no handbooks available that help social scientists to apply the techniques needed in order to translate dynamic systems conceptualizations into empirical research. This book aims to fill that gap. The main aim of this book is to explain the ideas and the application of a dynamic systems approach in such a way that it enables social scientists, especially researchers in the domain of adolescents, to apply the reasoning and the methodology in their own research.

In this chapter we start with an overview of the field of dynamic systems approaches. Since the first appearance of dynamic systems papers in the last two decades of the 20th century, the concept "dynamic systems approach" has found its way into numerous publications and also into different types of theory and methodology. This book covers only some of these publications and techniques. We start with a sketch of the broader field of dynamic systems thinking and then clarify how the approach of the present book relates to other approaches in this wider landscape.

The landscape of dynamic systems approaches

Two different ways of thinking in terms of dynamic systems

In several publications two main approaches to dynamic systems thinking in developmental psychology have been discussed: the Bloomington approach versus the Groningen approach (van Geert and Steenbeek, 2005), that is, contextualism versus organicism (Witherington, 2007). Van Geert and Steenbeek frame the division between both approaches mainly in terms of what phenomena are appropriate for dynamic systems modeling. Witherington perceives the difference between both approaches as more fundamental, in terms of a fundamental ontological division. Below we discuss both approaches in some detail.

Contextualism – the Bloomington approach

In developmental psychology, one of the most prominent representatives of dynamic systems theory is Thelen and Smith's theory of dynamic agents (Thelen and Smith, 1994, 1998). Thelen, Smith and colleagues have developed a dynamic systems theory as a special theory of embodied action. Starting with translating qualitative concepts of dynamic systems theory into a theory of human development, they focus on development as a process that takes place in real time and real action and involves a closed loop of interaction: it is a theory of embodied–embedded action that is highly empirically oriented. It also allows for dynamic modeling based on the physical parameters of space and time. Agents are acting systems, acting in a real environment, in real time (i.e. the time required to build up and perform a real action or behavior, e.g. grasping, walking stairs and so forth) and in the form of continuous loops of perception and action. According to Thelen and Smith (1994), human action is not the result of internal causal operators, or in general any internal representation of a particular domain of knowledge that is assumed to generate behaviors (Smith, 2005; Smith, Thelen, Titzer and McLin, 1999). That is, there are no such things as identity, self-concept or, in general, concepts that supposedly drive and govern our actions. Witherington (2007, p. 129) states that:

> One DSP camp, purely contextualist in orientation and associated most clearly with the writings of Thelen and Smith, address in their research the action in the context of the here-and-now, and reject higher-order forms as explanatory in the sense of formal and final cause, reduce developmental time to real time, regards as illusory the orderly, directional flow of development viewed in macroscopic terms, treats emergent patterns as epiphenomenal, and regards the process of self-organization in exclusively bottom-up terms.

The focus of the Bloomington approach on real time processes and on the importance of bottom-up processes is highly relevant also for the study of adolescent development. However, due to this focus on real time characteristics, this approach is considerably less suited for the study of more "psychological" phenomena such as meanings, cognitive abilities, attitudes or identity. Thus, the application of the theory tends to limit itself to – or particularly focus on – spatiotemporal action at a relatively early age. For the study of adolescent development this approach has severe limitations.

Organicism – the Groningen approach

Witherington (2007, p. 129) describes this approach as:

> representing an integration of metatheoretical approaches, specifically the contextualist and organismic world views, and finds its most cogent instantiation in the writings of Marc D. Lewis and Kurt Fischer and his colleagues [for a discussion of contextualist and organismic world view integration see Overton and Ennis, 2006]. This camp, by virtue of its world view merger, fully admits higher-order forms into its explanatory framework, integrates the emergent pattern into the nexus of causal relations, embraces all forms of causality – efficient, material, formal and final – as distinct but legitimate types of explanation, considers developmental time as emergent from but irreducible to real time and regards the process of self-organization in both bottom-up and top-down terms via circular or interlevel causality.

The Groningen approach is the basis of this book. We base our definition of what a dynamic system is on the *CRC Concise Encyclopedia of Mathematics* (Weisstein,

1999). Weisstein defines a dynamic system as "... a means of describing how one state develops into another state over the course of time" (Weisstein, 1999, p. 501). This type of dynamic systems approach is based on the view that complex human behaviors, which are meaning-laden and largely invoke the use of (verbal and non-verbal) symbols, should not be described as metaphorical entities, which thus remain vague, intangible and arbitrary, but must be described by means of Haken's notion of order parameters (Haken, 1999; Haken, Kelso, Fuchs and Pandya, 1990; Kriz, 2001; Latané, Nowak and Liu, 1994, van Geert and Steenbeek, 2005). We focus on the study of developmental processes defined by three main characteristics. First, development is concerned with long-term change, for instance change over the course of months, years or decades. These long-term changes can be observed in the form of events on the short-term time scale, namely the developing person's actions. Second, change on the long-term time scale (i.e. developmental processes) should be studied at the level of the individual system. Note that this does not necessarily mean an individual person; it can also refer to a dyad or even a group of people. The essence of this principle is that we study the sequence of values of the system itself, instead of aggregations over systems, such as mean values over groups. Third, the processes of change that form the topic of developmental study are complex. If we observe an adolescent acting in a context, we are in fact observing a complex multivariate stream, involving motor activity, perception, emotions, language and so forth, in a constant coupling with an environment that is affected by and, in turn, is affecting these events. However, we believe that we can meaningfully reduce this complexity to a few variables of interest, not because we believe these variables are the essential ones and the others just superficial, but because we assume that in the variables of choice the complexity of the system is in a sense preserved or represented. Essential for making a good selection of variables is that the basis of the selection consists of sound theoretical notions of how the development proceeds. In addition to these three theoretical characteristics, we restrict ourselves to approaches that use quantitative methods to try to grasp the developmental process.

Although this book – as stated – is based on the Groningen approach, we think that the integrated approach that Witherington proposes closely resembles the approach that is represented in this book. Witherington (2007, p. 149) describes this integrated approach as: "The lure of the organismic-contextualist DSP rests in its charge to capture both the domain-general and the domain-specific, the global order and the local variability, *without* reducing one to the other."

Although the name "Groningen approach" refers to the city where most contributors work, have worked or have visited frequently, the approach itself is not limited to that not-so-big city in the north of The Netherlands. There are other techniques and other authors whose work shows close resemblance to the approach we use. In the context of dynamic skills theory and hierarchic growth models, Kurt Fischer from Harvard University has applied dynamic growth modeling to the long-term development of cognitive skills in a way that is very similar to the Groningen approach (Fischer and Bidell, 2006). We also want to mention the Amsterdam group (van der Maas, Molenaar, Raijmaker). In addition to applying dynamic network modeling to the development of intelligence, in particular the emergence of the G-factor (Van der Maas, Dolan, Grasman, Wicherts, Huizenga and Raijmakers, 2006), the Amsterdam group has pioneered the application of catastrophe theory in developmental psychology (Van der Maas and Molenaar, 1992).

Catastrophe theory is probably best known in psychology for its formulation of so-called catastrophe flags. These flags are characteristics that indicate a sudden jump and can be observed before or during a sudden change or transition. Catastrophe theory is probably the oldest theory that describes sudden non-linear change. Zeeman (1976) applied the theory to describe sudden changes in animal behavior, and it was introduced to a broader audience in developmental psychology by Van der Maas and Molenaar (1992). Catastrophe theory in developmental psychology can be used to detect catastrophes or sudden jumps. The theory is based on the assumption that sudden change can be described by gradual changes in underlying parameters. The theory is especially applied for phenomena that are characterized by sudden shifts in behavior arising from small changes in circumstances. It demonstrates how the qualitative nature of equation solutions depends on the parameters that appear in the equation. Changes in the parameters may lead to sudden and dramatic changes in the observed behavior or psychological function. The construction of a real catastrophe model therefore starts with the identification of the underlying control parameter. In psychological research, such a variable is often hard to find. The mathematical backgrounds and techniques of catastrophe theory are a well documented and described domain of research, also in the social sciences. A thorough discussion would require more space (and specific knowledge) than is available here, therefore we will not describe the specific techniques needed for building catastrophe models.

However, catastrophe flags – phenomena derived from the catastrophe theory – will emerge throughout the book. These flags are especially important because they specify characteristics that are relevant in the study of developmental change in individual trajectories. We mentioned already that the flag "increase in variability" may indicate a transition. Several other flags – "divergence from linearity", "critical slowing down" and "anomalous variance" – are related to changes in variability. The flag "divergence" means that, following a transition, development can go in different ways but not any way: only a limited number of trajectories are available and crossing over from one trajectory to another is difficult or impossible. The flag "inaccessable zones" points to this phenomenon. The phenomena of divergence and inaccessable zones can be investigated by modeling developmental processes and simulating different trajectories, as discussed in Chapters 8 and 9. In addition to his work on catastrophe theory, and on the ergodicity problem that we will discuss in the next section, Molenaar introduced state space modeling to developmental psychology (1985; Molenaar and Ram, 2010; see also Chow, Ferrer and Nesselroade, 2007). By means of this technique the researcher can try to reconstruct an underlying state space by means of dynamic factor analysis. The state space concept will be discussed in the next chapter, and a simple technique to analyze development in a state space is discussed by Hollenstein in Chapter 6 of this book. However, the techniques that Molenaar developed are especially useful when the state space is more complex and consists of many variables. The approach can be extended to state space models in which the parameters vary arbitrarily over time, and in which the parameter changes are estimated on the basis of the overt variables (for further discussion see Molenaar, in press).

The person-oriented approach

Theoretically, there are close resemblances between the definition of the dynamic systems approach that we used in the previous section and the definitions of the person-oriented research as used for example by von Eye, Lerner and Bergman. The person-oriented approach focuses on individuals or homogeneous subgroups of individuals (von Eye, Bogata and Rhodes, 2006) and is often contrasted with variable-oriented research: the former stresses the relevance of differences between individuals and tries to distinguish between groups of individuals, whereas the latter focuses on general relations between variables in a population. Bergman and Trost (2006, pp. 603–604) define a person-oriented approach:

> The system is hierarchical and must be studied by carefully separating its different levels (from the molecular to the global). At each level, the system functions as an integrated, organized totality that is formed by the interactions among the elements, and the totality derives its meaning from these interactions and all elements considered simultaneously (Magnusson, 1990).... The focus is to understand development at the individual level by regarding the individual as a functioning whole with processes operating at a system level and its components jointly contributing to what happens in development. Considering the involved components all together and the principles guiding their evolvement as a system over time, on a developmental time scale, is the essence of the *theoretical* aspect of the person-oriented approach.

The person-oriented approach differs from the approach described in this book, especially in the choice of methods and techniques. It does focus (as we do) on groups of individuals, but not on the analysis of the individual process. For example, von Eye, Bogata and Rhodes (2006) state that groups can be identified using the means of statistics, (e.g. cluster analysis, latent class analysis or other methods of grouping of cases) or by crossing categorical variables. This latter method is commonly applied in the context of, for instance, log-linear modeling, correspondence analysis, latent class analysis or cross-factor analysis. In the same way, Lerner, Lerner, De Stefanis and Apfel (2001, p. 9.) state:

> Contemporary theories of adolescence stress developmental systems models that integrate both individual and contextual levels of analysis in a relational manner – ones that place substantive emphasis on understanding the diversity of adolescent development. This scholarship suggests that adolescence should

be investigated with multivariate longitudinal designs and change-sensitive measures and data analytic strategies.

Also Bergman and Trost (2006) illustrate their approach with an example of a study in which sample-based techniques are used (SLEIPNER, which is a statistical package for person-oriented analysis). These techniques start from a sample with different scores and try to differentiate between subgroups that show different developmental trajectories. This is a fundamental difference with the approach we present in this book: we start from theoretical assumptions and study the individual trajectories of development.

Although Luyckx and colleagues (Luyckx, Goossens and Soenens, 2006; Luyckx, Schwartz, Goossens, Soenens and Beyers, 2008) do not call their approach a person-oriented approach, the techniques in their approach, and the resulting knowledge, resemble the techniques and the orientation on differences between groups in recent longitudinal research on the development of identity in late adolescence that focuses on the description of different trajectories of identity development.

An important methodological question is whether it is possible to use inter-individual aggregation of data in order to arrive at models that pertain to processes that occur in individuals. According to Molenaar (2004) this is generally not possible, a conclusion that he bases on a discussion of the so-called ergodicity property. Ergodicity implies that the analysis of inter-individual variability yields the same statistical properties as an analysis of intra-individual variability, thus that the characteristics of group data are the same as characteristics of individual data over time. In psychology, the ergodicity property often turns out to be absent (for a detailed discussion of ergodicity in psychology, see: Molenaar and Ram, 2010; van Rijn and Molenaar, 2005). A simple example of the absence of ergodicity is the relation between speed and errors in typing. If we study this relation in a sample, we will find a negative relationship: people who type faster make less errors. Good typing skills mean high speed and few errors and thus this relation reflects that people differ in their typing skills. However, if we study the relation between speed and number of errors over time within one individual, the relation will be positive: higher speed is related to more errors. This reflects the individual experience that most people will have: if we try to type faster, we make more errors. The message in this example is that relations that are found in the analysis of group data may not be applicable to the individual. Thus, to gain knowledge about individual processes we need to assess individual processes as long as we have not demonstrated that the process under investigation is characterized by ergodicity.

Hence, validating dynamic systems models of change and development requires individual, time serial data collected with a frequency and total duration sufficient to capture the properties of the dynamics (Boker, 2002; Steenbeek and van Geert, 2005). According to Molenaar (2004), the shift from using data that are based on inter-individual variability to data on intra-individual variability may boil down to a Kuhnian paradigm shift in psychology. We might add that this methodological shift must go hand in hand with a theoretical and conceptual shift towards thinking in terms of dynamic systems.

Overview of the contents of this book

Now that we have sketched the location of our approach on the broad map of dynamic systems-related approaches, we will elaborate the contents of the present book.

We will start, in Chapter 2, with a description of the general characteristics of the dynamic systems approach that forms the basis of this book, and we explain why we think it is a fruitful approach for the study of adolescent development. Concrete examples of the specific techniques and their translation into a specific research design will follow in the rest of the book, which consists of two parts. The first part discusses different techniques that are meant to describe and assess process characteristics of development, such as variability, sudden jumps and attractor states. The application of these techniques is not limited to a dynamic systems approach, but can be applied in other types of process approaches as well. In each chapter we will focus on one type of process characteristic. Based on a specific example of its application in adolescent development, mostly from our own research group, we will discuss, step by step: the research question, the required design and data set, the application of the technique in our data set, the application to other types of data, the gain in knowledge when one applies this technique and, finally, the possibilities and restrictions of this technique. The techniques discussed are only a small selection of all the process analysis techniques that are available. Criteria for inclusion in this book were that: the techniques should be relatively simple; they should be applicable on many data sets and also on smaller data sets, data sets with only several measurement points and data sets with missing data; and they are not yet described in handbooks on statistical methods.

In the second part we discuss different techniques for building a dynamic systems model. By means of dynamic systems models the behavior of a system can be simulated, and in this way the mechanisms behind the processes can be investigated. In each chapter we will focus on one technique. Based on a specific example of its application in adolescent development, mostly from our own research group, we will discuss step by step how to develop a conceptual model, how to build a dynamic systems model, how to explore and simulate the modeled development, how to evaluate and validate the model, the gain in knowledge offered by this technique and, again, the possibilities and restrictions of this technique. But to start with, we will discuss in more detail what the dynamic systems approach is and why we think that this approach can fruitfully contribute to the field of research into adolescent development.

References

Bergman, L. R., & Trost, K. (2006). The person-oriented versus the variable-oriented approach: Are they complementary, opposites, or exploring different worlds? *Merrill-Palmer Quarterly, 52,* 601–632.

Boker, S. M. (2002). Consequences of continuity: The hunt for intrinsic properties within parameters of dynamics in psychological processes. *Multivariate Behavioral Research, 37,* 405–422.

Bosma, H. A., & Kunnen, E. S. (2001). *Identity and emotion: A self-organisational process*. Cambridge, UK: Cambridge University Press.

Bosma, H. A., & Kunnen, E. S. (2008). Identity-in-context and identity development-in-context are two different things. *Journal of Adolescence, 31,* 281–289.

Chow, S. M., Ferrer, E., & Nesselroade, J. R. (2007). An unscented Kalman filter approach to the estimation of nonlinear dynamical systems models. *Multivariate Behavioral Research, 42,* 283–321.

Fischer, K. W., & Bidell, T. R. (2006). Dynamic development of action and thought. In R. M. Lerner & W. Damon (Eds.), *Handbook of child psychology. Theoretical models of human development* (pp. 313–399). Hoboken, NJ: John Wiley & Sons.

Gottman, J. M. (1995). *The analysis of change.* Mahwah, NJ: Lawrence Erlbaum Associates.

Granic, I., Dishion, T. J., & Hollenstein, T. (2003). The family ecology of adolescence: A dynamic systems perspective on normative development. In G. Adams & M. Berzonsky (Eds.), *Handbook of adolescence* (pp. 60–91). New York: Blackwell.

Haken, H. (1999). Synergetics and some applications to psychology. In W. Tschacher & J.-P. Dauwalder (Eds.), *Dynamics, synergetics, autonomous agents* (pp. 3–12). Singapore: World Scientific.

Haken, H., Kelso, J. A. S., Fuchs, A., & Pandya, A. S. (1990). Dynamic pattern-recognition of coordinated biological motion. *Neural Networks, 3*, 395–401.

Kriz, J. (2001). Self-organization of cognitive and interactional processes. In M. Matthies, H. Malchow, & J. Kriz (Eds.), *Integrative systems approaches to natural and social dynamics* (pp. 517–537). Heidelberg: Springer.

Kunnen, E. S. (1992). *Mastering (with) a handicap*. Dissertation, University of Groningen, The Netherlands.

Latané, B., Nowak, A., & Liu, J. H. (1994). Measuring emergent social phenomena: Dynamism, polarization, and clustering as order parameters of social systems. *Behavioral Science, 39,* 1–24.

Lerner, R. M., Lerner, J. V., De Stefanis, I., & Apfel, A. (2001). Understanding developmental systems in adolescence: Implications for methodological strategies, data analytic approaches, and training. *Journal of Adolescent Research, 16*, p. 162.

Lichtwarck-Aschoff, A., & van Geert, P. L. C. (2004). A dynamic systems perspective on social cognition, problematic behaviour, and intervention in adolescence. *European Journal of Developmental Psychology, 1,* 399–411.

Luyckx, K., Goossens, L., & Soenens, B. (2006). A developmental contextual perspective on identity construction in emerging adulthood: Change dynamics in commitment formation and commitment evaluation. *Developmental Psychology*, *42*, 366–380.

Luyckx, K., Schwartz, S. J., Goossens, L., Soenens, B., & Beyers, W. (2008). Developmental typologies of identity formation and adjustment in female emerging adults: A latent class growth analysis approach. *Journal of Research on Adolescence*, *18*, p. 89.

Magnusson, D. (1990). Personality development from an interactional perspective. In L. A. Pervin (Ed.), *Handbook of personality: Theory and research* (pp. 193–222). New York: Guilford Press.

Molenaar, P. C. M. (1985). A dynamic factor model for the analysis of multivariate time series. *Psychometrika, 50*, 181–202.

Molenaar, P. C. M. (2004). A manifesto on psychology as an idiographic science: Bringing the person back into scientific psychology – this time forever. *Measurement: Interdisciplinary Research and Perspectives, 2,* 201–218.

Molenaar, P. C. M. (in press). Dynamic systems. In B. Laursen, T. D. Little, & N. A. Card (Eds.), *Handbook of developmental research methods*. New York: Guilford Press.

Molenaar, P. M. C., & Ram, N. (2010). Dynamic modeling and optimal control of intra-individual variation: A computational paradigm for nonergodic psychological processes. In: S. M. Chow, E. Ferrer, & F. Hsieh (Eds.), *Statistical methods for modeling human dynamics: An interdisciplinary dialogue* (pp. 13–37). New York: Routledge.

Nowak, A., & Vallacher, R. R. (1998). *Dynamical social psychology*. New York: Guilford Press.

Smith, L. (2005). Cognition as a dynamic system: Principles from embodiment. *Developmental Review*, *25*, 278–298.

Smith, L., Thelen, E., Titzer, R., & McLin, D. (1999). Knowing in the context of acting: The task dynamics of the A-not-B error. *Psychological Review*, *106*, 235–260.

Steenbeek, H., & van Geert, P. (2005). A dynamic systems model of dyadic interaction during play of two children. *European Journal of Developmental Psychology*, *2*, 105–145.

Thelen, E., & Smith, L. B. (1994). *A dynamic systems approach to the development of cognition and action.* Cambridge, MA: MIT Press.

Thelen, E., & Smith, L. B. (1998). Dynamic systems theories. In W. Damon & R. M. Lerner (Eds.), *Handbook of child psychology. Volume 1: Theoretical models of human development* (pp. 563–634). Hoboken, NJ: John Wiley & Sons.

Van der Maas H. L. J., Dolan, C. V., Grasman, R. P., Wicherts, J. M., Huizengd, H. M., & Raijmakers, M. E. J. (2006). A dynamical model of general intelligence: The positive manifold of intelligence by mutualism. *Psychological Review*, *113*, 842–861.

Van der Maas, H. L. J., & Molenaar, P. C. M. (1992). Stagewise cognitive development: An application of catastrophe theory. *Psychological Review, 99,* 395–417.

Van Geert, P. L. C. (1994). *Dynamic systems of development. Change between order and chaos*. New York: Harvester Wheatsheaf.

Van Geert, P. L. C., & Steenbeek, H. W. (2005). Explaining after by before: Basic aspects of a dynamic systems approach to the study of development. *Developmental Review, 25,* 408–442.

Van Rijn, P. W., & Molenaar, P. M. C. (2005). Logistic models for single-subject time series. In L. A. van der Ark, M. A. Croon, & K. Sijtsma (Eds.), *New developments in categorial data analysis for the social and behavioral sciences* (pp. 125–145). Mahwah, NJ: Lawrence Erlbaum Associates.

Vleioras, G., van Geert, P., & Bosma H. A. (2008). Modeling the role of emotions in viewing oneself maturely. *New Ideas in Psychology, 26,* 69–94.

Von Eye, A. Bogata, G. A., & Rhodes, J. E. (2006). Variable-oriented and person-oriented perspectives of analysis: The example of alcohol consumption in adolescence. *Journal of Adolescence, 29,* 981–1004.

Weisstein, E. W. (1999). *CRC concise encyclopedia of mathematics and concise encyclopedia of mathematics CD-ROM bundle edition*. Boca Raton, FL: CRC Press.

Witherington, D. C. (2007). The dynamic systems approach as metatheory for developmental psychology. *Human Development, 50,* 127–153.

Zeeman, E. C. (1976). Catastrophe theory. *Scientific American, 234*, 65–83.

2 General characteristics of a dynamic systems approach

Saskia Kunnen and Paul van Geert

In the previous chapter we sketched the basics of our approach as compared to related dynamic systems approaches. In this chapter we will discuss the general characteristics of a dynamic system. Dynamic systems theory conceptualizes a developmental process as a non-linear dynamic system. This system consists of various interconnected elements, and the behavior of the system is determined by these elements' interactions over time, with such interaction resulting in order behavior of the system. This sounds very general and abstract, so let us give some examples. In a new situation, a person's thoughts, emotions and perceptions of that situation interact. Perceptions affect emotions that affect thoughts, and vice versa, and this interaction results in an emerging appraisal of the situation. Or take a group of adolescents: they interact and influence each other and a group organization emerges. Or take a student who starts a new task: the characteristics of task and teacher and the competence, motivation and history of the adolescent interact, and from this interaction the task behavior of the student emerges. All these systems have in common that from the interacting elements something more organized emerges – an appraisal, a group or a coherent behavior. In all these examples, it is clear that whatever emerges is not there for eternity, but may be subject to change over time. In a dynamic systems approach we study how, from the interactions of the elements, higher, order phenomena emerge, how these phenomena may affect the interacting elements and how, over time, they may change themselves. In this chapter we will discuss the characteristics of this dynamic process and we will show how and why these characteristics are relevant in studying (adolescent) development.

The developmental process

A developmental process can be described as a sequence of states of a system over time. The state of a system at any moment in time can be described by a specific position on each of the dimensions, or characteristics, that are relevant for that system. These dimensions describe the higher order phenomenon of the system. For example, the identity state of an emerging adult in a specific domain can be described by means of two dimensions: the levels of exploration and commitment strength in that domain. One can imagine that these two variables together form a

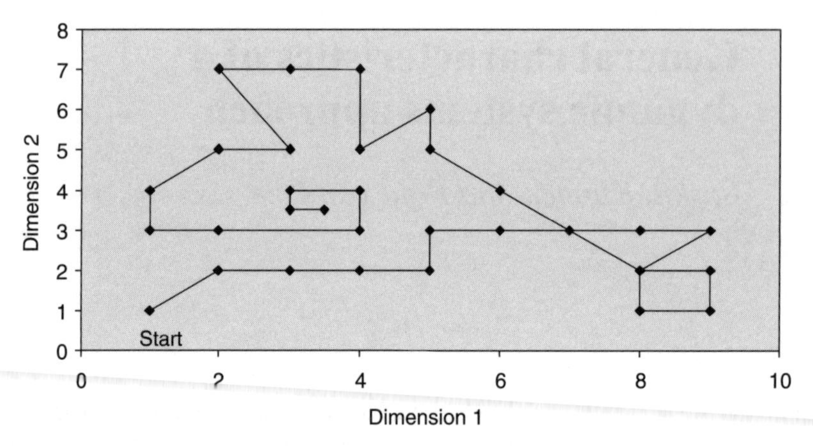

Figure 2.1 A two-dimensional state space.

surface that consists of all possible combinations of the values for exploration and for commitment. This surface (in the case of two dimensions) or space (in the case of three or more dimensions) is called the state space of a system. This state space contains all positions (i.e. combinations of values of the dimensions) that could theoretically be occupied by the system. Development of the identity state in that specific domain can be described as a path that is followed over time in that space, a path that can be described in terms of different positions on the surface that is formed by each of these two dimensions. So, if in an individual the level of exploration decreases, the system moves over the surface towards the position that belongs to that new set of values. Figure 2.1 shows a two-dimensional state space and the trajectory of the system that can be described by these two dimensions. The trajectory begins at point 1, 1 (start) and moves throughout the space.

A typical characteristic of developmental processes is that they are iterative, that is, they unfold step by step. For each step in a process, the starting point is the outcome of the previous step. For example, if we study autonomy development, we see that the adolescent acquires new autonomy gradually, in different pieces. Imagine a 12-year-old girl who, after some negotiations and struggles, is allowed for the first time to buy new clothes with a girlfriend instead of with her mother. While shopping with her friend, she finds out that the friend gets a monthly allowance for buying clothes, instead of having to ask her mother for every piece of clothing. So the next step for the 12-year-old is to ask her mother for an allowance as well. The mother, in turn, sees that her daughter came back happy and safe with more or less decent new clothes, and she will be more inclined than before to consider the request for an allowance. This is an illustration of the fact that the acquisition of each new piece of autonomy changes both the adolescent and her parents, and each step prepares them for the next step. Each new form of autonomy becomes attractive and is perceived to be within reach only because the previous steps in autonomy have been made. As Figure 2.2 shows, development over time is represented by small steps. In each step both the mother (M) and the daughter

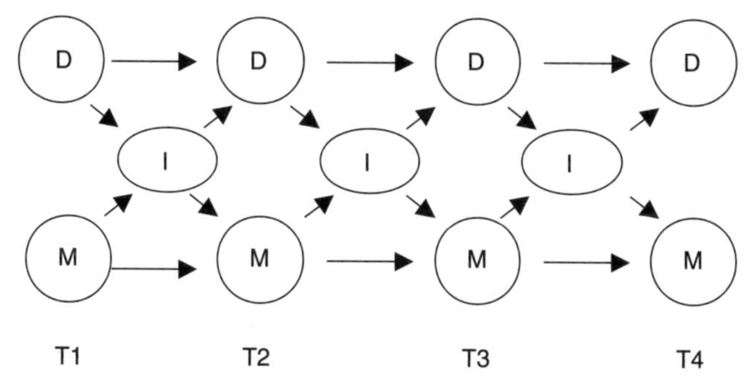

Figure 2.2 Development in mother–daughter interaction as an iterative process.

(D) contribute to the interaction (I) (e.g. the permission to go shopping with a friend). The outcome of that interaction affects both the mother and the daughter. This next interaction is the starting point for the interaction at T2, and so on.

This conceptualization of a developmental process as an iterative process is a core element in dynamic systems theory. It is the iterativity that is responsible for all types of non-linearity. Iterativity is therefore an important element in several techniques that are described in this book.

The importance of non-linearity

In living systems all change processes are non-linear because strictly linear changes would go on in the same way forever and processes in living systems do not (van Geert, 2008). Most linear models tend to forget this. A simple example concerns the model that describes the development of competence as a function of the person's motivation. Theories on motivation assume that a higher motivation results, via effort and invested time, in an increase in the level of competence. The level of competence, in turn, is assumed to have a positive effect on motivation, mediated by feelings of efficacy and competence. Most models show a mutual positive relation between both factors. However, something crucial is lacking in this simple model. Imagine a motivated child with moderate competence. The child's motivation increases his competence, the higher competence increases the motivation, higher motivation increases the competence still further, and so on forever. According to the linear model the child will become infinitely competent and infinitely motivated, but this is not what happens. Although there may be a positive relation between competence and motivation for some time, at some point the process changes and the motivation will decrease, regardless of the levels of competence. In addition, the level of competence will stop growing, regardless of the level of motivation. This implies a non-linear relation. At first sight, the example may seem a bit pointless. Of course, everybody knows that competence or motivation will not grow to infinity. However, the relevant questions are: What factors stop or slow down the process of mutual stimulation? And when do these factors become active? The answers to these questions may contribute to our understanding of the dynamics between motivation and competence. A dynamic systems approach does pay attention to the factors that account for the slowing down of growth by means of a so-called maximum growth capacity, which is nothing more than the translation of the notion that no growth can go on forever, due to limited resources such as time, energy, attention, etc.

Non-linearity can be seen in the relation between two variables, as described above, but also in the shape of a developmental trajectory of a variable. Many growth trajectories show a typical learning curve: they start slowly, speed up in the middle and slow down again. Other trajectories show a sudden jump: they start from a long-existing stable state, show a transition and then stabilize in a new stable state. Still others show a regression just before a period of rapid growth. These phenomena are well known in developmental science, but current linear models of development are not able to explain the how and the why of these different shapes of development, at least not as a characteristic that is inherent in the developmental process. Dynamic systems theory does help to explain this characteristic of change and development. We will elaborate one example to show how dynamic systems concepts may help to explain non-linear trajectories. Take the example of a typical learning curve: the number of words that an immigrant learns each day in the language of the new country. In describing the trajectory of "learned words" the concepts of iterativity and maximum growth capacity play an important role. In the beginning, in the first weeks, the number of newly learned words will be low because the immigrant has no understanding of pronounciation, grammar or the general flavour of the language, and auditive discrimination of resembling words is difficult. But gradually, depending upon the number of words that are mastered, short sentences are understood, variations are recognized and then new words fit in the newly learned grammatical structures. The number of newly learned words thus increases. But this does not go on forever, because after some time most common words are learned and few unknown words are left. In dynamic systems terms we see iterativity at work: The number of words already learned affects the number of words that will be learned today. And we also see maximum growth capacity at work: The number of words that can be learned plays a role in slowing down the maximum growth process. The concepts of iterativity and maximum growth capacity contribute to the understanding of, for example, differences in speed of learning at different points in time and between individuals. It offers possibilities to adjust teaching programs in such a way that they optimalize the learning curve.

Non-linearity will play an important role in this book. In the first part of the book we will discuss techniques to analyze non-linear characteristics in data sets, and in the second part we will describe how we can simulate the mechanisms underlying non-linearity.

System of interconnected elements

In the social sciences it is almost impossible to find a variable that is completely isolated, or a variable that is related just to one other variable. Social and psychological phenomena are typically characterized by broad networks of interconnected variables of elements. In fact, the whole social and non-social world can be seen as one enormous network of connected elements. For a researcher, that is not a practical conceptualization. All research focuses on small parts of that enormous network. Even Theories of Everything do so (Hawking and Penrose, 1996). So, in theory and in research, we always select a specific subgroup of elements. From a dynamic systems approach, that is not different as compared to other approaches. The main difference is that from a dynamic systems approach the researcher is forced to think about this and to make the chosen system explicit. It is important to realize that this selection is a choice made by the researcher. Systems do not simply exist out there – there are no predefined systems, we define them ourselves. Typically, we have theoretical or commonsense-based assumptions about specific elements that "belong" together – that are more strongly connected with each other than with other elements. These assumptions are strongly dependent on the type of research question we want to answer. If we want to study autonomy development in girls as a social construction that is determined by both peers and parents, we may define a system that includes the girl, her siblings, her parents and her friends or peers in school. However, if we want to study autonomy development as resulting from interactions between the mother and her daughter, we could define a system that consists of the girl's desired level of autonomy, her competence in autonomy issues and the mother's perception of her daughter's competence. For example, Lichtwarck-Aschoff, Kunnen and van Geert (2009) considered the mother–adolescent dyad as a system.

A logical consequence of defining a system is that we also, at the same time, define what is *not* the system. Strictly, the rest of that enormous connected network is not the system, and is thus the context of the system. Parts of that context may play a part in the conceptualization of the development of the system. The context may play a part because it provides the system with input. For example, the relevant context in the system of girl–parents–sibling–peers may be created by information from the media, role models, etc. In the second example the friend could be part of the context.

So far we have described four basic concepts in our definition of a dynamic system: the developmental process, iterativity, non-linearity and interconnectedness. In the next section we describe characteristics of a dynamic system that allow us to study developmental processes in new ways.

Systems at different time and aggregation levels

Although each study, per definition, focuses on a specific time scale, the topic of time scales, and of time in general, is only rarely discussed in developmental sciences. Hypotheses only rarely define whether and why specific changes are expected within a specified time frame. This is surprising, because time is the one and only common variable in all developmental research. In a dynamic systems approach time is the core variable. As a consequence, it offers possibilities to study how processes at different time levels influence each other.

In the example above, we showed how different research questions concerning autonomy development could result in the formulation of different systems. Depending on the research questions and the time scale, autonomy can be studied in the time span of hours (e.g. a discussion between an adolescent and her mother) or years (e.g. the developmental trajectories during adolescence). Thus, both the system and the context can be defined at many different levels of aggregation (Bosma and Kunnen, 2001; Steenbeek and van Geert, 2008; van Geert, 2008). These different systems are all related to each other. A system that focuses on real time interactions between a mother and her daughter can be seen as a subsystem in a broader system that includes peers and siblings. In the same way, we could define a system that is still more detailed and fine grained than the first one: for example a system that consists of emotions, thoughts and actions of the daughter. On a still more microscopic scale, we could define a system in terms of different neuropsychological processes, such as attention, and different types of information processing. And, on a more macroscopic level, researchers who are interested in fashion and group behavior could develop a system that consists of different girl groups or subcultures.

The lowest aggregation level that is common in psychological research on adolescent development consists of momentary components such as feelings, bodily sensations, cognitions, perceptions, appraisals, etc. This is a somewhat arbitrary choice of lowest level because these components, for example bodily sensations, can also be seen as higher order phenomena that emerge from components of an even lower order. The choice is purely based on what the common topics are in psychological research. The components on this lowest level are elements in a dynamic system: they are mutually related and continually interact with each other. From these interactions of momentary components emerges what is called "higher order behavior". The feelings, thoughts and perception of the adolescent girl self-organize in some form of coherent behavior, for example an act of rebellion against some parental restriction. This is the level that describes real time events. On a third level these events self-organize over time into enduring phenomena: roles, self-evaluations and self-representations. For example, the rebellious behavior of the girl and the reactions of her mother may self-organize in a way of arguing that is typical for that dyad. On a still higher level, self-organizing elements of the previous level give rise to abstract and stable concepts such as identity, sense of self or self-theory (Bosma and Kunnen, 2001). For example, the girl's experiences with conflict patterns with her mom, dad, brother and teachers may result in stable conceptions of herself as an assertive and self-confident kind of person.

The examples demonstrate some important principles of how one may define a system in actual research. First, it is not necessarily the person that is the system and the outer world that is the context. The context of the system can be part of the person. For example, the physical condition of the adolescent girl (such as a headache) could be defined as an influencing context factor of the system of conflict-related feelings and thoughts. In the same way, parts of the outside world can belong to the system, as in the mother–daughter dyad. Second, systems can be ordered in terms of aggregation level, which means that we can conceptualize a system of systems that is hierarchically ordered. We described already how the outcome of a system on a lower level may play a role as an element in a higher order system. This conceptualization of connected systems offers promising ways to study how long-term psychological development (as described by concepts such as autonomy or identity) shapes and, at the same time, is shaped by everyday events (Lichtwarck-Aschoff, van Geert, Bosma and Kunnen, 2008).

In summary, a dynamic systems approach can be used to study change on different levels and time scales, ranging from microseconds to decades. The foregoing implies that one of the first steps in a study based on a dynamic systems approach is the definition of the system and its elements. As may be clear from the examples, to choose elements, one needs a good theory of what one wants to study. One cannot define a system without theoretical notions about which elements play a role in it. Of course, this is true in any study, but in a systems approach it is clearly visible that one cannot select just two or three variables and neglect other, equally relevant, elements. In Chapters 8 and 9 we will demonstrate in detail how the elements and the relations of a system can be defined on the basis of theory. As mentioned before, the interconnectedness of systems of different hierarchical levels can be understood from the perspective of self-organization. Different techniques described in this book (especially grid techniques and model building) can be used to study how higher order patterns may emerge out of lower order connected elements. Chapter 11 will elaborate how a dynamic systems approach can be used to model and understand the connections between different time scales. In other words, a dynamic systems approach helps us to understand how long-term development emerges out of short-term day-to-day or minute-to-minute interactions, and vice versa.

Self-organization and emerging characteristics

Self-organization is one of the mechanisms that describe how systems at different time scales can be linked to each other. A typical characteristic of a system that consists of connected elements is self-organization – the emergence of stable higher order characteristics in the system (Bosma and Kunnen, 2001; van Geert, 2003). By higher order stability is meant that in the whole network of connected elements stable patterns arise: elements become connected (i.e. tend to appear together) with some other elements but not with specific other elements. For example, in theory a person's experience may consist of numerous uncountable combinations of thoughts, perceptions and emotions, and yet people have specific stable ways of perceiving the world. Specific emotions are connected to specific thoughts, perceptions and actions. How is it that out of an uncountable number of possibilities only a few patterns become true? This can be explained at least partly by a mechanism called the positive feedback loop. Different elements may trigger each other mutually because they have become related in a person's experience. These elements are described in the literature as scripts or schemata (Strayer, 2002). A positive feedback loop means that the emergence of a specific constellation of elements increases the chance that next time the same pattern will emerge. For example, in an adolescent with aggression problems the emotion "anger" , the thought "people want to hurt me", the perception "he wants to hurt me" and the belief "better that I attack first" may trigger each other and elicit an attack. Most probably, this results in a counterattack that confirms the thoughts and beliefs, thus strengthening the existing connections between the elements. Because of the idea that others want to hurt him, the adolescent interprets even the slightest sign of suspicious behavior in another person as "he is about to get me'. This increases the chance that this script will be frequently activated. As will be discussed in the next section, such a stable and dominant network of connections in dynamic systems theory is called an attractor.

Of course, this does not mean that the pattern is exactly the same in each activation. Small variations are possible, depending on the specific characteristics of each situation. For example, whether or not a physical attack is part of the script will depend on the other person or persons.

So, we could say that the aggressive adolescent has a stable behavioral pattern. However, that does not mean that there is some static state that resides as a kind of structure inside the adolescent. Patterns are stable because they emerge again and again. This means that, from a dynamic systems perspective, stability is a dynamic characteristic. Stability does not mean that there is no activity. A stable state can remain stable only because of many supporting processes and is thus in fact very dynamic. The pattern of anger and attributing bad intentions described above will vary according to the situation. It is fed by new experiences, where new connections with different elements may emerge.

From this view stability is thus not always synonymous with arrest or rigidity, although the aggression example suggests rigidity in the adolescent's experience. However, some stability is necessary in all living systems. The emergence of stable patterns allows the system to react adequately and fast in different situations and in this way the role of stability in development is as important as the role of variability and change.

Attractors and repellors

The concepts of attractors and repellors are especially useful to find answers to questions such as: What makes us see high stability on whatever characteristics in some individuals in some periods, while in other individuals or in other periods we see changes? What makes changes start after a stable period? What makes a new stability emerge after a period of change?

As discussed in the previous sections, self-organization may result in the emergence of stable patterns in a network of connected elements. A characteristic of such a stable pattern is that it tends to appear as soon as one or a few of the connected elements are triggered. In the previous section we mentioned the interconnectedness between feelings of anger and attributing bad intentions to others. Some aggressive children and adolescents tend – as the adolescent in our example – to interpret all kinds of social communications as an attack, as a result of the other's bad intentions (Visser, Singer, van Geert and Kunnen, 2009). For them, one small element, such as a way of looking, a movement or a remark, triggers the emergence of a complete pattern of experience (e.g. danger of humiliation or being attacked, anger and patterns of behavior such as a counterattack). Such self-organizing patterns that are "attractive" to the system are called attractors.

A more formal definition of an attractor is that it is a state – a specific place in the state space – to which the system tends to return. A common graphical way to represent the concept of attractors is to depict the behavior, (the change process of a system) as the movement of a ball over an irregular surface. The surface is the state space, and the trajectory of a system over time can be described by the movements of that system over the surface. The surface represents the possible combinations of values of the two variables in the system and (as shown in Figure 2.3) consists of hills and basins. The two black balls are systems, rolling over the surface. The hills and basins emerge because a third, vertical, dimension is added to the picture of the surface. This dimension represents how often a system remains at a specific place on the surface. For a better visual understanding, we assume that a lower position on that dimension (more to the bottom of the picture) means that the specific place is visited more frequently. Basins are thus attractors and they represent stable states of a system. Once a system is settled in an attractor, then it tends to remain there. Remember that each point on the surface represents a set of values for the variables that describe the surface. So we could say that in Figure 2.3 the set (10,10) describes an attractor.

Now, let us translate the example of the mother–daughter dyad in a graphical state space. For the sake of simplicity on a two-dimensional page, the surface is depicted in Figure 2.4 as a line, which means that each point on that line represents a specific value of the mother–daughter dyad.

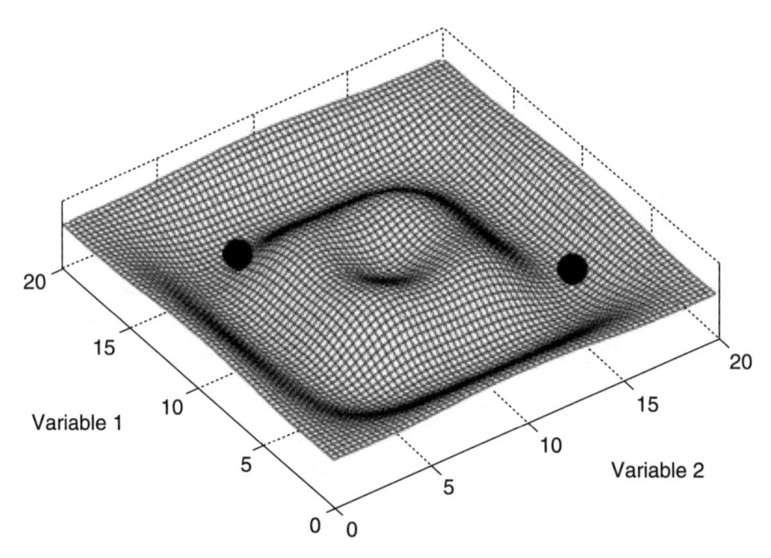

Figure 2.3 A two-dimensional state space as a landscape with hills and basins.

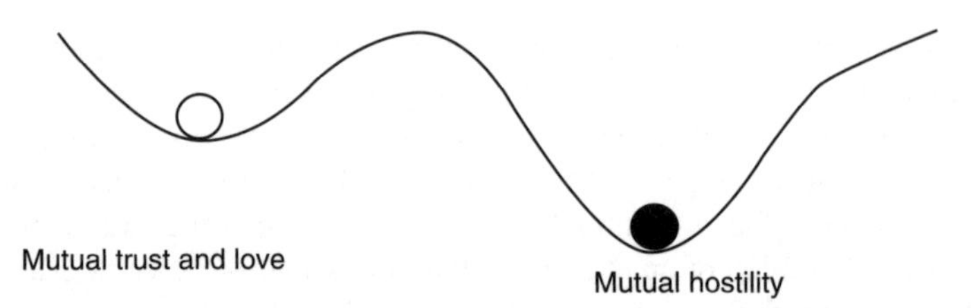

Figure 2.4 An attractor landscape of a mother–daughter dyad.

The line represents all theoretically possible states of the system, and the vertical dimension represents the likelihood that the system will remain at a specific point on the line. The line contains basins, and the ball tends to roll to the nearest low place in that basin (i.e. the basin is an attractor). In this example, the figure represents the possible states of a mother–daughter dyad. The dyad has lots of fights. Mutual hostility and distrust is therefore a strong attractor. Both partners in the dyad readily interpret small behavioral elements, such as a remark or way of looking, as an attack and thus react in a hostile way. A behavioral element can be seen as a location somewhere on the steep side of the right basin. Once the system is there, it rolls into the hostility basin. In the system in this figure there is another attractor, in which mother and daughter love and trust each other. It might be that they share some interest, say the love for their baby cats, in which they can show each other mutual trust. The ball may roll in any of both attractors. However, the hostility attractor is the steepest one, and once there it is more difficult to get out as compared to the trust attractor. The surface has hills too. The ball will never stay longer than a very short time on the top of such a hill and then it rolls away. In this picture, there is a hill between the two attractors. This hill may represent the condition in which there is trust from one participant and hostility from the other. In this dyad such a combination never lasts long: once one of them shows hostility, the other follows. Thus, there are states that are practically impossible for the system to occupy, and such states are called repellors (Hollenstein, 2007).

The concept of attractors is especially useful when we want to understand rigidity in behavior and experience. Rigid ways of behaving and experiencing continue to exist despite clear disadvantages and pain for the person, and despite strong attempts to intervene. Attractors and repellors can be investigated especially well by means of the grid techniques in Chapter 6 and the model-building techniques discussed in Chapters 8, 9 and 10. These methods can demonstrate how rigid states emerge, and probably more importantly they help in understanding how and when dysfunctional, unwanted rigidity may be influenced.

Transitions and bifurcations

Transitions and bifurcations are relevant concepts if we want to understand how stable (and rigid) systems may change. When imagining a ball rolling in a steep basin, escape seems to be very difficult. However, the surface itself may be subject to change as well, which means that specific places on that surface may become more or less attractive. Such changes in the system can be triggered by changes in other variables in the system, by changes in the connections between variables in the system or by the emergence of new relevant variables.

Especially in adolescence there are many examples of this, because in adolescence many fundamental characteristics change. One example concerns cognitive development. Young adolescents develop new forms of abstract thinking. These new cognitive capacities affect many other variables, such as their self-esteem, their moral reasoning and their thinking about parents, relationships, school, and so on. This means that during such a period the relevant dimensions in the state space may change. In other words, the landscape itself changes. Old attractors disappear, which may mean that connected elements become disconnected and new connections are formed. For example, strong attractors in the adolescent's belief system may become subject to reflection and questioning and thus lose their strength. Over time, new connections will be formed and new attractors and repellors may appear in the new state space (Hollenstein, 2007; Lichtwarck-Aschoff and van Geert, 2004).

A clear example of a changing state space is the emergence of attributional thinking in early adolescents' perceived competence. Younger children base their perceived competence on the outcomes of performances, thus on success or failure. However, around age 10–12 children start to recognize that the cause of success is important as well. They recognize that failure that can be attributed to a lack of effort is less damaging for one's self-worth than failure attributed to a lack of competence. In this period, self-handicapping strategies emerge as a way of coping with fear of failure (Kunnen, 1993; Nurmi, Salmela-Aro and Ruotsalainen, 1994). This cognitive change affects the whole state space. New basins of attraction emerge, with self-handicapping being one of them.

Another example of changes in the attractor landscape concerns the changes in parent–adolescent relationships. In Figure 2.4 we showed the attractor landscape of a mother–daughter system at a specific moment in time. The dyad was amidst a period of many conflicts. However, in most dyads this is a temporary phase that is followed by a gain in autonomy and a repair of the mutual trust. Figure 2.5 shows a graphical representation of this development over time. Gradually, the hostility basin becomes less steep – it happens less often that only small remarks push the system in the basin. After 1 month there is not really a steep basin, which means that interactions become rather unpredictable and can go in any direction. After 6 months the hostility basin has completely vanished. Of course, this does not mean that the dyad is never angry anymore, but it means that there is no attractor that pulls them into a hostile state with little opportunity to escape.

Such a change in the state space can be described as a transition: a relatively stable situation becomes unstable and chaotic, and from that chaos a new stability arises.

A concept that is often used in this context is the concept of bifurcation. Bifurcation means that the system is on the point where development can take different pathways.

In this mother–daughter dyad, development moved in the direction of mutual trust, but in some cases development goes another way. The hostility basin may

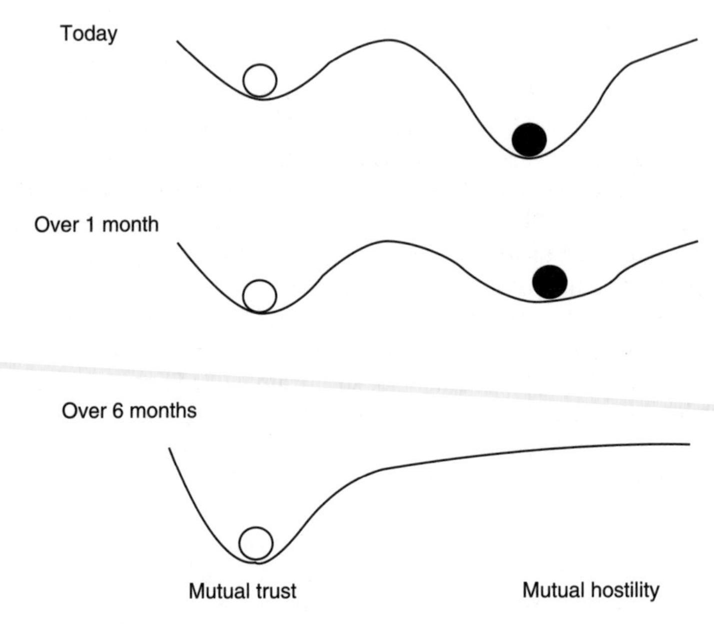

Figure 2.5 Transition – the change in attractor landscape over time.

become steeper and steeper, while the trust basin disappears. Such a development may end up with the daughter running away or being put into childcare following reports of severe fights.

Another example, concerning a child with fear of failure, is that the child develops the ability to integrate attributions in her perceived competence. This offers several new opportunities. She may continue in a pattern of low perceived competence and fear of failure and strengthen this pattern by developing a self-handicapping strategy as attractor in her task behavior. However, the change in state space also offers her the opportunity to reconsider the old associations between failure and consequences. She may develop the trust that she can succeed as long as she puts in enough effort. Periods of transition offer opportunities to change the direction of development. This implies that transitional periods may be especially suited for intervention (Magai and McFadden, 1995; Magai and Nussbaum, 1996).

Transitions and bifurcations are thus relevant phenomena in developmental studies. A technique that is especially well suited to look for them is the grid technique discussed in Chapter 6. In the second part of the book we will elaborate techniques to investigate the mechanisms underlying these phenomena.

Variability

A concept that is especially relevant in a transitional period is the concept of variability (van Geert & van Dijk, 2002). As mentioned before, stability is not a rigid state, and living systems are never completely stable. Living systems interact with their environment and these interactions cause perturbations. Perturbations

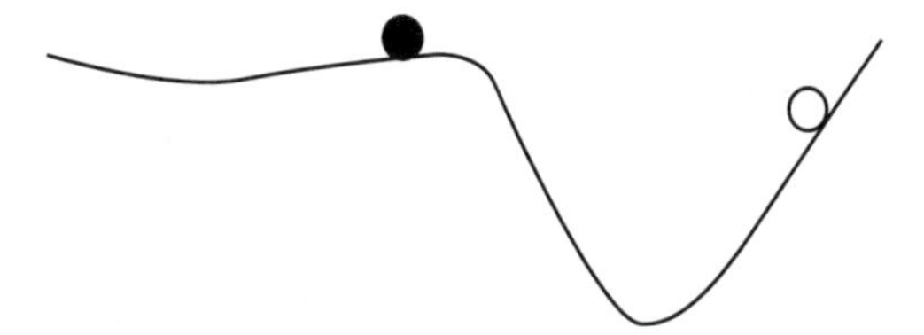

Figure 2.6 Differences in return time depend on the strength of the attractor.

cause the system to move around in the attractor basin, or to move temporarily out of the basin. In research, fluctuations are often considered as irrelevant noise and are neglected. For example, differences in daily self-esteem measures are often seen as indicative of a "real" underlying stable level of self-esteem. However, variability (the amount of fluctuation over time) and especially changes in this variability can be very important and informative characteristics of a system. For example, Kernis, Comell, Sun, Berry and Harlow (1993) found inter-individual differences in individuals' stability of self-esteem as well as in their level of self-esteem. Combining the two self-esteem characteristics results in a much better understanding of the role of self-esteem in cognitive and emotional reactions to evaluative events. Kuppens, Oravecz and Tuerlinckx (2010) found that the average level of emotion was only one of three relevant measures in emotions, the others being variability and return time to attractor.

In such research variability measures are studied as stable characteristics that were found to be relevant to understand the person. In developmental studies, however, variability is found to be especially relevant in understanding the process: it is an indication that the system is in the neighbourhood of a transition. One of the earliest signs of a transition is an increase in the variability of a system (van der Maas and Molenaar, 1992). Variability can be studied in different ways. A well known aspect of variability is the variance. Although most studies focus on variance within groups, one can also study the variance within one system, for example in an individual time series of autonomy scores. However, other aspects of variability are important as well. An indication that an attractor basin is becoming less steep is an increase in the so-called return time: the time it takes after a disturbance before a system returns to the attractor. It is clear that in Figure 2.6 the return time of the black ball will be much longer than that of the white ball.

But also in other situations the variability can give important information about a system. It tells us something about the strength of attractors and about the existence of one or more attractors. In Chapter 5 several techniques are discussed that are well suited to assess variability.

What are the advantages of studying adolescence from a dynamic systems view?

As demonstrated above, dynamic systems theory offers different concepts and tools to study changes over time, and more knowledge about change is what we need in the study of adolescence. We know quite a lot about the differences between pre-adolescents, adolescents and post-adolescents, but questions concerning hòw individuals change and where the huge differences between them come from are still largely unanswered. The dynamic systems conceptualizations can be used to gain qualitatively better knowledge about the processes of development and the mechanisms that drive these processes. In other words, we gain insight into the *why* and *how* of the developmental process itself. We have discussed features of developmental processes such as attractors, sudden changes, emergence of new characteristics, variability, etc. These features can be explained and studied well from a dynamic systems perspective. In classic research, these features have not received much attention, mainly because they are characteristics of individual trajectories and are only visible if we study individual trajectories. Most research, also in developmental studies, is so-called sample-based research and has focused on groups and changes in groups. Such research may reveal global changes over time but not the individual patterns of development, therefore much of the developmental knowledge from this classical view concerns not the process itself but the outcome of developmental processes in groups. This has an additional disadvantage because findings from sample-based research, such as the type of relation between two variables, cannot automatically be extrapolated to the individual level. As discussed in the previous chapter, a relation that does exist on a group level may be absent or different if we investigate that same relation within an individual over time.

A dynamic systems approach can be used and has been used to study all kinds of development, such as the development of economies, of bird populations and of a wide range of human development. This book focuses on adolescent development. There are several reasons to assume that adolescent development is especially well suited for a dynamic systems approach. Adolescence is a time of transition in which major changes take place in all domains of development (Lichtwarck-Aschoff and van Geert, 2004). Some authors describe the period of early adolescence as a transition period between one stable state and another (Granic, Dishion and Hollenstein, 2003). In adolescence much change takes place, and this change is often sudden, non-linear, stepwise, etc. Adolescence is definitely a period in which state transitions take place on different levels. It is also a period in which the relationship between the adolescent and different aspects of the context changes, so new types of systems can be defined and may become relevant. A dynamic systems conceptualization of adolescent development draws attention to new questions, such as the role and nature of variability, and thereby enhances our understanding of adolescent development. Within a dynamic systems approach the critical questions concern the process level and the temporal unfolding of interaction patterns over time.

The application of a dynamic systems approach to adolescent development is not entirely new, with several studies appearing in the last decade (e.g. Bosma and Kunnen, 2001; Granic, Dishion and Hollenstein, 2003; Lichtwarck-Aschoff and van Geert, 2004; Vleioras, van Geert and Bosma, 2008).

Why are models so important in dynamic systems building and in simulating developmental processes?

We see model building and simulation as important tools to learn about developmental processes (Franken, in preparation). Contrary to the social sciences, in most beta sciences the development of theory-driven models and the study of their behavior is an important source of scientific knowledge (Dyson, 2004; Hawking and Penrose, 1996). In the social sciences, models are mainly used to describe patterns of outcomes. The model itself is not related to the processes of the phenomenon under study. These models typically describe distributions in a population in relation to independent variables. Dynamic systems models are completely different, aiming to represent and to model the mechanisms underlying the developmental process. Such a model provides a kind of map of the actual (hypothesized) mechanisms. In the previous sections we stressed the major role of non-linearity and iterative processes in developmental processes. Typical of iterative non-linear processes is that their development cannot be predicted in a global way. How the development will proceed cannot be predicted on the basis of independent variables at the beginning of the process. It can be predicted only by actually simulating each step (i.e. each iteration) of the developmental process for a specific constellation of values of the variables. Dynamic systems models thus enable experimental theoretical psychology, which means that we can build models that represent (part of) a theory. By studying the behavior of the model we can test hypotheses about what kind of behavior should be generated in specific conditions. A specific application concerns the possibility of testing hypotheses that could not, for ethical reasons, be tested empirically. By means of models, the result of different aversive conditions and what factors could counterbalance the negative effects of aversive conditions can be tested. In Chapters 8 and 9 we will give examples of the application of models in experimental theoretical psychology.

Of course, for dynamic systems models it is also important that the generated outcomes fit with the empirically found data. But the primary aim of these so-called "toy models" is that they help us to sharpen our thinking about development (our insight into non-linearity and its implications for development) and to explore and test whether conceptual and theoretical models and their assumed relations between variables result in plausible trajectories of development (Broer and Krauskopf, 2000). Outcomes of simulations help to elaborate and fine-tune theoretical models. The building and application of quantitative dynamic systems models will be the topic of the second part of this book.

How to choose a technique?

This book consists of two parts. The first part focuses on methods that help to grasp different aspects of the change process by new and creative ways of analyzing data. It describes different techniques to analyze dynamic systems phenomena such as attractors (grid techniques), variability and sudden non-linear change. The second part of the book focuses on the building of dynamic systems models that can be used to simulate developmental processes. This focus on the actual building of quantitative models is a specific characteristic of a dynamic systems approach. Different types of quantitative dynamic systems models are discussed. Thus, the book presents different techniques to analyze processes and to simulate development. For readers who are not yet familiar with these techniques, it may be difficult to know which technique is best suited for their specific research. In this section we will discuss how a suitable technique can be selected, what you need for it and what it may bring you. The answers to these questions depend on the research question and on the type of data. In an ideal case, the type of data can be chosen on the basis of the research question, but of course research circumstances are not always that ideal. Nevertheless, the choice of a technique depends primarily on the research question. What do you want to know? Does the research question address characteristics of a data set, such as whether a sudden change appears following an intervention, (e.g. whether a skill develops faster after a new way of teaching is introduced)? In this case the type of techniques described in the first part of the book can do the job. When the research question addresses mechanisms and processes of development, then the application of the model-building techniques discussed in Chapters 8–11 may be more suited than the other techniques. For example, if one wants to explore how a specific skill may develop in different circumstances and teaching methods, the building of a dynamic systems model is best suited because such a model offers possibilities to build-in the assumed effects of the specific characteristics of these different teaching methods on a real time level, and to explore their effects on developmental trajectories in different types of persons and contexts.

Another factor that is important in choosing for data analysis or for model building is the knowledge that is available about the topic under study. If a topic is new and there is very little knowledge about, for example, the factors that may be important in the developmental process, the conditions for more and less optimal development, the development over time or the distribution of levels over age, then the best step may be to carry out observational studies.

To give an example, some years ago we were in a program for career choice and were confronted with young adults instead of the expected adolescents. Our initial impression was that the type of process, the problems and the optimal intervention in this group differed from the processes, problems and successful interventions in a group of adolescents. But we did not know how, it was just that we suspected a difference. We started to do some case studies, which provided us with new insights about the processes in young adults with career choice problems (Kunnen, Holwerda, Bosma and Bosman, 2009). As a next step in the study of a specific unexplored phenomenon, it may be easiest to start with analyzing process characteristics: to gather longitudinal data about the process and analyze, for example by means of grid techniques (Chapter 6), what the individual trajectories look like. The outcomes from these analyses may help to develop more concrete ideas about the mechanisms underlying a developmental process.

If the research question concerns the characteristics of data, then one can choose from many different techniques. Of course, the choice of just one technique depends again on the question and on the characteristics of the data. State space grids are very easy to apply for data that are paired and either belong to a limited number of qualitative categories (such as different emotions) or can be expressed in an ordinal or ratio scale with a limited number of categories. Also, a combination of three or more variables is possible but it is simpler to start with two – observation categories in a parent–child dyad or two variables within one individual.

The techniques described in Chapter 5 address in different ways the question of the shape of individual longitudinal trajectories. The techniques differ with regard to the type of data available: qualitative and variable, a small number or a large number with highly irregular and fluctuating data. In Chapter 5, analyzing trajectories with a limited set of data points, such as four or five, is possible with the technique described in the section on searching for change; grasping inter-individual differences and intra-individual differences in qualitative data sets can be handled by techniques of the kind described in the section on searching for variability; and for analyzing intensive data sets and trying to figure out whether and where in the long and irregular time series sudden changes take place, the techniques in the section on searching for discontinuity can be used.

Quantitative dynamic systems models can be used to model the development of one variable and also the development of different variables that are somehow related to each other. The models are especially suited if the research question addresses mechanisms of development (e.g. how and when different variables affect each other in the developmental process) or the developmental shape of a specific variable over time.

Building a model requires that one has notions about the characteristics of the process on a micro level, and of the type of relation between the variables. By micro level we mean the level of one small step in the process, thus the term "micro" is relative as compared to the developmental level one aims to simulate. This requirement does not mean that there should be a thorough empirical basis for the characteristics at the micro level. In general, there is no such knowledge. As will be demonstrated in Chapters 8 and 9, an educated guess based on common sense and theoretical knowledge suffices to formulate the micro-level relations. Of course, the relations that are formulated are hypotheses themselves, and by comparing models with different assumptions on the micro level more insight is gained in the mechanisms.

The model described in Chapter 8 is an example of how almost any developmental process can be modeled. Such a model describes the development of one variable or of several variables that are continuously interacting with each other. Also the influence of stable factors can be integrated in the model. The techniques of conditional growth that are discussed in Chapter 9, (describing stage-wise development) are especially useful in the simulation of development that is assumed to be dependent on the emergence of other skills or attributes. In such a model theoretical notions concerning sufficient and necessary conditions can be translated in IF–THEN statements and in that form incorporated in a dynamic systems model. Also, hypotheses concerning the presence and content of sufficient and necessary conditions can be tested by making different models that include different conditions.

Agent models (Chapter 10) are applied most often in studies that address the interactions between people. Examples of studies in which it has been used recently are studies into the interactions between adolescents in a peer group or a class room, or into pre-school children playing together. However, the technique can be applied in other studies as well. The main characteristic of the model is that it models the continuous interactions between two or more agents over time. These agents may be people, groups of people or characteristics within one person. For example, based on the theory of the dialogical self (Hermans and Kempen, 1993) one might use different voices within one individual as the different agents. A major difference with a dynamic systems growth model is that the equations that describe the changes in each agent over time are generally simpler and do not contain logistic growth equations.

The techniques in Parts I and II differ with respect to the need for theory and for data. The techniques in Part I require both theory and data. The theory is needed to guide the exploration process. It is useless to try to find attractors or sudden changes if there are no hypotheses or expectations concerning the how and why of the developmental process. For building a dynamic systems model, one does not need data. They are handy, but not strictly necessary. What one needs are theoretical notions about what the mechanisms in the development under study may look like. As discussed, most often there is no empirical evidence for the kind of mechanisms available. Thus, one has to rely on theory, good observations, descriptions or case studies and educated guess. However, once a model is developed, data are needed to validate the model. The best type of data is of course longitudinal time series of individuals. However, as a second best option, group data offer possibilities for a first validation as well. In short, to build a good dynamic systems model a good theory is much more important than a good data set. In our experience, the theories that offer most inspirations and insight for developing notions about developmental mechanisms are the older and broader developmental theories. The theories of psychology's founding fathers such as Piaget, Vygotsky, Erikson, Bowlby and William James are rich in qualitative descriptions of how development may work, which are the building blocks of a dynamic systems model.

We hope that the directions given above help in selecting a technique. The starting point for that selection should be the specific research question one wants to address and a sound theoretical basis. But often there is not just one suitable technique, and depending on the specific requirements of each technique one can choose from several possibilities.

References

Bosma, H. A., & Kunnen, E. S. (2001). *Identity and emotion: A self-organisational process*. Cambridge, UK: Cambridge University Press.

Broer, H. W., & Krauskopf, B. (2000). Chaos in periodically driven systems. In B. Krauskopf and D. Lenstra (Eds.), *Fundamental issues of nonlinear laser dynamics* (Vol. 548; pp. 31–53). New York: American Institute of Physics.

Dyson, F. (2004). A meeting with Enrico Fermi. *Nature, 427*, 297.

Franken, D. *Modeling cognition.* In preparation.

Granic, I., Dishion, T. J., & Hollenstein, T. (2003). The family ecology of adolescence: A dynamic systems perspective on normative development. In G. Adams & M. Berzonsky (Eds.), *Handbook of adolescence* (pp. 60–91). New York: Blackwell.

Hawking, S., & Penrose, R. (1996). De *aard van ruimte en tijd (The nature of space and time).* Amsterdam: Prometheus.

Hermans, H. J. M., & Kempen, H. J. G. (1993). *The dialogical self: Meaning as movement.* San Diego: Academic Press.

Hollenstein, T. (2007). State space grids: Analyzing dynamics across development. *International Journal of Behavioral Development, 31,* 384–396.

Kernis, M. H., Cornell, D. P., Sun, C.-R., Berry, A., & Harlow, T. (1993). There's more to self-esteem than whether it is high or low: The importance of stability of self-esteem. *Journal of Personality and Social Psychology, 65*, 1190–1204.

Kunnen, E. S. (1993). Ervaren controle en waargenomen competentie op de basisschool (Perceived control and perceived competence in primary school). *Kind en Adolescent, 14,* 194–204.

Kunnen, E. S., Holwerda, N., Bosma, H. A., & Bosman, S. (2009). Career choice in adolescence and emerging adulthood, In M. Kuijpers & F. Meijers (Eds.), *Career learning: Research and practice in education* (pp. 103–118). Hertogenbosch, The Netherlands: Euroguidance.

Kuppens, P., Oravecz, Z., & Tuerlinckx, F. (2010). Feelings change: Accounting for individual differences in the temporal dynamics of affect. *Journal of Personality and Social Psychology, 99,* 1042–1060.

Lichtwarck-Aschoff, A., & van Geert, P. L. C. (2004). A dynamic systems perspective on social cognition, problematic behaviour, and intervention in adolescence. *European Journal of Developmental Psychology, 1,* 399–411.

Lichtwarck-Aschoff, A., Kunnen, E. S., & van Geert, P. L. C. (2009). Here we go again. A dynamic systems perspective on emotional rigidity across parent–adolescent conflicts. *Developmental Psychology, 45,* 1364–1375.

Lichtwarck-Aschoff, A., van Geert, P. L. C., Bosma, H. A., & Kunnen, E. S. (2008). Time and identity: A framework for research and theory formation. *Developmental Review, 28*, 370–400.

Magai, C., & McFadden, S. H. (1995). *The role of emotions in social and personality development: History, theory, and research.* New York: Plenum Press.

Magai, C., & Nusbaum, B. (1996). Personality change in adulthood: Dynamic systems, emotions, and the transformed self. In C. Magai & S. H. McFadden (Eds.), *Handbook of emotion, adult development, and aging* (pp. 403–420). San Diego: Academic Press.

Nurmi, J. E., Salmela-Aro, K., & Ruotsalainen, H. (1994). Cognitive and attributional strategies among unemployed young adults: A case of the failure-trap strategy. *European Journal of Personality, 8,* 135–148.

Steenbeek, H. W., & van Geert, P. L. C. (2008). The empirical validation of a dynamic systems model of interaction: Do children of different sociometric statuses differ in their dyadic play interactions? *Developmental Science, 11*, 253–281.

Strayer, J. (2002). The dynamics of emotions and life cycle identity. *Identity, 2,* 47–79.

Van der Maas, H. L. J., & Molenaar, P. C. M. (1992). Stagewise cognitive development: An application of catastrophe theory. *Psychological Review, 99,* 395–417.

Van Geert, P. L. C. (2003). Dynamic systems approaches and modeling of developmental processes. In J. Valsiner and K. J. Conolly (Eds.), *Handbook of developmental psychology,* (pp. 640–672). London: Sage.

Van Geert, P. L. C. (2008). Complex dynamic systems of development. In R. A. Meyers (Ed.), *Encyclopedia of complexity and system science. Vol. 2 Applications of physics and mathematics to social science* (pp. 1872–1916). New York: Springer.

Van Geert, P. L. C., & van Dijk, M. W. G. (2002). Focus on variability: New tools to study intra-individual variability in developmental data. *Infant Behavior and Development, 25,* 340–374.

Visser, M., Singer, E., van Geert, P. L. C., & Kunnen, E. S. (2009). Inner logic of children with aggressive behaviour. *European Journal of Special Needs Education, 24,* 1–20.

Vleioras, G., van Geert, P., & Bosma H. A. (2008). Modeling the role of emotions in viewing oneself maturely. *New Ideas in Psychology, 26,* 69–94.

Part I

Describing development: The assessment of process characteristics

3 The search for process characteristics

Saskia Kunnen

As we discussed in the previous chapter, the dynamic systems approach is attractive because it can explain all kinds of developmental characteristics that cannot be explained otherwise. We have mentioned non-linearity, stability and (sudden) changes, variability (and variability in variability), attractors and bifurcations. The chapters in this first part of the book describe techniques that help to detect such process characteristics in data sets.

In research into adolescent development, interest in dynamic systems, self-organization, processes and process characteristics is growing. However, this holds especially for introductory and discussion sections. Thus, the research questions concern processes and the data are interpreted in terms of processes but often the analysis of the data does not allow for conclusions concerning process characteristics (Bosma and Kunnen, 2008). This is not surprising because many standard statistical tools are not well suited for the analysis of processes. Most statistical techniques are sample based and focus on differences between groups or, in longitudinal studies, changes in groups over time. In the conclusions of papers reporting on such research the changes that are found are often assumed to hold for individuals as well. As discussed in the previous chapter, this is based on the often incorrect assumption that ergodicity is present in the phenomena under study.

In this first part of the book we will discuss several simple techniques that are well suited for analyzing the typical process and dynamic systems characteristics of variability, (dis-)continuity and attractors and stability.

Looking for variability

In a dynamic systems approach variability, especially differences and changes in variability, is considered relevant for understanding the developmental process. As mentioned, the increase of variability is an indicator of increasing instability of the system and one of the first signs of a transition (van der Maas and Molenaar, 1992). Also the catastrophe flags "divergence from linearity" and "critical slowing down" refer to the changing variability of a system in reaction to perturbations. They refer to the phenomenon that shortly before a transition the system reacts more strongly to perturbations (divergence from linearity) and takes more time to return to the stable position (critical slowing down).

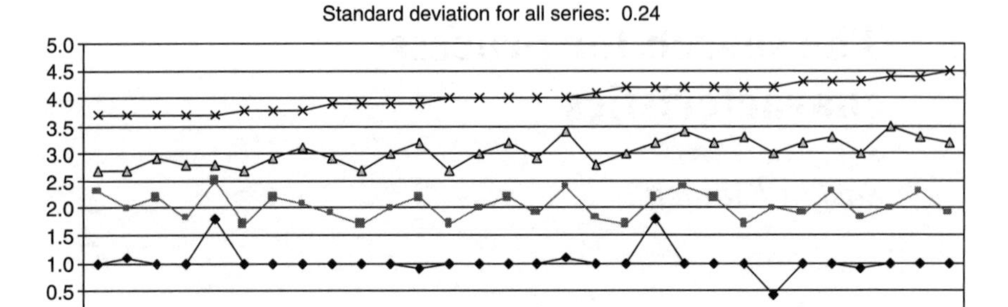

Figure 3.1 Different data series with the same standard deviation.

All these phenomena describe changes in the variability that require specific techniques to analyze them. The variability in the value of one single variable, either in group data or in individual time series, can sometimes be expressed in a simple way by means of (changes in) the standard deviation. However, to test differences in standard deviations one needs long data series. Moreover, a standard deviation is a rather global measure. Different patterns of variability may result in the same standard deviation. Figure 3.1 shows four different individual data series that all have the same standard deviation. The upper three series all consist of the same raw data and only their sequence differs. The lowest series is a very homogeneous pattern with a few peaks. The huge differences in the trajectories show that there is much about variability that is not grasped by the standard deviation.

For other types of variability standard deviations are not applicable at all. For example, in complex processes variability often means that different variables (e.g. emotions, cognitive styles, behaviors) occur together in different constellations, and one may want to know whether there are differences between individuals or over time in the amount of variability of these patterns. Lichtwarck-Aschoff, Kunnen and van Geert (2009) investigated variability in emotional reactions following conflicts by analyzing a series of reactions on an individual basis. In that study, subsequent reactions sometime consisted of exactly the same emotions, but more often they were partly the same. In such data sets, one needs other techniques to grasp the differences in variability.

Looking for (dis-)continuity, attractors, sudden changes and jumps

Continuity, discontinuity, attractors, sudden changes and jumps in a developmental trajectory are process characteristics that can be observed especially in individual longitudinal data. However, most current statistical tools are designed for the analysis of group data. In the analysis of process characteristics, group data are often not very helpful. As an example, imagine adolescents who develop some type of new skill that develops all of a sudden. One moment the level of skill is zero and the next moment the skill has a level of 1. However, not all adolescents

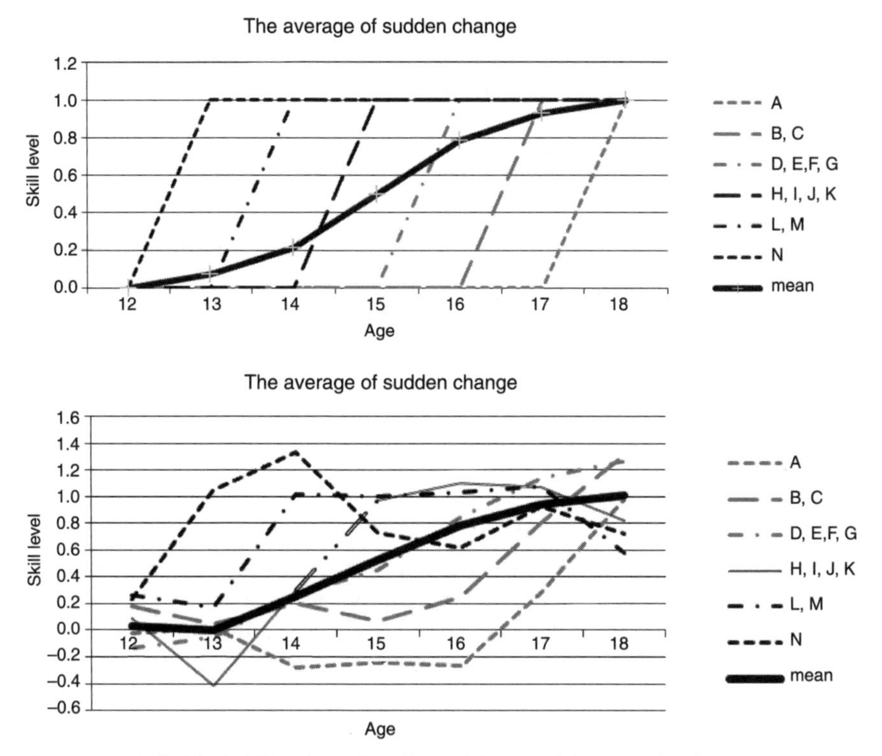

Figure 3.2 Individual skill trajectories of 14 subjects and the mean level.

"jump" at the same time. Most adolescents jump between age 13 and age 17. The distribution of the time of the jump is more or less normally distributed. For 14 adolescents we assess the skill level each year between age 12 and age 18 and compute the group mean for each age. We find that at age 12 the mean level is zero, which gradually increases to 0.5 at age 15 and then to 1.0 at age 18. Figure 3.2(a) shows the individual trajectories of our 14 subjects and the mean level of the skill. It is clear that based on the mean scores we may easily but wrongly conclude that the skill under study shows a nice gradual development during adolescence. But what are other ways to analyze these data? How can we assess whether there is really a jump in each individual data set? Remember that in reality data are never that smooth. Figure 3.2(b) shows the same data as in Figure 3.2(a) but with some random variation added. For such a data set, specific techniques are required to analyze whether there is a discontinuous jump in the individual data.

This example makes clear that analysis of the shape of developmental change should be based on the analysis of sequences of individual data. Time series analysis offers these techniques but they often require large numbers of data, and in psychological research we tend not to have enough data points. A short scan of developmental psychology journals shows that studies with more than four measurement points are scarce, and often this is not just a matter of bad design.

In studies that use time-consuming measurements such as extensive rating scales or interviews, a more frequent assessment is often not possible. Thus, we need techniques to detect changes in rather short time series.

Techniques to study variability, attractors, (dis-)continuity and sudden change

In the first part of the book different techniques will be described to analyze (differences in) variability, attractors, (dis-)continuity and non-linear and sudden change. We will present the different techniques in Chapter 5. First, we will show how we were able to demonstrate that, following a specific event, sudden change occurred in individual trajectories of aggressive behavior with only four or five measurement points. A complicating factor in that study was that the sudden event concerned a change of schools, which took place at different times for different children in the sample. Second, we describe three techniques that address the question of whether a specific aspect of early language development is a continuous or a discontinuous process. Finally, we discuss how the level of variability can be assessed in a series of emotional reactions, in which the number of emotions and the intensity of each emotion may be different for each data point.

Chapter 6 describes the technique of using state space grids in order to analyze a variety of process characteristics. Grid techniques are especially suited to study the movements of a system through the state space. One can imagine a data set that consists of a sequence of interactions between an adolescent and his parent, where each data point describes the emotional expressions of both the parent and the adolescent. By means of grids one can analyze whether dominant patterns of interactions can be found, whether specific expressions of one partner are followed by specific expressions of the other, which of the partners initiates changes in the interactions, etc. In a more abstract way, grids offer possibilities to study (changes in) variability, the strength of attractors in individuals and the return time, and to compare differences in attractor strength between individuals and changes within individuals. Grid techniques can also be used to analyze differences in variability, such as in the four data series depicted in Figure 3.1.

However, before we start with these techniques in Chapters 5 and 6, Chapter 4 addresses the question of how to assess significance in process data. Describing variability in a set of data is one thing, but to compare this variability in different time periods and decide whether the differences found are significant is still another. In several of the analyses described in Chapter 5, Monte Carlo permutation techniques are used to determine statistical significance. Permutation techniques are very simple methods to determine whether any difference found in empirical research is coincidental or systematic: caused by chance or not. The reason why we discuss them in this book is that they are applicable in irregular, sloppy data sets with all kinds of weird characteristics such as partial dependencies – the same type of data sets that we typically have when we analyze differences in trajectories.

References

Bosma, H. A., & Kunnen, E. S. (2008). Identity-in-context and identity development-in-context are two different things. *Journal of Adolescence, 31,* 281–289.

Lichtwarck-Aschoff, A., Kunnen, E. S., & van Geert, P. L. C. (2009). Here we go again. A dynamic systems perspective on emotional rigidity across parent–adolescent conflicts. *Developmental Psychology, 45,* 1364–1375.

Van der Maas, H. L. J., & Molenaar, P. C. M. (1992). Stagewise cognitive development: An application of catastrophe theory. *Psychological Review, 99,* 395–417.

4 Monte Carlo techniques

Statistical simulation for developmental data[1]

Paul van Geert, Henderien Steenbeek and Saskia Kunnen

Developmental studies often result in data sets that are far from ideal. First, many longitudinal studies are small, unbalanced (it rarely happens that the sample is truly representative), show dependencies, consist of qualitative data, and so forth. Second, the questions that developmental psychologists ask are often difficult to answer by means of the standard statistical techniques. For instance, they want to know whether a longitudinal data set shows a discontinuity or whether the variability of the data has truly changed. Such questions are often avoided, not because they are found to be uninteresting but because they are too difficult to answer. For example, one of our studies addressed the frequency of different types of trajectories in identity development in different domains. We wanted to know whether one specific domain was characterized by a different patterning of trajectory types. This question could not be answered by using conventional statistical techniques. In this chapter we will discuss statistical techniques that are very well suited for dealing with small and unbalanced data sets and for answering the kind of questions that we should ask if we are really focusing on the developmental process. These techniques, known as Monte Carlo methods, random permutations or random sampling techniques, are highly flexible. They can be used to check virtually any test statistic (e.g. not only averages, but also extremes, distributional characteristics, and so forth). They can test explicitly formulated null hypotheses (and in fact force the researcher to be as explicit as possible about the null hypothesis). They can be used in procedures that are conceptually rather complicated, while preventing such procedures becoming too complicated in the statistical or mathematical sense. In several of the following chapters these techniques have been used.

The basic principle of these techniques is that they determine the chances that a result is just accidental. They determine the probability that an observed result is caused by chance alone by simulating that chance – that is, they make a very large number of accidental distributions (e.g. of autonomy scores of 15- and 16-years-olds, under the assumption that the scores come from the same distribution) and simply count the number of times that the observed phenomenon (or an even "stronger" one) occurs in the accidental distributions. In the remainder of the chapter, we will use terms such as permuted, shuffled or resampled, which all refer to these permutation techniques. The application of random permutation methods is not difficult, but it requires some space to explain them. For that reason we have included the next section, which describes how to apply these techniques in a step-by-step way.

Step-by-step application of permutation techniques

For the instructions in this text we use a spreadsheet, in this case Excel. Other spreadsheets may in principle do the job too, but two add-ins are required and these are written especially for Excel. For that reason, you will need Excel to follow the instructions. The two add-ins you need are:

1. Poptools.xla. This add-in can be downloaded from the internet (e.g. from http://www.cse.csiro.au/poptools/index.htm).
2. Paul's functions.xla. This add-in can be downloaded from the website (www.psypress.com/dynamic-systems-approach/appendices). Both add-ins are opened after Excel is opened. Once they are opened, they will each place a new drop-down menu on the menu bar: Poptools and functions.

Basic techniques

Statistical simulation techniques largely use two different principles of randomization. The first is based on the notion of a finite set, for instance a set of 20 scores on a measure of autonomy in adolescents (obtained from 20 subjects). Let us assume that this set is divided into two, with 12 observations for the 15-year-olds and 8 for the 16-year-olds. We want to know whether there is a significant difference between both age groups. The technique will then calculate all possible re-orderings of the 20 scores over a group of 12 and a group of 8 (or approximate all possible re-orderings by calculating a great many of such distributions). This is the principle of *permutation* or *random permutation*. It is also known as random drawing from a sample without replacement. It is done in Excel/Poptools by means of the *Reshuffle* function.

The second principle of randomization draws all possible (or an approximation of all possible) samples from a given distribution that in principle contains an infinite number of members. This is the *resampling* principle. Such a distribution can be represented by a finite sample, such as the 20 scores from our example. If we draw randomly from that sample with replacement of the randomly drawn cases, we act as if the distribution has an infinite number of members (it is never exhausted, because we take only a "copy" of the case that we have drawn, so to speak). We can randomly draw cases from a finite sample with replacement by means of the Excel/Poptools formula *Resample*. This distribution can be represented by a finite sample and also by an equation that describes the form of that distribution. For instance, we can specify an equation for a normal distribution with a given mean and standard deviation. We can randomly draw a case from this distribution by just using its mathematical properties. This procedure is carried out by means of formulas for a host of random distribution forms contained in Excel/Poptools.

Working with the basic techniques

Open the program Excel (version 97, 2000 or later versions). Create a new file and call it "resampling". Enter +1 in cell B1, +2 in B2, ... until +6 in B6. Now you have a column with the numbers 1 to 6. As an exercise, we will reshuffle this neat row.

Permutation principle

Select a range as big as the range you want to shuffle (randomly permute). In this example it is a column of six cells, for example C1 to C6. Type *=shuffle (*and "select the data range that needs to be shuffled (i.e. B1 to B6) and close with a final bracket)". Finalize the equation with *Ctrl + Shft + Enter*, which is the procedure for entering an array formula. The shuffle formula is an example of an array formula. Click *F9* several times and observe the nature of the changes. You will see that the numbers in array C1–C6 are randomly shuffled following each click. In the Excel file "demo chapter 4 resample.xls" on the website you will find this in *tab demo 1*.[1]

Resampling principle

Select a range as big as the range you want to resample; in our example select D1 to D6. Type *=resample* (and select the data range that needs to be resampled (B1 to B6) and close with a final bracket")". Finalize the equation with *Ctrl + Shft + Enter*. The resample formula is also an example of an array formula. It can also be entered as a normal formula, by just clicking Enter. In that case, the formula will appear in one cell only and then needs to be copied to other cells. Try this by entering the equation =resample(B$1:B$6) in cell E1. Then, copy E1 to E2 to E6. Click F9 several times and observe the nature of the changes in the columns C1 –C6, D1–D6 and E1–E6.

When you compare the changes in C1–C6 with D1–D6, you will see that following each recalculation (F9) in C1–C6 each number appears once, while in D1–D6 some numbers may appear more than once and others are absent. This is the consequence of the difference between reshuffling (without replacement) and resampling (with replacement).

In general, we recommend that you first give a name to the range of data that you will reshuffle or resample. Select the data set, then click on the Name Box and type a name, for instance *data1*, and then close with Enter (Figure 4.1). You can now write down your resample equation by simply typing *=resample(data1)* and clicking Enter. This equation can be copied and pasted without changing the reference to the original data range. In the Excel file on the website we have demonstrated this in the range G1:G6 (contains data1) and H1:H6 (resampling of data1).

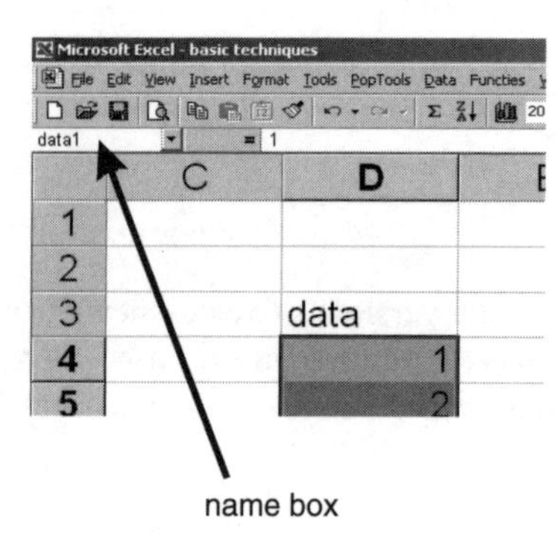

Figure 4.1 Screen print showing how to give a name to a range.

A simple example: Comparing means

Theory

One of the most common tasks for statistical testing is to determine the chance that a difference between groups, for instance a difference in the average scores of two groups, is just a matter of chance. A standard method is to use a *t*-test. However, the same thing can be accomplished by means of a random permutation procedure. This will lead to (an approximation of) the exact *p* value, that is, the probability that the observed difference is due to chance, based on the properties of the sample itself. A major advantage of this technique is that even if the sample is very small, skewed or extremely unbalanced (contains a number of outliers), the resulting *p* value will very closely approach the exact *p* value and will thus be reliable, irrespective of the strangeness of the sample. The technique can also be used with sets of (partly) dependent data. Another major advantage of the permutation technique is that it is not limited to testing the probability that a difference in averages is statistically significant (or, to put it differently, due to chance). For instance, we might be interested in the question of whether the differences in the standard deviations in two samples are due to chance, or we might want to know whether the occurrence of a relatively high number of extreme scores in one sample and not in the other is due to chance. In order to answer these questions, we do not have to make any assumption about the "true" underlying distribution (which we do not know anyway).

Application

Open a new file and call it "Compare samples". We want to compare the test scores of two groups of children, say of boys and of girls. Enter the scores from Table 4.1 into columns B and C of the spreadsheet: with the labels "Boys" in B1 and "Girls" in C1. As you will see, we have missing data: one of the girls was ill during the test. From these data we want to know two things: whether boys and girls differ

Table 4.1 Scores for boys and girls

Boys	*Girls*
1	4
14	9
3	5
2	3
5	9
12	8
11	1
2	4
5	9
4	8
11	7
4	
7	9
15	8

significantly from each other, and whether boys have extreme scores (defined as "higher than 10") significantly more often.

Testing the significance of differences in average scores

Are the differences between boys and girls statistically significant (i.e. what is the probability that such differences arose randomly)? Randomly means that the two groups do not have different scores. Of course there are individual differences among the children, but they are not related to their sex (that is the null hypothesis). Another way of describing this null hypothesis is to think about the data as *labeled numbers*. Thus, the numbers in the column under boys carry the label *boy*, those under girls have the label *average*, and so forth. According to the null hypothesis, the assignment of a label to a number is completely arbitrary. Any assignment is as good as any other, since the numbers (the percentages positive emotions) are not systematically linked to any of these labels. Any random assignment will produce average scores and differences between these scores. The null hypothesis predicts that many of those differences will be as great as the differences found in the data set, which implies that the differences from the data set cannot be distinguished from differences that are due to chance alone. It is an illusion to think that the observed differences reflect something meaningful about boys or girls. To determine the mean scores of both sexes, type in cell B16 *=average(B2:B15)*, and in cell C16 *=average(C2:C15)*. You will see that the average score of boys is higher: 6.857143 versus 6.461538 for the girls. In cell D16 you type *=B16-C16*. This cell thus shows the difference between the averages of both groups: 0.395604.

We will now test whether the null hypothesis is correct. First, select the entire range of cells from B1 to D16 (this will cover all the relevant data cells and equations). Copy and paste the range to F3. Select the range of copied data from F4 to G17 and delete them. Select the range of the deleted data, type *=shuffle(B2:C15)* and press Ctrl + Shft + Enter. (Ctrl + Shft + Enter is used to define a block of cells as an array.) Press F9 several times and observe the results. The shuffle equation now randomly assigns each number to one of the two columns. Each time you press the F9 button and the shuffle formula reshuffles all the data, you see the averages for this reshuffled set in the cells F18 and G18, and the difference between them in cell H18. Press F9 a thousand times and write down the difference between the averages of boys and girls, then determine how often this difference is the same as or bigger than the empirical difference in cell D16. Or use an automatical procedure that does the same thing.

Open the file *Paul's Functions.xla* (if it is not open yet). This will add an item to your menu bar, named *Functions*. Click on Functions/Monte Carlo Procedure. A pop-up window will appear that looks like Figure 4.2. Click on the barred button of the first input box (to the right of the question "Which values do you want to

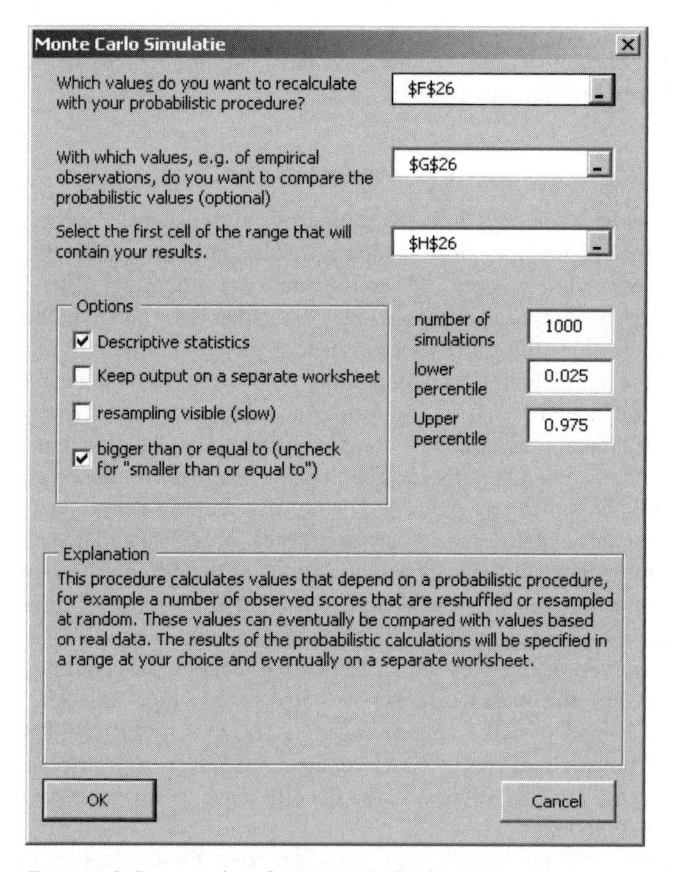

Figure 4.2 Screen print of a Monte Carlo simulation.

recalculate with your probabilistic procedure") and select the cell *H18* (this cell contains the reshuffled difference between boys and girls). Then click on the barred button of the second input box and select the cell *D16* (this cell contains the differences between the *observed* averages of boys and girls). Click on the barred button of the third input box and select cell *J5*. The remaining options can be left unchanged. After pressing the OK button, the program will do the reshuffle for you a thousand times; it will calculate the 2.5 percentile value of the simulated differences and the 97.5 percentile value. These values will specify the 95% interval for the differences between averages in positive emotions, based on the null hypothesis. The "bigger than" checkbox will count the number of times the differences in averages found on the basis of chance are *as big as or bigger than* those from the real data set.

After a while, the program will print out a range of numbers over two columns. The first column contains the names of the statistical criteria that were calculated. The second column contains the results for the test statistic, which is the difference between the boys and the girls. Look at the row with the title "P-value". This gives you the number of times the simulated differences were as big as or bigger than the observed differences, divided by the number of simulations. It should be around .42. Repeat the whole procedure a few times to get a feeling for how strongly the p values can fluctuate over sessions consisting of a thousand runs (for really serious work, 10,000 runs are recommended). In summary, the random permutation procedure shows that the difference between boys and girls is not statistically significant, with $p \approx .42$.

Beyond averages

It appears as if the boys show more extreme scores than girls. For instance, it looks as if the number of scores above 10 is greater in the boys than in the girls. We will first calculate the number of high scores. What is high? Given the distribution of the data, a high percentage is anything higher than 10 (this is just an option; other limits are also possible). How many cases higher than 10 are there in both groups? In order to account for the different number of subjects in each of the groups, we should divide this number by the number of subjects in each group. This can be accomplished by selecting cell B18 and typing *=COUNTIF(B2:B15;">=10")*. This formula will count the number of cases in the range B5:B15 that are bigger than 10. Do the same for the girls by selecting cell C18. In cell D18 type *=B18-C18*. This is the difference in frequency of high scores between boys and girls. Then type *=COUNTIF(C2:C15;">=10")*. Repeat the whole procedure for the reshuffled data (in cells F20:H20). Now repeat the Monte Carlo procedure for these new test statistics (the differences in the amount of extreme scores). You will find a p of around .027. Thus, the boys do have higher scores significantly more often. It is best to try to do this yourself. If you want to check whether you did it OK, or if you get stuck, you can cheat under the tab "boys/girls" in the file "demo chapter 4 resample.xls".[1]

Complex, irregular, dependent data sets

In the example above we might have used a *t*-test to test the difference between boys and girls as well, assuming the distribution of the data is more or less normal. Resampling techniques are especially useful if the data set does not meet the criteria for the common tests, or if the research question cannot be answered by simply comparing group means. In this example we demonstrate how resampling can be used in answering a complex question in a data set that is partly dependent. It is based on our research on identity trajectories. In this research we distinguished between different types of trajectories. For each subject in our sample we classified identity trajectories in six different domains in one of five types. Most subjects had comparable trajectories in five out of six domains plus one incongruent domain – the "outlier". Our research question was whether there are specific domains that are incongruent more frequently. The data set for this computation can be found in the file "resampling demo.xls", under the tab "outliers".[1] The data set consists of a table with, for each subject, a code for each domain: 1 for the outliers, 0 for all other domains. For each domain it is counted how often that domain was the outlier. As can be seen in row 15, most outliers occur in the philosophy of life domain (5). We tested the null hypothesis that our finding was a chance finding in a random distribution and that in fact the philosophy of life domain does not have more outliers than the other domains. We did this by repeatedly shuffling the data per subject. For example, if you place the cursor on call K3 you will see the equation *=shuffle(D3:I3)*. If you press F9 repeatedly you will see that the "1" in each row in the range K3:P14 is in a different position every time. In the row K15:P15 the frequency of outliers is computed. In a Monte Carlo procedure we test how often the simulated number of outliers in the philosophy of life domain (K15) is as high or higher than the empirically found number of outliers in that domain (D15). The Monte Carlo output shows that in about 0.036% of cases the simulated frequency was higher than the empirically found frequency. This means that $p < .05$ and we can reject the null hypothesis that there is no difference in frequency of outliers between the domains.

Applying permutation techniques

In this chapter we have described how to apply permutation techniques. The application itself is really simple. The main task is to formulate what exactly you want to know, what your null hypothesis is and find out how the information you need can be extracted from the data. Often, the analysis will not be done on the scores that are gathered but, for example, on the differences between two data points or on the maxima of a series of data, and so on. In the techniques that are described in the next chapter you will see several examples of the way in which permutation techniques can be used. More information about resampling techniques can be found in Todman and Dugard (2001).

Note

1 A demonstration file for this chapter can be found at www.psypress.com/dynamic-systems-approach/appendices.

Reference

Todman, J. B., & Dugard, P. (2001). *Single-case and small-n experimental designs. A practical guide to randomization tests.* Hove, UK: Lawrence Erlbaum Associates.

5 The search for variability and change[1]

Saskia Kunnen, Marijn van Dijk, Anna Lichtwarck-Aschoff, Marieke Visser and Paul van Geert

In this chapter we describe a variety of techniques that are well suited for analyzing processes and individual trajectories in developmental psychology. As discussed in Chapter 3, characteristics such as variability, sudden change and non-linearity are important in developmental processes. Common statistical techniques in the social sciences are not optimally suited to analyze these characteristics. Many statistical techniques focus on detecting differences in means between groups. Not coincidentally, "Compare means" is one of the main categories in the well-known statistical program SPSS. However, important questions in developmental psychology do not only concern whether (groups of) children differ on average from each other at a given point in time. Relevant questions if we want to understand the process of development concern the shape of the developmental process (e.g. whether language development is a gradual process or whether it shows discontinuities and sudden changes), the effects of a specific event (e.g. effect of school transition on the trend of aggression development) or differences and changes in variability over time and between individuals.

In the physical sciences many techniques exist that focus on the analysis of these questions. However, contrary to physicists, developmental researchers in general do not have reliable and complete data sets with thousands of measurement points. Typically, we have to work with repeated assessments of tests, self-reports, classroom assignments or observations, our data sets often contain less than ten assessment points or have missing values and we have to face loss of subjects over time.

In this chapter we will discuss techniques that focus on the analysis of change in trajectories, on (dis-)continuities and on differences in variability, techniques that are applicable in irregular, incomplete data sets with a relatively small number of subjects and data points. The collection of techniques we describe are by no means exhaustive. They are meant as examples of how typical developmental research questions can be addressed. The three techniques chosen cover different research questions and different types of data sets. First, we describe a technique for analyzing changes in developmental trends. The example concerns classroom aggression ratings in a group of pre- and early adolescents and analysis to determine whether the trends in aggression change after a school transition. The data set consists of only four or five measurement points. Second, we describe techniques that address the question of whether a specific aspect of early language development is a continuous or a discontinuous process. This analysis requires a denser data set but it can be applied on an individual level. The paper in which the study has been published describes the data of four individuals. Although the example concerns early language development in toddlers, the technique can be easily applied to, for example, second language acquisition in adolescents. The third technique described is for analyzing differences in variability in the emotional experience of adolescent girls. This data set is characterized by irregularity in the number of assessments and by qualitative categories that differ per subject.

Searching for change

In this section we will describe a method to analyze whether trajectories change following a specific event. In studying development, a relevant question is whether events affect the course of development. Think for example of the effects of an intervention – the introduction of a new teaching method, parental divorce or a change of school. To answer such a question, a method is needed by which we can assess whether the slope of the trajectory before the event differs from that after the event. This technique compares the slope before and after the event within each child, and huge inter-individual differences in directions and steepness of the slope are not a problem.

We illustrate this technique by means of a study that aims to answer the question of whether trajectories of aggressive behavior in pre- and early adolescents change after a school transfer from special to regular education. The data are from the dissertation research of Visser (2011); see also Visser, Kunnen and van Geert, (2010), who investigated the aggressive behavior of special school children with aggression problems over a period of 2 years (five waves). The data in this example are from 59 children, for whom at least four waves of teachers' observations were available (scores on the Aggressive Behavior Checklist). We considered the impact of change in the classroom environment by studying the behavioral trajectories of children who transferred from special education to regular education. Because the special education classrooms in the study comprised mostly aggressive or at least behaviorally disturbed children, negative peer group effects are more likely to occur within the special classrooms than in classrooms in regular education. We expected that children who transferred from special to regular education would show a decrease in aggressive behavior after they transferred, relative to what would be expected from their individual trajectory in aggressive behavior during the special school period. The aim was to investigate whether the individual trends in aggressive behavior changed when children transferred to a school of regular education as compared to another special school. Thus, we wanted to test whether the trajectory of aggressive behavior, calculated for the period before school transition, changed after a school transition. It is important to note that such trajectories can show considerable individual differences: some children may show a downward change, others an upward change and still others are likely to be constant. Thus, our test focused on the effect of the school transition on the direction and magnitude of the trajectory. For instance, if before the transition to a regular school a child showed an upward trajectory, then we expected to find a *decrease* in the upward trajectory, if not a complete change in the trajectory direction. In a child with a downward trajectory, we expected to find an even stronger downward trajectory than before. These expectations were statistically tested by means of random permutation methods and statistical simulation. In order to check the changes in observed trend before the school transition, we proceeded as follows.

First we determined the linear model of aggressive behavior for each child during the pre-transition period. To test whether the direction changed following the transition, we calculated whether the aggression after transition was lower than what could be expected on the basis of the child's own trend of aggression change. The null hypothesis (see Box 5.1) was that the new environment did not add anything to the trend already initiated, and thus that the data points after transition would organize randomly around the trend line calculated on the basis of the data points before transition. In Figure 5.1 we show an example of how (the signs of) the residuals before and after transition are determined for one child. This was done for each child in the sample, after which the average of the residuals after transition was calculated.

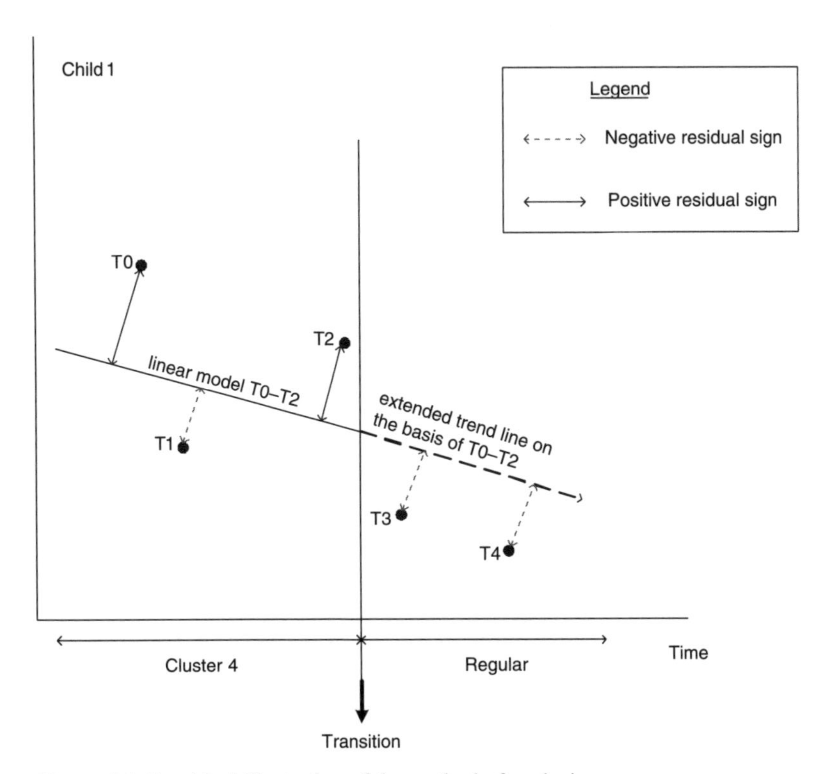

Figure 5.1 Graphical illustration of the method of analysis.

Box 5.1

Null hypothesis: The data points after transition organize randomly around the trend line calculated on the basis of the data points before transition, in other words the trajectory of aggressive behavior does not change after transition to a regular school.

Alternative hypothesis: The data points after transition organize significantly more below the trend line calculated on the basis of the data points before transition compared to the data points before transition, in other words the trajectory of aggressive behavior shows a significant descent after transition.

Under the assumption that there would be an equal chance of positive and negative residuals after transition compared to before, the signs of the residuals before transition were randomly permuted and each time multiplied with the absolute residuals after transition. The average of these residuals was compared with the average of the empirical distribution of residuals (after transition) with the use of random permutation tests. We repeated the analysis with an alternative null hypothesis (see Box 5.1), based on a 50 : 50 distribution of signs (there is an equal chance of a positive or a negative residual sign after school transition). We did this because the empirical distribution of signs before transition is slightly negatively biased. A 50 : 50 distribution gave us a more correct testing of the null hypothesis that the observed scores after the transition have an equal probability of falling above or below the observed trend. The children who transferred to a regular school (*Regulars*) were compared with the children who transferred to another special school (*Changers*).

The central question was: Did the children who transferred to a regular school show a change towards less aggression after their transition, more than would be expected from the individual trajectory that started during the special school period? For the *Regulars*, our statistical tests indicated a systematic decrease in aggression after the school transition relative to the child's expected aggression on the basis of its observed trend line during the special school period (residuals are –25.32, $p = .01$ and .009). The group of *Changers* however did not show a change towards less aggressive behavior relative to the expected levels based on the children's trajectories (average of residuals = –2.68, $p = .46$ for both tests). So we found that a transfer from special to regular education resulted in a decrease in aggressive behavior, whereas a transfer to another special school had no effect on aggression.

Application to other studies and data sets

From our example it is clear that the technique is very flexible because we tested different alternative hypotheses based on the specific distribution of residuals in our sample. The formulation of the right hypothesis is the main challenge in applying this technique. We think that this challenge is actually an advantage because it forces the researcher to formulate exactly what she wants to know and what the data may reveal. With such a flexible technique, there are few restrictions, the main ones being that we need at least four measurement points (given that the target event is in-between the second and third measurement) and at least 40–50 subjects.

Searching for discontinuity

When analyzing individual change over time from a dynamic systems perspective, one relevant question is whether irregularities in an individual trajectory represent fluctuation in a more or less gradual process, or whether they are a sign of a real discontinuity such as a sudden change in the developmental process. In this section we discuss how discontinuity can be found in a time series of data. This section is based on a publication by van Dijk and van Geert (2007), who analyzed time serial language data on the development of preposition use collected from four participants. Their aim was to analyze whether the time series showed a real discontinuity. In this chapter our aim is to clarify the techniques that were used. We focus therefore on the description of the methods, using the data and results only to demonstrate these techniques.

The concept of discontinuity that was adopted in this study was a transition from one variability pattern (range) to a different variability pattern, in the sense that these patterns are separated by a gap. Variability is thus a core concept in this approach, and the testing criteria are designed to be sensitive to changes in variability patterns. The authors aimed to explore whether the empirically found data ranges were produced by a continuous model or a discontinuous model. The smaller the probability that a continuous model (plus random variability) reproduces the data, the less likely it is that the observed differences in the participants are an accidental outcome of an undivided, continuous developmental trajectory.

The first step in these analyses was to formulate null hypotheses, based on various continuous models: a linear model; a quadratic model; a non-linear model with symmetric noise based on Loess smoothing; a non-linear model with moving average smoothing. Each of these models follows the trend in the data in a continuous fashion and variability is considered as noise. Consequently, for each of these models a noise component was estimated by fitting a regression model to the residuals (the differences between the observed values and the values estimated by the continuous curves). The regression model specifies the expected variance of the noise for each point in time, under the assumption that the noise follows a normal distribution. A continuous null hypothesis model can thus be simulated by adding a Gaussian noise component to any point of the estimated continuous curve.

First, these continuous models will be estimated on the basis of characteristics of the observed data. Then, these models are used to simulate data sets. Each of these simulated data sets will therefore, by definition, be produced by the continuous model. If these simulated models are capable of producing the statistical indicators of discontinuity that were observed in the participants, the null hypothesis of underlying continuous development cannot be rejected.

The criteria

The analyses aimed to detect indicators that are likely to occur in the case of discontinuity. The first indicator is the existence of an anomaly in the data at the moment of the discontinuous shift. We expect that such an anomaly can be observed in the form of an unexpectedly large, local peak or "spike" in the data. The peak results from the (presumed) sudden emergence of some new form. In the paper on language development (van Dijk & van Geert, 2007) this concerned the emergence of rules governing the use of spatial prepositions, but of course this could be any newly emerging skill or form. In addition, there is a fair chance that new forms are likely to be abundantly used immediately after their initial discovery (a sort of novelty effect). The second indicator – the membership procedure – is based on the assumption that the discontinuity corresponds to the fact that the data consist of two discontinuous sets of scores, expressed in terms of degree of membership to a set.

Criterion 1: The peak model[2]

With this criterion we aim to identify a discontinuous transition if the trajectory shows an unexpectedly large peak, or spike, at some point in time. This peak might reveal the moment at which the system loses its stability and shifts into a different variability pattern. As mentioned earlier, there is a fair chance that the sudden emergence of a new skill or ability is characterized by a (probably short) time of abundant use of that new skill or ability. This transient performance peak, if any occurs, will be added to the sudden shift in the subpatterns described in the previous section, and thus marks the underlying transition even more clearly.

This criterion focuses on the aspect of the "gap" at the moment of the transition, and this gap might be conceptualized as a "sudden change" in the curve.

STATISTICAL PROCEDURE

A peak is defined as the maximal positive difference between an expected and an observed value in the trajectory. Two types were distinguished: an absolute peak and a relative peak. In the case of the absolute peak, variability at a specific point in time is defined as the absolute difference between the observed (or simulated) data point and the expected point, based on the underlying continuous model. This difference is the residual value, which is used to define the absolute peak. In the case of the relative peak, these residuals (for all points in time) are divided by the expected value – the value of the continuous model at the corresponding point in time. We have made the distinction between absolute and relative peaks because the degree of variability is often strongly related to the central tendency in a distribution. As an illustration, assume a trajectory that shows a simple increase from value 1 to value 50. In this example, a residual of 4 is considered to be more salient if it occurs around an observation with value 5 than when it occurs around value 45.

While the absolute peak is strictest and signals unexpected spikes in the data, the relative peak criterion is sensitive to smaller peaks that might be meaningful in the context that they appear in. With "context" we especially refer to the mean level of the variable in a given time frame. It is a well-known fact that variability is related to the general mean. For instance, a data series with a mean of 100 is expected to have a larger range (expressed in terms of standard deviation, SD) than a data series with a mean of 5, therefore it is to be expected that the variability in a data set increases when the mean level increases. In our statistical procedure, we take the peak (the maximal value of either absolute or relative residual) in the data as our key value and test it against the peaks found on the basis of a great many (5000) simulated continuous models, with distribution characteristics similar to those of the data.

Criterion 2: Membership procedure[2]

Previously, we have postulated that if a discontinuity occurs it shows itself in the form of two distinct subpatterns. A discontinuous curve contains a gap between the two stages or phases, however close they are to each other in time. However, time-serial data from developmental studies consist of sets of separate data points – that is, there are gaps everywhere. Does it make sense to apply the gap definition to something where gaps are everywhere? The trick is to consider a set of developmental, time-serial data as a single object, which in this case is the range. Continuity can be defined as set membership, as belonging to the range. Any two data points within the range are, by definition, continuous. Any two data points, one of which lies in the range and one of which lies not in the range, are by definition discontinuous. The set of observed data points is of course just a small subset of all the possible points that could lie within the range. Thus, how do we decide whether a particular, new data point lies in the range or not?

To make this decision we envisage an imaginary magic bug that can jump from any point in the range to any other but cannot do anything else (see Figure 5.2). Thus, the range is in fact defined by the set of possible jumps the magic bug can make, and whatever point lies within the bug's radius of action is a potential member of the range. Let us proceed by adding a new data point to the series, in this case a new measurement of some developing variable. Does this new data point correspond to continuity or a discontinuity? We can ask the bug. If he has a jump in his repertoire that can bring him from anywhere in the range to the new point or beyond, then there is no gap from the bug's point of view between the range and the new point. Thus, the new point is continuous to the range. If the bug has no such jump in his repertoire and thus cannot reach the new data point from somewhere in the range, then there is a gap from the bug's point of view and the new data point is a discontinuity. The magic bug metaphor maps directly onto a mathematical definition of (dis)continuity in ranges defined by sets of data points.

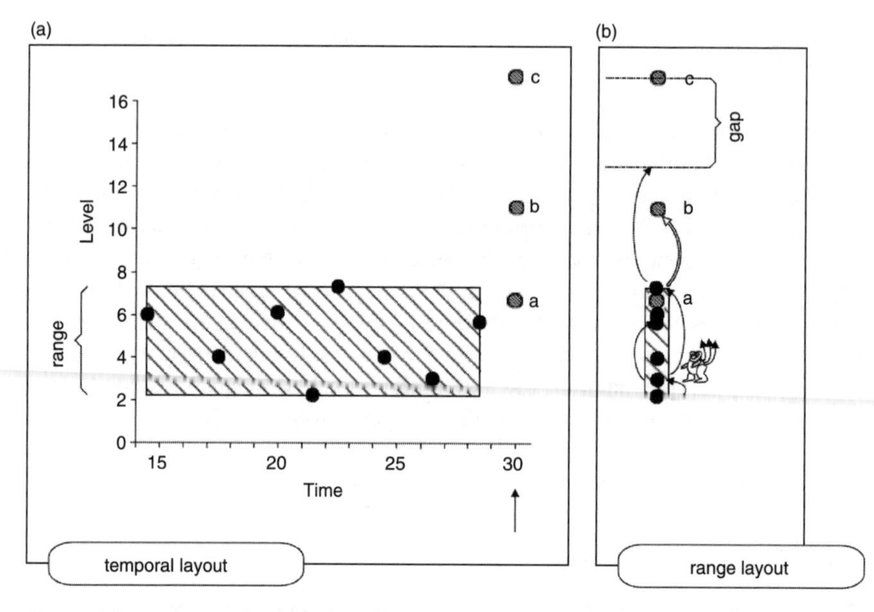

Figure 5.2 A scheme of the jumps that are and are not included in the continuous range as defined by "the magic bug'. (a) The range covered by the hatched rectangle is continuous at time 30: the measurement at time 30 can be "reached' from the range and there is no gap. (b) The hatched ranged is discontinuous at time 30: the measurement at time 30 cannot be "reached' from the range, hence ther is a gap at time 30 (the formal definition of reachability is given in the text).

Central to the argument is the definition of a range of data points by the set of possible "jumps" from one point to another within the range.

Formally speaking, the bug's jumps define a set of data that are within reach of the bug. All data points within reach of the bug are members of the set and have a set or range membership equal to 1. All data points that are within reach of the bug's repertoire of jumps are also members of the set, and those that are not within reach are not members of the set or range. This criterion relates the existence of a gap to the concept of set membership that stems from fuzzy logic (McNeill & Freiberger, 1993). Fuzzy logic rests on the idea that all things are characterized by the degree to which they are members of a class. In modern fuzzy logic, "objects" (observations, objects, properties, etc.) are assigned a degree of membership to a particular category (see Ross, 1995, for a particularly clear technical introduction; a highly accessible introduction is given by Kosko, 1993, 1997; McNeill & Freiberger, 1993; Nguyen & Walker, 1997; von Altrock, 1995). In mutually exhaustive classes, objects have a degree of membership of either 1 or 0. For instance, a particular piece of furniture is either a chair or not a chair (for instance, it is a bench). In fuzzy logic, an object can have any degree of membership between 0 and 1. For instance, the piece of furniture is a chair that looks like a bench – it has a degree of membership of .8 to the category "chair". Maximal ambiguity arises if an object has a degree of membership equal to .5. In this case, the object is 50% part of a category and 50% not. According to the membership criterion, we conceive of the data set as either a single "set" or a series of "sets" (in principle, two). All data values can be assigned a degree of membership to each set. In the simplest case, the case of continuity, the data consist of a single set and thus all values in the data set have a degree of membership of 1 to that set. If the data are truly discontinuous, the data are cut into two consecutive sets if a new data point emerges that is not a member of the set of data points already present (say at time t). A data point belongs either to the first or to the second set, thus a data point has a degree of membership of 1 to the first set and 0 to the second set. Data points can also be somewhere in-between and thus have a degree of membership of, for instance, .5 to the first and .5 to the second set.

STATISTICAL PROCEDURE

Set membership is easy to define. The first step in defining a set S consists of taking an initial set. Let us take the first five data points, ranging from time $t1$ to $t5$). Data points 1, 2, 3, 4 and 5 are members of set S. Now we collect a new data point, data point n, and wish to know if it also belongs to the set. Recall that the magic bug defined set membership by its possible jumps. A possible jump is, for instance, the jump from point 1 to point 3, which is a jump of length 3 – 1. Any member of the set is a possible starting point for the bug. Now take the point in the set with the highest value (name it h) and select the "biggest jump", thus the largest distance between two values in the set (name it max–min).

Since all points that can be reached by the bug are members of the set, the point that lies at distance $h \pm |\text{max–min}|$ is also a member of the set. The degree of membership of (potential) members of the set is defined as follows. If h is the set's maximal value, if |max–min| is the set's greatest distance and if n lies not within reach of $h \pm |\text{max-min}|$, the degree of membership of n to the set S is 0. More precisely, there exists a gap between n on the one hand and the set S on the other hand.

All points that have been assigned to the initial set (1–5) have, by definition, a degree of membership of 1. All points that lie between any two possible members of the set have, by implication, a degree of membership of 1. All other points have a degree of membership that is equal to the likelihood that such points are within reach of the bug (lying within reach refers to the membership by implication: remember that if a is a member and b is a member, a new point n is also a member if it lies between a and b). Thus, the degree of membership of n is defined by the sum of probabilities of all the possible "jumps" for which n lies within reach. Since a jump is defined mathematically as $m1 \pm |m2–m3|$ (for $m1$, $m2$ and $m3$ arbitrarily chosen full members of the set), the degree of membership is defined by the sum of probabilities of such triplets. A practical way of calculating degrees of membership is by randomly sampling triplets of values from a data set S, calculating the resulting $m1 \pm |m2–m3|$ value and repeating that value a great many times. By doing so we can numerically approximate the likelihood of occurrence of any possible value and thus determine its degree of membership to the set.

The set *S* can be specified by taking an initial set (e.g. data points 1–5, ranging from time *t*1 to *t*4), determining if the first data point outside the set (i.e. the point at time *t*5) is a member, adding it to the set if its degree of membership is satisfactory (e.g. > .8 > .95 or whatever seems reasonable) and continuing until we meet a data point whose degree of membership is smaller than some pre-established value (in this case .05). This data point defines a discontinuity in the data.

Illustrations

In order to get an impression of the results generated by this type of analysis we describe the data for Lisa, one of the four subjects in the study. Lisa is the subject with the clearest indications of a discontinuous trajectory (see Figure 5.3).

On the basis of visual inspection, a first major peak in the trajectory was chosen. Using this representation, the participant shows her first major "jump" at point zero on the x-axis. The other numbers on the axis represent the number of days between the other observations and this point zero. Solely on the basis of visual inspection, trajectories of this participant (and the others in the study as well) may be described in terms of two distinct phases: an initial phase in which there are only a restricted number of prepositions-in contexts; and a more advanced phase in which prepositions are used in many different contexts but the usage is highly variable, depending on context.

Results for the peak criterion

Table 5.1 shows that most of the positions of the discontinuity estimated with both the relative and the absolute peak methods correspond with those based on visual

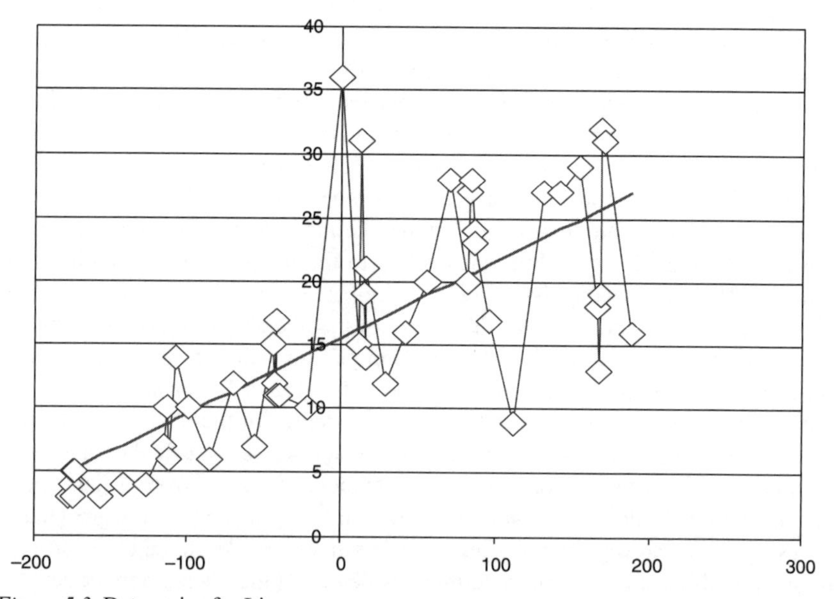

Figure 5.3 Data series for Lisa.

Table 5.1 *p* Values of the peak method for Lisa, based on 5000 simulations

Peaks	p *Values of peak method for Lisa*				
	Estimated position	*Linear model*	*Quadratic model*	*Symmetric residuals model, Loess*	*Symmetric residuals model, moving average*
Relative	0	.004	.04	.09	.36
Absolute	0	.23	.17	.01	.05

inspection. More importantly, the analysis reveals that the peak criterion is less robust or consistent than the subpattern criterion. Using the relative peak as a criterion, peaks greater than expected on the basis of the continuous model occur with Lisa's data but only for the linear and quadratic continuous models. Using the absolute peak as a criterion, greater than expected peaks occur ($p<.05$). For further illustration, see Part 2 of the appendix on the website.

Results for the membership procedure

Figure 5.4 shows a sharp drop in the degree of membership with the initial data set. Such a drop is a strong indication for a discontinuity at that point in time. The degree of membership fluctuates dramatically between 0 and 1 after point 0. This means that after the values that are discontinuous, values occur that are continuous with the initial set. This points to a combined model (continuous and discontinuous) in which certain values belong (and others do not belong) to the initial set. The existence of a fluctuation between an original level or range and a new, more advanced level or range is comparable to the flag of "bimodality" in the catastrophe model. To test the likelihood of a sharp drop in membership against the null hypotheses we have discussed earlier, we must run similar randomization tests to

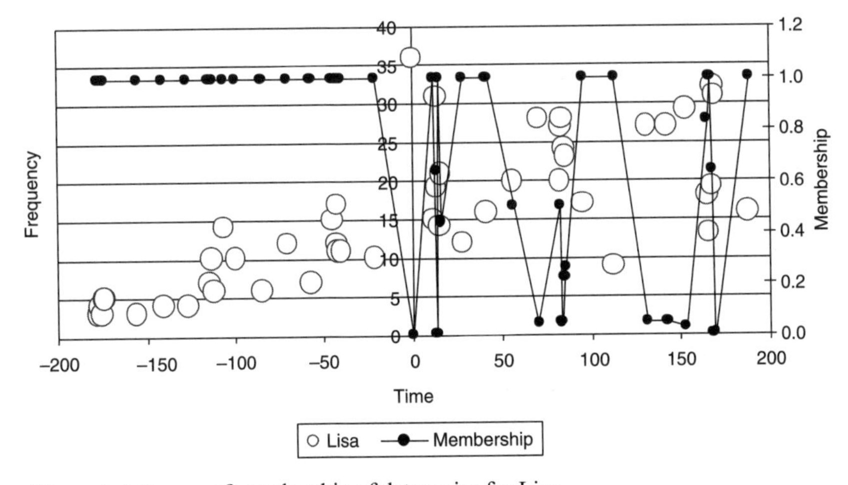

Figure 5.4 Degree of membership of data series for Lisa.

Table 5.2 *p* Values of the membership method for Lisa

p *Values of membership method for Lisa*			
Linear model	*Quadratic model*	*Symmetric residuals model, Loess*	*Symmetric residuals model, moving average*
.06	.04 .	07	.09

those in the preceding sections. The results of these tests are presented in Table 5.2, which shows one *p* value below .05 and thus that this procedure produced only one significant result.

Application to other studies and data sets

In this section we have presented procedures that can be used to test for the presence of a discontinuity in time serial data. Compared to the other techniques discussed in this chapter, these are the most rigid and the most critical. They are the most rigid in that they are meant to answer one specific question: Is there discontinuity or not? They are the most critical in that they need a time series of data that consists of at least 40 measurement points. Nevertheless, one can think of a broad range of topics, also in adolescent research, in which this technique could be very useful. One could think of the learning of skills and abilities that require a kind of insight and for that reason can be assumed to show a discontinuous learning curve, or one could hypothesize sudden effects of specific events (e.g. new reward and punishment regimes, or transitions to another school). Collecting many data points is often not as difficult as it seems because, for example, skills can be assessed not only by means of extensive tests but also by continuous success and failure registration in the performances during the learning process. Short reports or beeper techniques (Larson and Csikszentmihalyi, 1983) that can be gathered daily or even more frequently generate long series of data points in a rather easy way. Even identity can be assessed on a daily basis by means of one short question (Klimstra, Luyckx, Hale, Frijns and van Lier, 2010). As the example study shows, one does not need large groups. In fact, the technique can be used in a case study, and relevant conclusions can be based on only one subject. Commonly three or four subjects are used in such a study, because this gives a first impression of the possible generalization of the findings.

The question of which criterion is "the best" depends on the specific question of the researcher and the data at hand. The peak criterion is simpler, but more restricted, because it focuses specifically on variability, whereas the membership procedure can be applied in a broad range of research topics. The methods presented here are certainly not exhaustive. The aim was not to provide a full overview of all possibilities, but primarily to serve as an inspiration for researchers to adjust the procedures and develop their own to fit the specific details of their own data.

Searching for variability

In this section we describe a technique that can be used to detect variability in data sets that consist of irregular data. With irregular data we mean that the subjects and/or the data points differ in the type and in the number of characteristics. This is often the case in observation studies, where the kind and the number of observed categories may differ for each time point, and in (repeated) self-report, where subjects describe themselves in terms of a not predefined set of characteristics. The data set we use to illustrate this technique consists of a longitudinal series of reported emotions following a conflict (Lichtwarck-Aschoff, Kunnen and van Geert, 2009). The subjects differed with regard to the kind and the number of emotions they reported, and the subjects reported different kinds and numbers of emotions in subsequent conflicts. Our aim was to compare the subjects with regard to their emotional variability. In this longitudinal study of mother–daughter interactions, the hypothesis was that girls with high numbers of conflict with their mother would have lower levels of emotional variability (i.e. they would show less variation in the emotions they felt during the conflicts). The underlying idea of this hypothesis is that dyads with a lot of conflicts are stuck in a certain conflict pattern and therefore more often feel the same in response to a conflict. In this section we focus on the techniques that were used to assess the intra-individual variability in emotional states during the conflicts.

The data consisted of the girls' diary reports on these emotional states. The girls reported on their naturally occurring conflicts during each of six 2-week episodes. The consequence of this design is that the number of conflicts and thus data points is different for each girl. The girls were provided with an exhaustive list of 14 different emotions (angry, frustrated, disappointed, ashamed, afraid, guilty, sad, lonely, hurt, regret, hopeful, relieved, happy and proud). Additionally, they were allowed to add emotions if the list did not represent their feelings. Feeling "misunderstood" and "not taken seriously" emerged out of these open entries. For each conflict episode, the girls indicated which of these emotions they had experienced during the conflict.

In order to determine the intra-individual variability in emotional states three different measures were used, based on the idea of symbol dynamics (Daw, Finney and Tracy, 2003; for a comparable approach see the Karnaugh maps in Dumas, Lemay and Dauwalder, 2001). The basic rationale underlying this approach is transformation of the system's trajectory or geographical movement in time into a sequence of specific symbols corresponding to partitions within the state space (Dale and Spivey, 2005). First, we computed the emotional state space for each girl, containing all reported emotions across all her conflict episodes. Every state within the space represents how a girl felt during a particular conflict (see Table 5.3).

The girls could choose as many emotions as they wanted to describe how they felt during the conflict. This means that we have to deal with multiple emotions that describe an emotional state during the conflict (which makes it different from the state space grids described by Hollenstein in the next chapter). In our calculation, an emotional state can therefore take the form of a single emotion or

Table 5.3 Example calculation of the emotional codes and the sequential Hamming distance

	How did you feel during conflict?					
Conflict episode	*Angry*	*Sad*	*Hurt*	*Afraid*	*Code*	*Sequential Hamming distance*
1	1	0	0	0	A	–
2	0	1	1	1	B	4
3	1	0	0	0	A	4
4	1	0	1	0	C	1
5	1	0	1	0	C	0
6	0	0	1	0	D	1

Note: This example of emotion data entry is based on six conflict episodes and four emotions. The last two columns indicate the code for the emotional state (e.g. A stands for anger alone, B stands for sad, hurt and afraid) and the sequential Hamming distance between the preceding states.

a combination of different emotions – that is, every emotional state is represented by a set of emotions present (1) or absent (0) in the string that represents the emotional state. The mathematical representation of every state consists of a particular string of "1"s and "0"s. We computed the emotional space for every girl and counted the number of different states. States with exactly the same emotion or pattern of emotions were given the same nominal code, and states with different emotions or combinations thereof were given different codes (the codes are denoted by letters; see Table 5.3). The emotional variability was defined as the number of different emotional states.

The second and third measures were based on the Hamming distance (Hamming, 1950; Teşileanu and Meyer-Ortmanns, 2006). The Hamming distance is used to calculate the distance (absolute difference) between two symbolic strings, which in our study is two emotional states. The distance between the emotional states indicates by how much the emotional states differ from each other and in this sense represents the variation between the states (compare this with the intergrid distance used by Lewis, Lamey and Douglas, 1999). We computed two forms of the Hamming distance. The first one, called the *sequential* Hamming distance (see Table 5.3), indicates the distance between the preceding states – the distance between emotional state at time t and at $t + 1$. Thus, this measure indicates by how much a girl varies from one conflict to the next. The second one, which we call the *overall* Hamming distance (see Table 5.4), specifies the distance between all pairs of states that are different, regardless of the time order.

This measure represents an overall value of the emotional variability because it describes by how much all the existing states differ from each other. The calculation in both cases is based on the same principle and is as follows: If two emotional states contain exactly the same emotions, the Hamming distance is zero; for each emotion that is different (absent or present compared to another or preceding state) the Hamming distance is raised by one (see Table 5.3 for the sequential Hamming distance and Table 5.4 for the overall Hamming distance). In the case of the sequential Hamming distance the preceding states are compared and for the overall

Table 5.4 Example calculation of the overall Hamming distance

Difference between states	*Overall Hamming distance*
A – B	4
A – C	1
A – D	2
B – C	4
B – D	2
C – D	1

Note: This example is based on the data of Table 5.3. The overall Hamming distance neglects the time order by computing the difference between all pairs of states that are different.

Hamming distance the differences between all pairs of different states are computed. The resulting Hamming distance represents the sum of the absolute differences. As one can see in Tables 5.3 and 5.4, the values of the overall Hamming distance, are higher than the values of the sequential Hamming distance. Nevertheless, in both cases the lower the value of the Hamming distance, the more similar the states are and the smaller the emotional variability.

The number of emotional states as well as both Hamming distances were used as measures for the intra-individual emotional variability. In order to explore the link between the emotional variability measures and the number of conflicts, we used the Curve procedure of the statistical program SPSS (version 14). Two models – a linear model and a quadratic model – were fitted to the data. We want to emphasize that the curve-fitting procedure used here is different from general growth modeling approaches (e.g. latent growth curve analysis). The data that we use to fit the linear and quadratic curves are inter-individual difference measures that represent the degree of intra-individual variability (i.e. the data are aggregated across each individual's conflict episodes). Thus, we fit a model that describes the relation between the number of conflicts and the emotional variability on a group level, and not a model of individual development. Based on a comparison of the explained variances, the model that best describes the data was chosen. Table 5.5 shows the means and standard deviations of the three emotional variability measures and Table 5.6 gives the results for the linear and quadratic models.

As one can see in Table 5.6, for all three emotional variability measures the quadratic relationship fits the data much better than the linear relationship. The variance explained by the linear model for the overall Hamming distance is considerably higher compared to the other two emotional variability measures but

Table 5.5 Means and standard deviations of the three emotional variability measures

	Mean	*Standard diviation*
Number of different emotional states	5.47	2.37
Sum of sequential Hamming distances	16.82	8.30
Sum of overall Hamming distances	77.82	51.88

Table 5.6 Comparison between a linear model and a quadratic model for the relationship between the emotional variability measures and the number of conflicts

	Linear model		*Quadratic model*	
	F	R^2	*F*	R^2
Number of different emotional states	0.52 (1, 15)	.03	9.38 (2, 14)	.57**
Sum of sequential Hamming distances	0.64 (1, 15)	.04	8.27 (2, 14)	.54**
Sum of overall Hamming distances	10.44 (1, 15)	.41*	13.11 (2, 14)	.65**

Note: Statistically significant values: $^{*}P < .05$; $^{**}P < .01$.

still below the level of explained variance of the quadratic model. All three measures of the intra-individual variability in emotional states showed a reversed U-shaped relationship with the number of conflicts (see Figure 5.5).

A valid objection could be made with regard to the size of the emotional space that we used in this study. The defined space contains many different state terms (i.e. different emotions) that are probably not evenly distributed across the state space (i.e. some emotions are closer to each other than others), therefore one might wonder whether the variability measures are inflated by differences between emotional states that are actually nearly synonymous. In order to check for this we collapsed the 16 emotional entries into seven relatively broad emotional categories (anger, negative internal emotions, fear, shame, guilt, feeling misunderstood and positive emotions). Based on this collapsed data set we again calculated the three emotional variability measures. First, these new collapsed emotional variability measures were strongly correlated with the original variability measures (Pearson correlations ranging from .89 to .93). Next, we looked at the relationship between the collapsed emotional variability measures and the number of conflicts. The results were highly comparable with the results described above, with all three measures again showing the reversed U-shaped relationship. Hence, the variability measures were not inflated by the high number of emotions or different distances between the emotions and the results could be confirmed with a collapsed data set. Thus, using the techniques discussed in this section we were able to assess differences in variability in a sequence of self-reported emotions (highly irregular within and between subjects) and to demonstrate that the amount of variability was related to other variables (e.g. the number of mother–daughter conflicts).

Application to other studies and data sets

The techniques used in the search for variability were especially designed to cope with an extremely irregular data set. The main challenge was that each emotional state could be entirely different with regard to both the number and the type of emotions; moreover, the number of data points also differed between the subjects. Such irregular data are common in longitudinal studies that use observations, free reports, diaries and self-description where the respondents are not restricted in their way of reporting. Because each study and data set is different, it is not that

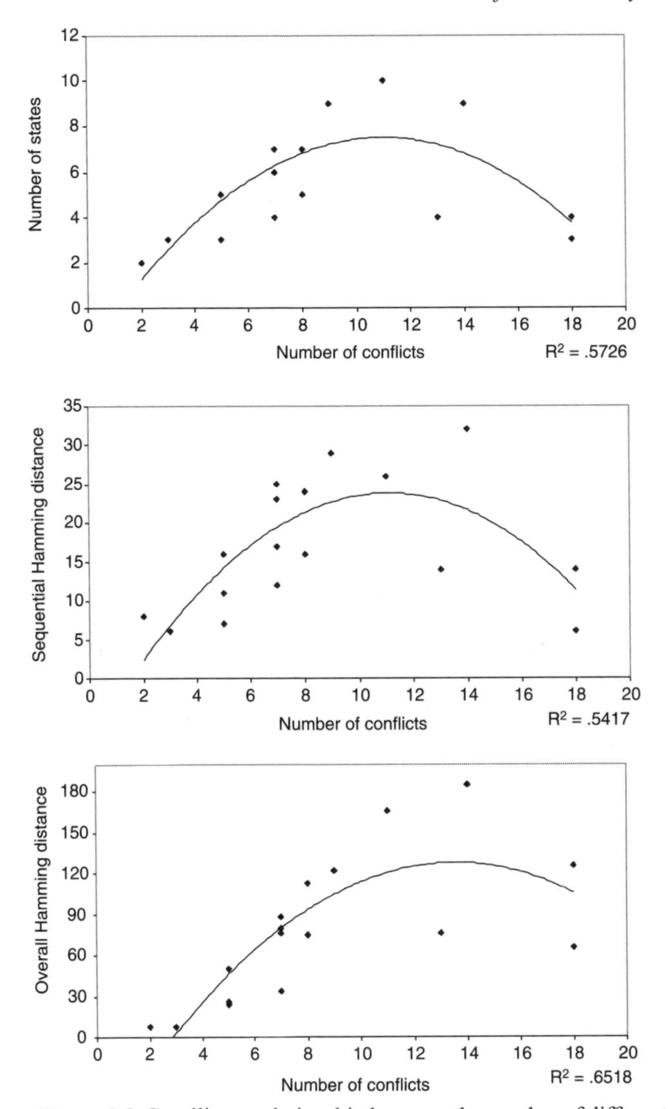

Figure 5.5 Curvilinear relationship between the number of different emotional states, the sequential Hamming distance and the overall Hamming distance and the number of conflicts.

easy to apply the technique described here to another study. However, several steps in the approach can be distinguished that can be translated easily. The most important step concerns the translation of the relevant aspects of the actual data to a more formal level. In this study, we recoded all kinds of different data into a simple set that just described whether a data point was the same or different from the previous one. In this form, the technique can be used for analysing variability in all kinds of data sets. Of course, depending on the data and the research question, operationalization of "the same" and "not the same" can vary. In this study "the same" means "all elements are the same", but another definition could be "at least two common elements". Also, one could define "not the same" as "no common element". But the translation of the data points in a binary system (or a system with three or four conditions) offers still more possibilities. Instead of "the same" versus "not the same" other characteristics can be used. For example, in a study that focuses on increase in complexity, the criterion could be whether each new data point is more complex than the previous one or not, with codes for "more complex" and "the same or less complex" as compared to the previous data point. This formal translation of data requires thorough theoretical thinking because there is a huge loss of detail. Thus, one has to define specifically what one really wants to know and what formal information one wants to extract from the data.

Conclusion

In summary, the techniques described in this chapter are practical and useful examples of techniques that can provide us with knowledge about changes that can be acquired with other methods only if we have very large and reliable data sets, which we generally do not have in the social sciences. The application of such techniques does not demand high levels of technical, mathematical and statistical knowledge. Instead, they demand a thorough theoretical thinking of what one's study is exactly about, what one's hypotheses are and a creative way of thinking in how one's data can be analyzed in order to answer these theoretical questions.

Notes

1 Two demonstration files and one appendix for this chapter can be found at www.psypress.com/dynamic-systems-approach/appendices.
2 The complete technical description of this technique can be found in the "appendix chapter 5 searching for discontinuity.doc", on the website www.psypress.com/dynamic-systems-approach/appendices.

References

Dale, R., & Spivey, M. J. (2005). From apples and oranges to symbolic dynamics: A framework for conciliating notions of cognitive representation. *Journal of Experimental and Theoretical Artificial Intelligence, 17,* 317–342.

Daw, C. S., Finney, C. E. A., & Tracy, E. R. (2003). A review of symbolic analysis of experimental data. *Review of Scientific Instruments, 74,* 915.

Dumas, J. E., Lemay, P., & Dauwalder, J. P. (2001). Dynamic analyses of mother–child interactions in functional and dysfunctional dyads: A synergetic approach. *Journal of Abnormal Child Psychology, 29,* 317.

Hamming, R. W. (1950). Error detecting and error correcting codes. *Bell Systems Technical Journal, 25,* 147–160.

Klimstra, T. A., Luyckx, K., Hale, W. W., Frijns, T., & van Lier, P. A. C. (2010). Short-term fluctuations in identity: Introducing a micro-level approach to identity formation. *Journal of Personality and Social Psychology, 99,* 91–202.

Kosko, B. (1993). *Fuzzy thinking: The new science of fuzzy logic.* New York: Hyperion.

Kosko, B. (1997). *Fuzzy engineering.* Upper Saddle River, NJ: Prentice-Hall.

Larson, R., & Csikszentmihalyi, M. (1983). The experience sampling method. *New Directions for Methodology of Social and Behavioral Science, 15,* 41–56.

Lewis, M. D., Lamey, A. V., & Douglas, L. (1999). A new dynamic systems method for the analysis of early socioemotional development. *Developmental Science, 2,* 457.

Lichtwarck-Aschoff, A., Kunnen, E. S., & van Geert, P. L. C. (2009). Here we go again. A dynamic systems perspective on emotional rigidity across parent–adolescent conflicts. *Developmental Psychology, 45,* 1364–1375.

McNeill, D., & Freiberger, P. (1993). *Fuzzy logic.* New York: Simon & Schuster.

Nguyen, H. T., & Walker, E. A. (1997). *A first course in fuzzy logic.* Boca Raton, FL: CRC Press.

Ross, T. J. (1995). *Fuzzy logic with engineering applications.* New York: McGraw-Hill.

Teşileanu, T., & Meyer-Ortmanns, H. (2006). Competition of languages and their Hamming distance. *International Journal of Modern Physics C: Computational Physics and Physical Computation, 17,* 259–278.

Van Dijk, M. W. G., & van Geert, P. L. C. (2007). Wobbles, humps and sudden jumps: A case study of continuity, discontinuity and variability in early language development. *Infant and Child Development, 16,* 7–33.

Visser, M. (2011) The tip of the iceberg and beyond. Doctoral dissertation, University of Groninge, The Netherlands.

Visser, M., Kunnen, E. S., & van Geert, P. L. C. (2010). The impact of context on the development of aggressive behavior in special elementary school children. *Mind, Brain and Education, 4,* 34–43.

Von Altrock, C. (1995). *Fuzzy logic and neurofuzzy applications explained.* Upper Saddle River, NJ: Prentice-Hall.

6 Using state space grids for understanding processes of change and stability in adolescence[1]

Tom Hollenstein

Adolescents are often characterized by what appear to be mutually exclusive characteristics. On the one hand, they are seen as intransigent, fixated on some aspects of their experience (e.g. peers) at the expense of others (e.g., parents) or easily stuck in emotional states (e.g. Lichtwarck-Aschoff, Kunnen and van Geert, 2009). On the other hand, adolescents are also described as fickle, in flux, unpredictable, disorganized or emotionally labile (e.g. Larson, Moneta, Richards and Wilson, 2002). The usual focus on only one of these two aspects of adolescent behavior without the other is therefore incomplete. From a dynamic systems perspective, however, these characteristics are consistent with a system undergoing a phase transition (Granic, Hollenstein, Dishion and Patterson, 2003; Hollenstein, 2007; Hollenstein and Lewis, 2006). In this chapter, a graphical and quantitative dynamic systems technique – state space grids – will be described as a way to better understand the dynamics of adolescence. After describing the method, examples of how adolescence can be better understood through state space grid analyses will be provided at several time scales: micro (moment-to-moment), meso (context-to-context and day-to-day) and macro (developmental time scale of months to years). The appendix (on the website[1]) contains details of how to prepare and use the state space grid technique with the software program GridWare (Lamey, Hollenstein, Lewis and Granic, 2004).

State space grids

Based on the abstractions of state space and attractors, Lewis, Lamey and Douglas (1999) developed state space grids (SSGs), a graphical approach that utilizes ordinal data and quantifies these data according to two dimensions that define the state space for the system. This technique was first used for analyzing two dimensions for one individual (Lewis et al., 1999; Lewis, Zimmerman, Hollenstein and Lamey, 2004) but was adapted to study dyadic behavior, specifically observable affect in parent–child interactions (Granic and Lamey, 2002; Granic et al., 2003; Granic, O'Hara, Pepler and Lewis, 2007; Hollenstein, 2007; Hollenstein, Granic, Stoolmiller and Snyder, 2004; Hollenstein & Lewis, 2006). Recent adaptations have explored other two-dimensional state spaces, such as left–right versus up–down eye gaze direction (McCarthy, Hollenstein, Muir and Lee, 2007), ventral versus dorsal EEG activation during children's processing of emotion faces (Todd, Hollenstein and Lewis, 2009) and preschooler versus peer group interactions (Martin, Fabes, Hanish and Hollenstein, 2005). Current work is being done to combine state space dimensions of psychophysiology (e.g. heart rate, galvanic skin response), self-reported emotional states and observed self-conscious affect to examine the real-time concordance of these aspects of the emotion system (Hollenstein, Lanteigne, Glozman, Flynn and Mackey, submitted). Thus, defining the state space of a system as the intersection of two or more dimensions is at the discretion of the researcher based on theory, the research question, time scale and measurement constraints (Hollenstein, 2007).

With the SSG method, the system's behavioral trajectory (i.e. the sequence of behavioral states) is plotted as it proceeds in time on a grid representing all possible behavioral combinations. Each cell of the grid represents the simultaneous intersection of the categories within each dimension or axis, much like a temporal scatter plot. For dyadic parent–adolescent systems, for example, the parent's behavioral categories (e.g. negative, neutral, positive affect) may form the x-axis and the same behavioral categories from the adolescent form the y-axis. Any time there is a change in either person's behavior a new point is plotted in the cell representing that joint behavior and a line is drawn connecting the new point and the previous point. Thus, the grid represents a sequence of dyadic events. For example, a hypothetical trajectory representing 15 seconds of parent–adolescent behavior is presented in Figure 6.1. The state space is formed by the intersection of an ordinal set of affect categories for both parent and adolescent: High negative

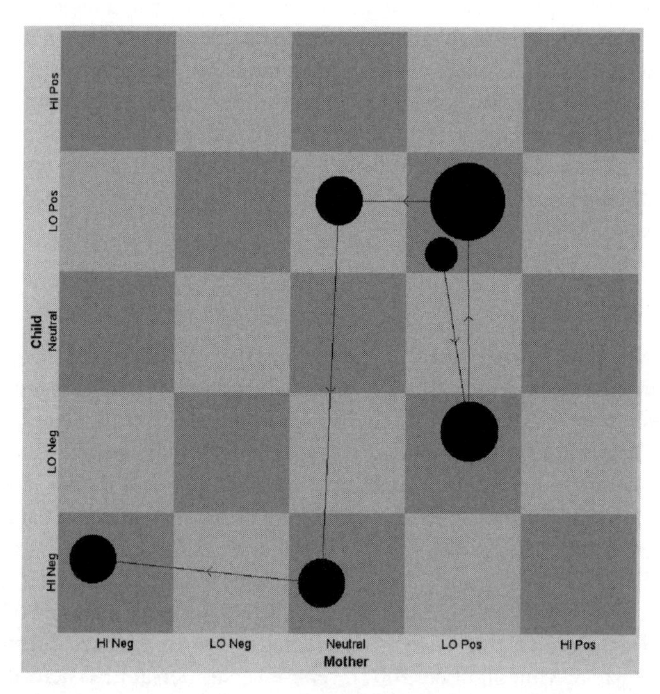

Figure 6.1 Hypothetical state space grid depicting 15 seconds of parent–adolescent affect.

(HI Neg), low negative (LO Neg), Neutral, Low positive (LO Pos) and High positive (HI Pos). The size of the plot point corresponds to the duration of each dyadic behavior. The sequence depicted begins in the mutually LO Pos cell followed by 3 seconds in the Mother LO Pos/Adolescent LO Neg cell, 4 seconds in the mutually LO Pos cell again, 2 seconds in the Mother Neutral/Adolescent LO Pos cell, 2 seconds in the Mother Neutral/Adolescent HI Neg cell and finally 2 seconds in the mutual HI Neg cell.

Using the SSG software GridWare (Lamey et al., 2004), measures can then be derived from SSGs that index the content and structure of the system behavior (for a description of how to use this program, see the appendix on the website). In dynamic systems terms, these content and structure values would correspond to attractors/repellors and patterns of variability, respectively. For example, a dyad that got "stuck" in a state of mutual negativity (i.e. conflict) would have high duration values in the HI Neg/HI Neg cell (see Figure 6.1). Moreover, if mutual negativity was an attractor, the trajectory would return to that cell more quickly and frequently. Thus, high durations and short return times are useful measures of attractors. Because any measurement period is necessarily a brief snapshot of an ongoing dynamic, these indices of attractors are not as precise as those based on longer time series or those derived from more formal mathematical calculations (see Hollenstein, 2007, for a discussion of attractor detection). However, the pattern of the trajectory in a state space does reflect the underlying attractors and repellors of the system. A state space with very few and/or deep attractors would have trajectories with very limited ranges and few changes from state to state. Conversely, a system with many and/or shallow attractors would give rise to trajectories that cover more of the state space and change states more frequently. In this way, the structural properties of a trajectory within the state space (e.g. number of cells visited, number of transitions) will be consistent with the structure of the system itself – that is, in contrast to the conventional idea that variability is the result of error that should be minimized or controlled, SSG variability is an informative signal and not just noise (Granic and Hollenstein, 2006; Thelen and Ulrich, 1991; van Geert & van Dijk, 2002).

Any exploration of dynamics is necessarily an examination of changes over time, thus the time scale of SSG analysis is a critical factor. Neural processes occur on the scale of milliseconds and life-span development occurs over the course of years. SSG analysis can be applied to any time scale; here, examples are presented at a few scales that are relevant for adolescent development. First, the most obvious and intuitive scale of time with the moment-to-moment changes in affect for two interacting partners will be described. Next, slightly longer spans of time will be considered in order to examine changes across interpersonal contexts or days. Finally, changes at a developmental time scale of years will be considered in light of the dynamics revealed at the other, shorter, time scales.

SSG analysis at the micro scale

The variability of emotional or behavioral states is one of the few long-recognized structural characteristics of mental health, well-being and adjustment (Bonanno,

Papa, Lalande, Westphal and Coifman, 2004; Cattell, 1935; Cheng, 2001; Chown, 1959; Granic et al., 2003, 2007; Hollenstein and Lewis, 2006; Kuppens, Allen and Sheeber, 2010; Leach, 1967; Lichtwarck-Aschoff et al., 2009; Schultz and Searleman, 2002). This relationship between variability and positive outcomes is curvilinear such that being extremely variable or not variable enough are both problematic. In fact, this kind of variability is often interpreted along a rigidity–flexibility continuum. Many of the psychopathologies that arise or accelerate during adolescence (e.g. depression, anxiety, antisocial behavior) have been characterized by greater rigidity (Bylsma, Morris and Rottenberg, 2008; Friedman, 2007; Granic et al., 2007; Johnson and Nowak, 2002). Thus, the relative flexibility of adolescent emotions and behavior in real time (or across contexts; see the next section) can be examined as an index of emerging problems.

Figure 6.2 displays a contrast between low variability (rigidity) and high variability (flexibility) in real time using the same state space depicted in Figure 6.1. Rigidity is characterized by longer durations of states (larger plot points), fewer transitions from state to state and fewer cells occupied. In contrast, flexibility is characterized by shorter durations, more transitions and greater dispersion across the state space. For example, the observed affect of mothers and their 13–14-year-old daughters during a conflict discussion was used to create SSGs (Hollenstein, 2005). *Dyadic* rigidity was correlated with both girls' aggression ($r = .35$) and depression ($r = .30$) scores, although the amount of negative affect was unrelated to either. Thus, although the mothers and daughters were locked in conflict, as is common at this age (Steinberg, 2001), the negativity of this conflict did not relate to outcomes; rather, the real-time *structure* of the interaction was a better predictor. Parent–child rigidity as measured with the SSG technique has been found to be associated with both externalizing and internalizing outcomes at other ages as well, including early childhood (Hollenstein et al., 2004) and pre-adolescence (Granic et al., 2007).

Another way in which SSG analyses can be useful for examining dynamics in adolescence is as a complement to simulations and other modeling techniques. Simulation models offer a direct way to test hypothesized underlying processes that give rise to observed behavior and are an under-used method in developmental science. A dynamic simulation model imitates the time course of a real process in a reduced, shortened and idealized way (Gilbert and Troitzsch, 1999; Schmidt, 2000; Steenbeek and van Geert, 2005). Hence, a researcher can specify parameters that reflect expected rates of change and the mutual influence of two or more processes over time to create a time series that should be quite similar to the corresponding real-world time series if the theory-based parameters were accurate. These comparisons between simulated and real-world data are often the only way to converge on the underlying properties of a dynamic system. For example, Steenbeek and van Geert (2005, 2007) utilized an agent-based model to explain patterns of interaction among dyads of different sociometric status. The model simulated data based on several parameters, including concerns, drives, emotional appraisals, emotional expressions and behavior. The simulated time series for each

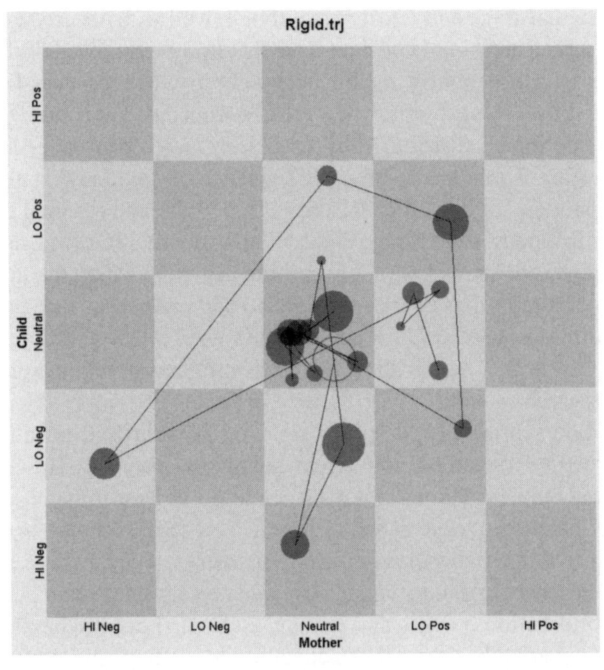

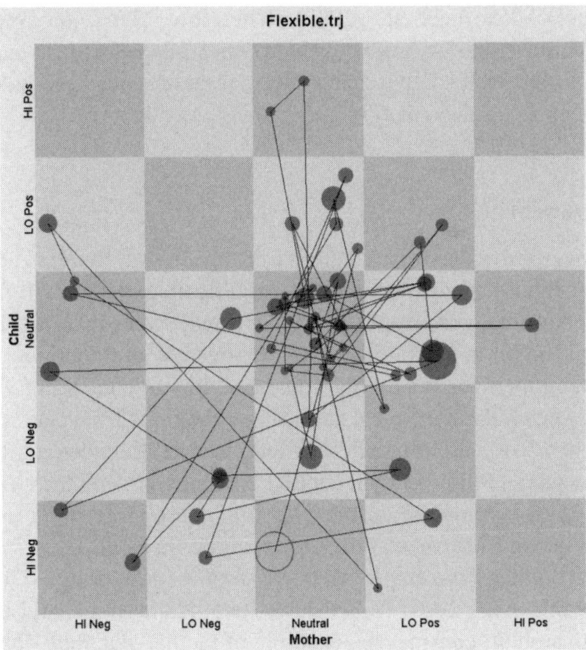

Figure 6.2 Examples of dyadic interactions characterized as rigid (top) and flexible (bottom).

combination of popular, average and rejected children fit well with observed data. Because both the observed and simulated data were dyadic, graphing and deriving measures via SSGs is a potentially useful accessory to such process-based modeling. Figure 6.3 shows two example SSGs created from data generated by the Excel and Visual Basic model distributed by van Geert (www.paulvangeert.nl/articles_appendices.htm). These grids show the sequence of emotional states of the two interacting partners, one dyad consisting of a popular and rejected child and the other dyad of a popular and average child. Similarities to SSGs from actual dyadic play interactions (not shown) would reveal the degree to which the theory was viable, whereas dissimilarities between simulated and real-world trajectories would require updating the theoretical model. In this way, direct and dynamic modeling, especially in combination with SSGs, is a fruitful but as yet unexplored area of adolescent research.

Interpreting real-time variability as either rigid or flexible is a promising research direction for understanding adolescent behavioral patterns. However, focusing solely on real-time properties is not sufficient for at least three reasons: (1) dynamic systems function at several scales of time and organization – in fact, it is the relations across these scales through which systems self-organize (Lewis, 2000, 2005); (2) the best way to understand system dynamics is to observe before, during and after a perturbation (Granic and Lamey, 2002); (3) rigidity/flexibility requires both real-time variability as well as adaptation to shifting environmental demands (Lichtwarck-Aschoff et al., 2009). Therefore, dynamic systems examinations of real-time variability rarely exclude context-dependent changes or developmental trajectories. Instead, dynamic systems research considers multiple time scales simultaneously, as described in the following two sections.

SSG analysis at meso scales

The challenge to any system occurs when there is a change in underlying structure or a shift in environmental demands. An adaptive and flexible system will make such changes fluidly to effectively respond to the current, rather than previous, circumstances. A rigid system, in contrast, will perseverate and continue with previous dynamics long after the context has changed. For an adolescent, these changes may happen frequently in a typical day as he or she shifts from classroom, to peer interactions, to a work environment, to a long stretch of concentration on homework or a video game, followed by a conflict with a parent and then a long phone conversation with a romantic partner. Each of these shifts requires an adjustment of behavior and affect. In order to examine these changes across contexts, several SSG studies have employed a two- or three-task design (Granic and Lamey, 2002; Granic et al., 2007; Hollenstein, 2005; Hollenstein and Lewis, 2006). To illustrate this point, consider the example of mother–daughter conflict data derived from Hollenstein (2005) and reported in Hollenstein and Lewis (2006) described next.

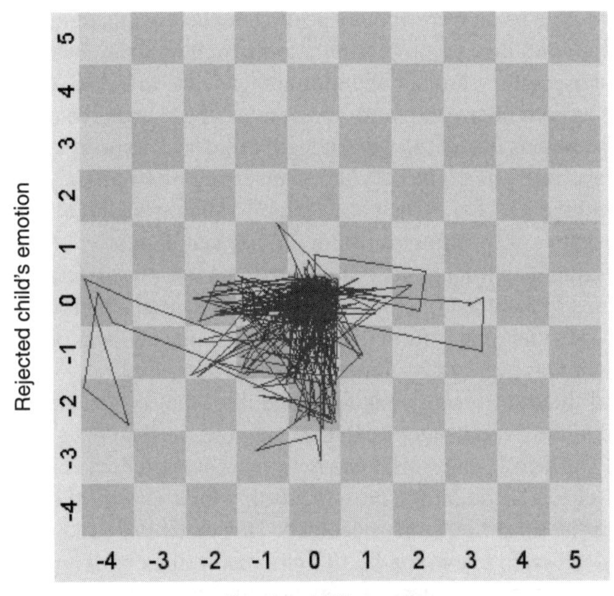

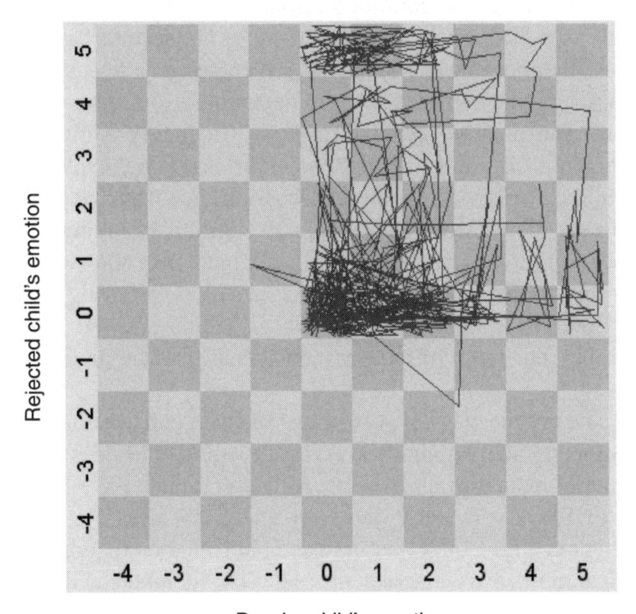

Figure 6.3 Examples derived from data simulated by an agent model. Positive values reflect the intensity of positive emotion and negative values reflect the intensity of negative emotion.

Mothers and their adolescent daughters were observed across three discussions. The first and the third discussion were about a positive topic (e.g. planning a party or vacation) but the second discussion was on a topic that the dyad had rated as the most contentious issue they argued about at home. Thus, this A-B-A design allowed for analysis at both micro and meso time scales: the changes in real-time variability across discussions from positive to negative and back to positive topics. The state space in this case was created by the intersection of 10 affective states from the SPAFF (Gottman, McCoy, Coan and Collier, 1996) arranged in a quasi-ordinal sequence, negative to positive, for both mother and daughter: contempt, anger, anxiety/fear, sadness, whining, neutral, interest, humor, joy, affection. Two measures were derived: transitions (number of changes in dyadic affective states) and dispersion (an index that ranges from 0, meaning only one cell was occupied, to 1, meaning behavior was evenly distributed across all cells equally). Figure 6.4 shows an example of the three discussions from one dyad that is consistent with the pattern observed in the overall sample. In this example, vertical lines indicate a change in the girl's affective state, whereas horizontal lines reflect changes in mother's affective state. The default state is neutral, which is why the central neutral/neutral cell is the most frequently occupied. This particular dyad engaged in the first positive discussion (1) with a bit of humor as well as brief anxiety on the girl's part; most likely this was nervous laughter, which is common for girls this age. During the first half of the conflict discussion (2a), the dyad exhibited brief anxiety as well as a flash of mother affection. In the second half of the discussion (2b), the mother became angry and the girl expressed a relatively long duration of sadness. The dyad repaired in the final positive discussion (3) by maintaining a neutral and positive affect throughout, including another brief mother affection moment. It is not the content, however, that is most interesting. The structural variability changed across these discussions in a way that reflected the constraining effects of negative emotions and conflict. Breaking up the discussion sequence into four 4-minute segments (see Figure 6.4) allowed values to be determined for the number of transitions (43, 23, 9, 39, respectively) and the overall dispersion (.60, .38, .35, .52, respectively), which showed that the variability or flexibility during conflict was considerably lower than during positive discussions.

At another meso scale of time, day-to-day changes in affect and behavior can be traced as a trajectory on an SSG. Variability at this scale would reflect descriptions of the fickle or mercurial nature of adolescents. Although to date there has been limited application of SSGs with daily data, any study that uses diaries (e.g. Lichtwarck-Aschoff et al., 2009), the experience sampling method (e.g. Larson et al., 2002) or ecological momentary assessments (e.g. Silk, Steinberg and Morris, 2003) would be appropriate. Consider the example given by Lichtwarck-Aschoff, van Geert, Bosma and Kunen (2007), in which mothers and adolescent daughters each recorded whether they had a conflict and, if so, how they felt both during the conflict and at the end of the day when completing the diary. The state space consisted of 15 emotional states that were arranged in a quasi-ordinal fashion from

1

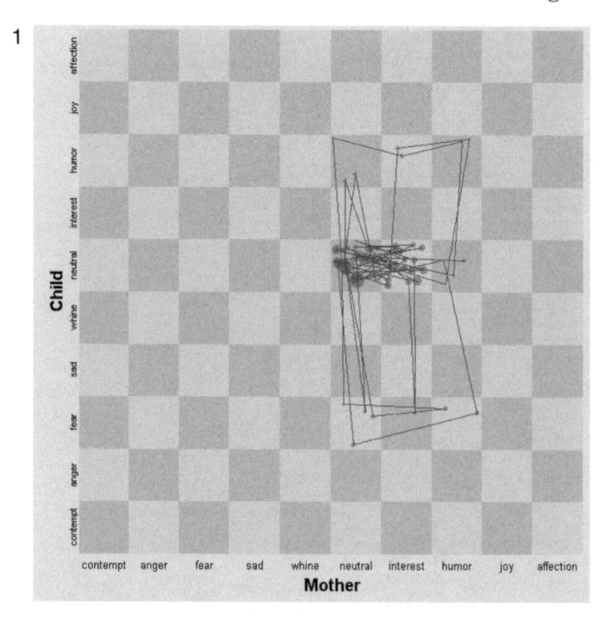

2a

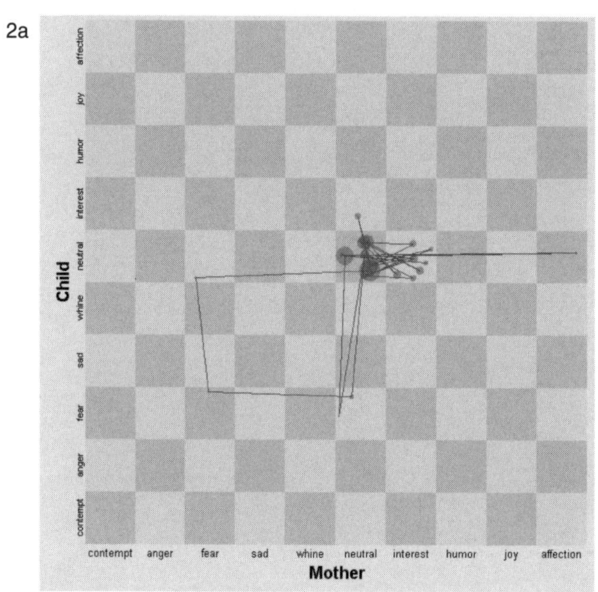

Figure 6.4 State space grids for one dyad across three discussions. The 8-minute conflict discussion was broken down into two 4-minute segments (2a and 2b) for better comparison with the positive discussion (1 and 3), which were each 4 minutes long. *(Continued)*

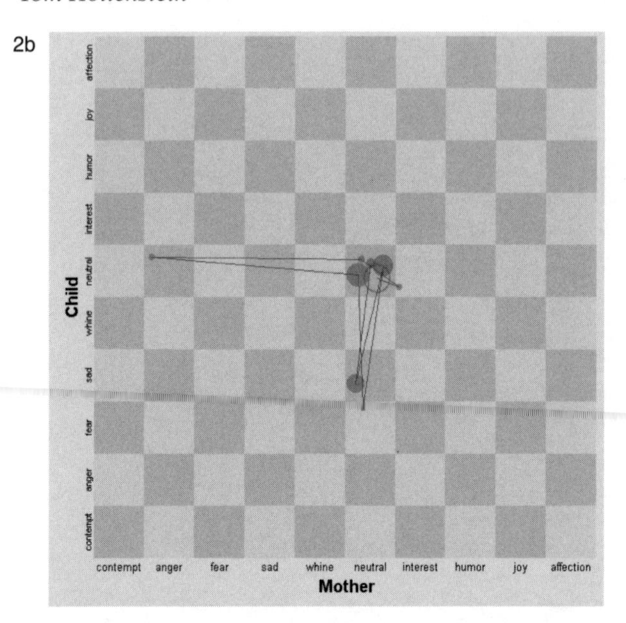

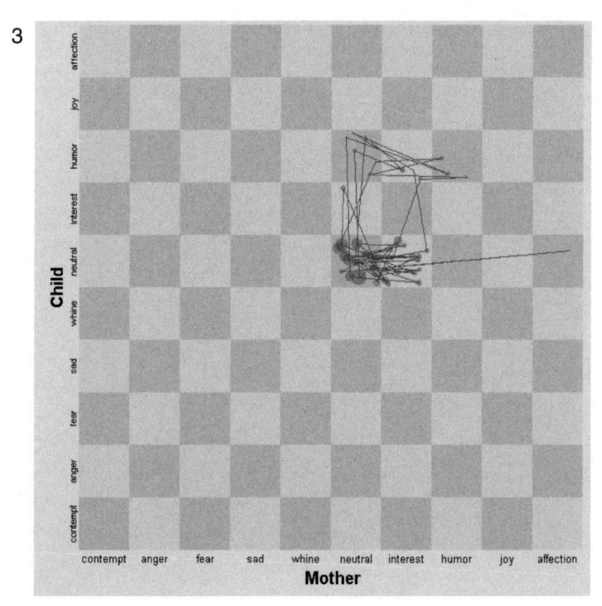

Figure 6.4 (Continued)

negative to positive (see Figure 6.5). Each conflict event was a two-step trajectory, with the mother's and daughter's self-reported emotions during the conflict as the first plot point (open circles) and their self-reported emotions at the end of the day as the second plot point (filled circles). Most of the conflicts begin in the lower left of the state space (mutual negativity) and move toward more positive emotions (i.e. they "repair"). However, differences in whether the repair is unilateral can be seen in these three examples. In Figure 6.5(a), there are more vertical transition lines, indicating that the mother repaired from the conflict but the daughter tended to have lingering negative emotions. In contrast, Figure 6.5(b) has more horizontal transition lines, indicating that the mother was more likely to maintain negative emotions after the conflict. Mutual repair is exemplified in Figure 6.5(c), where the dyad frequently returns to the mutually positive portion of the state space.

There are potentially many more ways in which adolescent behavior can be examined at time scales between real time and developmental time. Dynamics of peer and romantic relationships, academic and behavioral coincidences or markers of physical development (hormones, pubertal status) and emotions/behavior are other examples of SSGs that might help to answer research questions at the meso scale.

SSG analysis at the developmental scale

At the core of any basic developmental question is the attempt to understand both stability and change. The adolescent transition is of particular interest because it is a period of upheaval in which change occurs in virtually every domain: neural, hormonal, physical, cognitive, behavioral, interpersonal, academic, emotional. From a dynamic systems perspective, this level of developmental change reflects a phase transition, a period of temporary instability as the system re-organizes structurally. Granic et al. (2003) tested this *adolescent phase transition hypothesis* using SSGs. One of the most direct and observable features of a phase transition is a marked increase in variability as the systems shifts from one stable set of attractors to a new one. Thus, Granic et al. (2003) hypothesized that the dyadic behavioral variability of parent–adolescent interactions would peak in early adolescence at the height of the transition. In this study, parents and adolescent boys engaged in discussions about their most heated conflicts five times: every other year from ages 9–10 through to ages 17–18. The third time point coincided with the boys' entry into adolescence at age 13–14. The dyads' developmental trajectories of real-time variability across the five time points were analyzed using two SSG measures: number of cells occupied and number of transitions. Both of these measures showed a significant quadratic peak exactly at the hypothesized transition point (Figure 6.6). Moreover, conflict (mutual negativity) did not peak until the boys were older, aged 15–16, indicating that the peak variability preceded the most intense parent–boy conflict.

A similar developmental analysis was conducted on a sample of girls who changed to a new school at the same time as the female adolescent transition

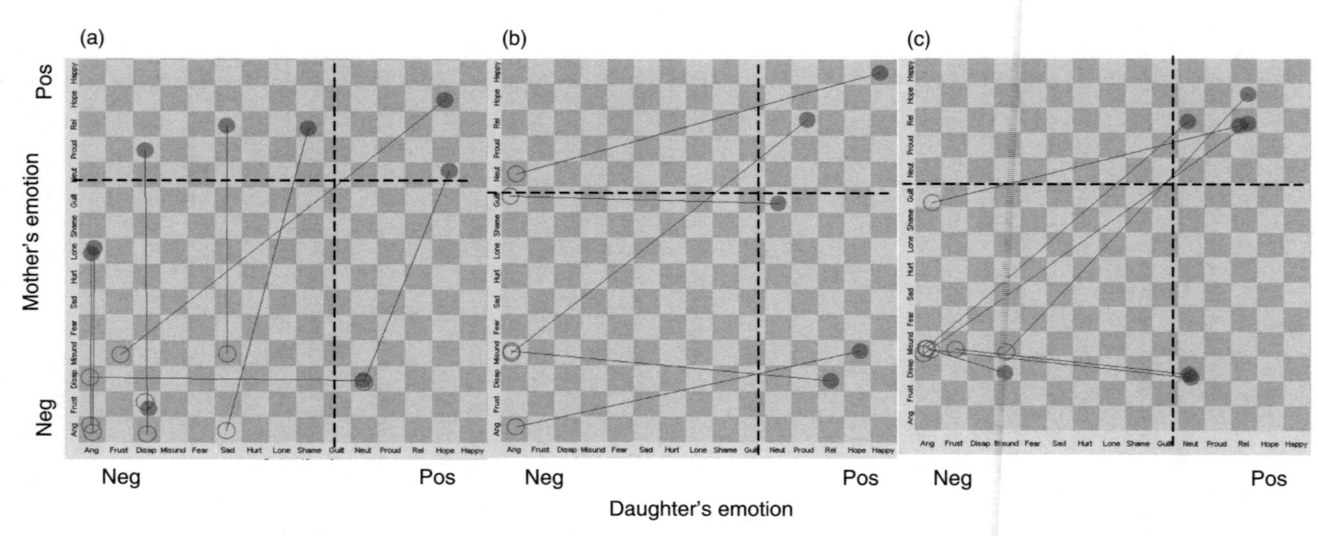

Figure 6.5 Examples of mother–daughter conflicts in three dyads across 12 non-consecutive weeks. The dashed line separates the negative emotional states from neutral and positive states.

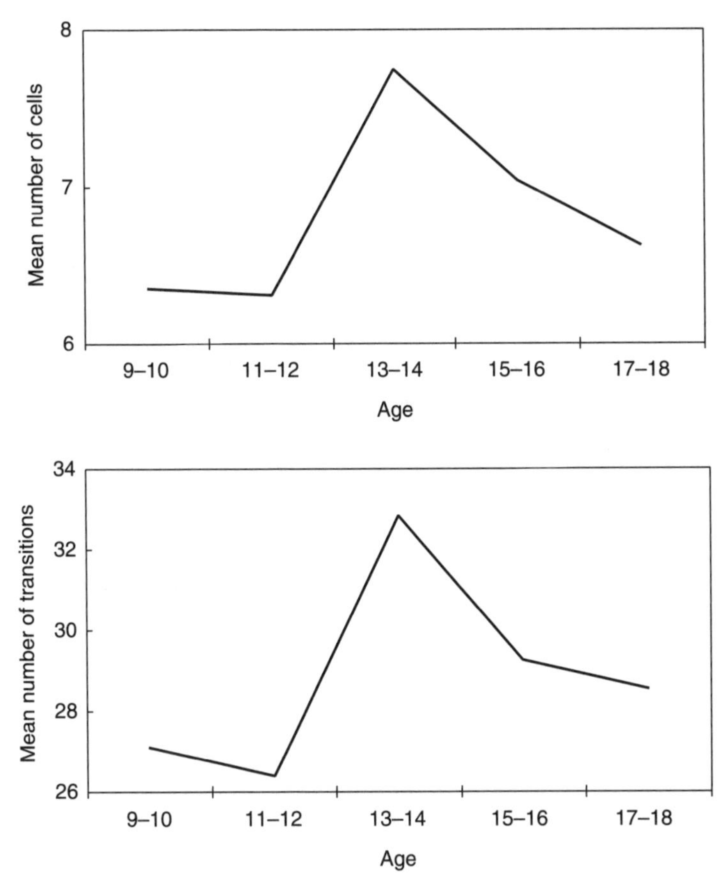

Figure 6.6 Longitudinal profiles of two SSG measures (number of cells and number of transitions) across five waves of parent–boy interactions (from Granic et al., 2003).

(ages 11–12). In this study (Hollenstein, 2005, 2007), mothers and daughters engaged in conflict discussions at four time points: once before the transition and then every 6 months after. The SSGs were the same as shown in Figure 6.4. What distinguished the developmental profiles was the amount of stress the girls were experiencing at the same time as they made the transition into a new school.[2] Those with low stress exhibited the hypothesized quadratic profile consistent with a phase transition, whereas the dyads with stressed girls showed the opposite pattern of lowered variability during the transition phase (Figure 6.7). Interestingly, negative emotions during conflict increased linearly and equally for both groups over time, so once again there is evidence for the independence of structure and content across this transition.

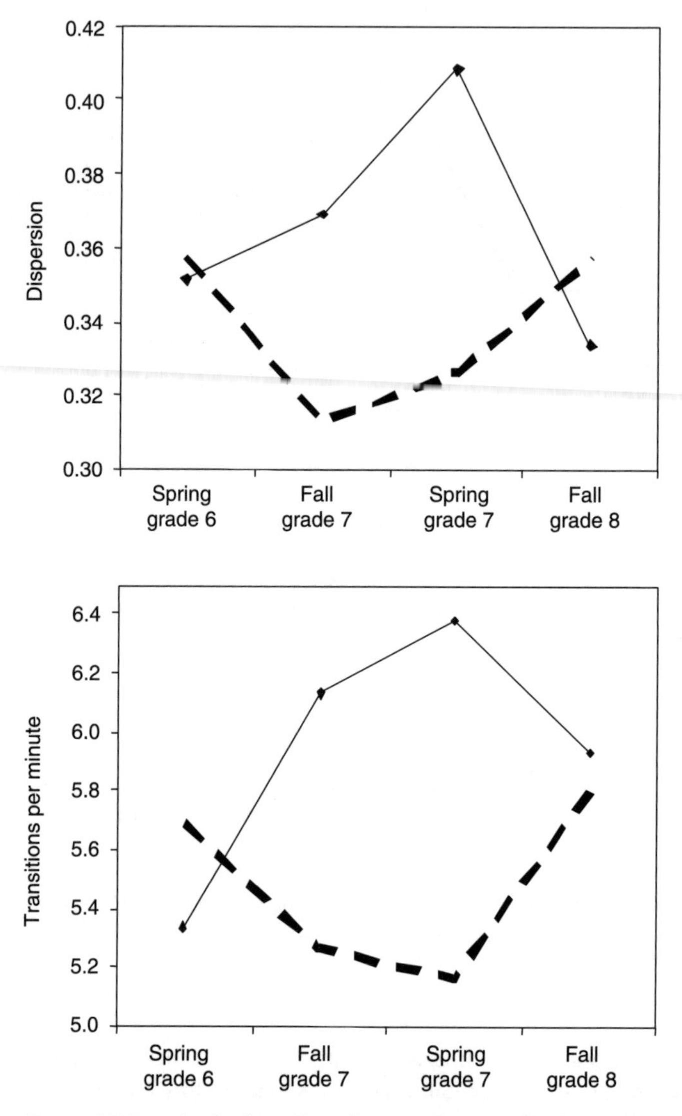

Figure 6.7 Longitudinal profiles of two SSG measures of variability (dispersion and number of transitions per minute) across four waves of mother–daughter conflict discussions. The solid line represents the low stress group and the dotted line the high stress group.

Conclusions

So far, the use of SSGs for the study of adolescence has only scratched the surface of all that is possible. Further tests of the adolescent developmental phase transition hypothesis, for example, would go a long way to understanding this period of vulnerability and opportunity (Dahl and Spear, 2004). The SSG technique is also quite adaptable, so a range of systems (intra-individual, dyadic, groups) can be explored at one or more time scales. Furthermore, the examples shown here have depicted only simultaneous behaviors. SSGs can reflect lagged relationships, with one axis being a step before or after the other. Finally, although GridWare (Lamey et al., 2004) is limited to two dimensions, mostly due to display restrictions, state space analyses are not constrained to two dimensions. Interactions among peer triads (Lavictoire, 2010) and groups of children (Martin et al., 2005) have been attempted and work is being done to make this more accessible. Thus, as one of the most dynamic periods of development, our understanding of adolescence may be enhanced by dynamic systems analyses such as SSGs.

Notes

1 A demonstration file and on appendix for this chapter can be found at www.psypress.com/dynamic-system-approach/appendices.

2 In Canada, it is somewhat common for elementary schools to only have classrooms up to grade 6 (approximately age 11) and then have “middle school” or junior high school for grades 7 and 8.

References

Bonanno, G. A., Papa, A., Lalande, K., Westphal, M., & Coifman, K. (2004). The importance of being flexible: The ability to both enhance and suppress emotional expression predicts long-term adjustment. *Psychological Science, 15*, 482–487.

Bylsma, L. M., Morris, B. H., & Rottenberg, J. (2008). A meta-analysis of emotional reactivity in major depressive disorder. *Clinical Psychology Review, 28*, 676–691.

Cattell, R. B. (1935). On measurement of perseveration. *British Journal of Educational Psychology, 5*, 76–91.

Cheng, C. (2001). Assessing coping flexibility in real-life and laboratory settings: A multimethod approach. *Journal of Personality and Social Psychology, 80*, 814–833.

Chown, S. M. (1959). Rigidity: A flexible concept. *Psychological Bulletin, 56*, 195–223.

Dahl, R. E., & Spear, L. P. (2004). *Adolescent brain development: Vulnerabilities and opportunities*. New York: New York Academy of Sciences.

Friedman, B. H. (2007). An autonomic flexibility–neurovisceral integration model of anxiety and cardiac vagal tone. *Biological Psychology, 74*, 185–199.

Gilbert, N., & Troitzsch, K. G. (1999). *Simulation for the social scientist*. Buckingham, UK: Open University Press.

Gottman, J. M., McCoy, K., Coan, J., & Collier, H. (1996). *The specific affect coding system (SPAFF) for observing emotional communication in marital and family interaction*. Mahwah, NJ: Lawrence Erlbaum Associates.

Granic, I., & Hollenstein, T. (2006). A survey of dynamic systems methods for developmental psychopathology. In D. Cicchetti & D. J. Cohen (Eds.), *Developmental psychopathology* (pp. 889–930). New York: Plenum Press.

Granic, I., Hollenstein, T., Dishion, T. J., & Patterson, G. R. (2003). Longitudinal analysis of flexibility and reorganization in early adolescence: A dynamic systems study of family interactions. *Development Psychology, 39*, 606–617.

Granic, I., & Lamey, A. V. (2002). Combining dynamic systems and multivariate analyses to compare the mother–child interactions of externalizing subtypes. *Journal of Abnormal Child Psychology, 30*(3), 265–283.

Granic, I., O'Hara, A., Pepler, D., & Lewis, M. D. (2007). A dynamic systems analysis of parent-child changes associated with successful "real-world" interventions for aggressive children. *Journal of Abnormal Child Psychology, 35*, 845–857.

Hollenstein, T. (2005). *Socioemotional development across the early-adolescent transition*. Unpublished doctoral thesis, University of Toronto, Canada.

Hollenstein, T. (2007). State space grids: Analyzing dynamics across development. *International Journal of Behavioral Development, 31*, 384–396.

Hollenstein, T., Granic, I., Stoolmiller, M., & Snyder, J. (2004). Rigidity in parent–child interactions and the development of externalizing and internalizing behavior in early childhood. *Journal of Abnormal Child Psychology, 32*, 595–607.

Hollenstein, T., Lanteigne, D., Glozman, J., Flynn, J. J., & Mackey, A. (submitted). The dynamics of discordance: Relations among heart rate, observed affect, and self-reported distress during a spontaneous speech.

Hollenstein, T., & Lewis, M. D. (2006). A state space analysis of emotion and flexibility in parent–child interactions. *Emotion, 6*, 656–662.

Johnson, S. L., & Nowak, A. (2002). Dynamical patterns in bipolar depression. *Personality and Social Psychology Review, 6*, 380–387.

Kuppens, P., Allen, N. B., & Sheeber, L. B. (2010). Emotional inertia and psychological maladjustment. *Psychological Science, 21*, 984–991.

Lamey, A., Hollenstein, T., Lewis, M. D., & Granic, I. (2004). GridWare (Version 1.1). [Computer software]. http://statespacegrids.org.

Larson, R. W., Moneta, G., Richards, M. H., & Wilson, S. (2002). Continuity, stability, and change in daily emotional experience across adolescence. *Child Development, 73*, 1151–1165.

Lavictoire, L. (2010). *The dynamics of social rejection in triadic peer interactions in early childhood.* Unpublished Master's thesis, Queen's University, Canada.

Leach, P. J. (1967). A critical study of the literature concerning rigidity. *British Journal of Social and Clinical Psychology, 6*, 11–22.

Lewis, M. D. (2000). The promise of dynamic systems approaches for an integrated account of human development. *Child Development, 71*, 36–43.

Lewis, M. D. (2005). Self-organizing individual differences in brain development. *Developmental Review, 25*, 252–277.

Lewis, M. D., Lamey, A. V., & Douglas, L. (1999). A new dynamic systems method for the analysis of early socioemotional development. *Developmental Science, 2*, 457–475.

Lewis, M. D., Zimmerman, S., Hollenstein, T., & Lamey, A. V. (2004). Reorganization in coping behavior at 1½ years: Dynamic systems and normative change. *Developmental Science, 7*, 56–73.

Lichtwarck-Aschoff, A., Kunnen, E. S., & van Geert, P. L. C. (2009). Here we go again: A dynamic systems perspective on emotional rigidity across parent–adolescent conflicts. *Developmental Psychology, 45*, 1364–1375.

Lichtwarck-Aschoff, A., van Geert, P. L. C., Bosma, H., & Kunnen, E. S. (April, 2007). *Mothers' and daughters' perceptions of conflicts: The role of emotional repair*. Paper presented at the biennial meeting of the Society for Research on Child Development, Boston, MA.

Martin, C. L., Fabes, R. A., Hanish, L. D., & Hollenstein, T. (2005). Social dynamics in the preschool. *Developmental Review, 25*, 299–327.

McCarthy, A., Hollenstein, T., Muir, D., & Lee, K. (April, 2007). *Children's eye gaze pattern during thinking and its relation to their knowledge about thinking-related gaze behavior*. Poster presented at the biennial meeting of the Society for Research on Child Development, Boston, MA.

Schmidt, B. (2000). *The modelling of human behaviour.* Ghent, Belgium: SCS-Europe BVBA.

Schultz, P. W., & Searleman, A. (2002). Rigidity of thought and behavior: 100 years of research. *Genetic, Social, and General Psychology Monographs, 128*, 165–207.

Silk, J. S., Steinberg, L., & Morris, A. S. (2003). Adolescents' emotion regulation in daily life: Links to depressive symptoms and problem behavior. *Child Development, 74*, 1869–1880.

Steenbeek, H., & van Geert, P. (2005). A dynamic systems model of dyadic interaction during play of two children. *European Journal of Developmental Psychology, 2*, 105–145.

Steenbeek, H. and van Geert, P. (2007). A dynamic systems approach to dyadic interaction in children: Emotional expression, action, dyadic play, and sociometric status. *Developmental Review, 27*, 1–40.

Steinberg, L. (2001). We know some things: Parent–adolescent relationships in retrospect and prospect. *Journal of Research on Adolescence, 11*, 1–19.

Thelen, E., & Ulrich, B. D. (1991). Hidden skills: A dynamic systems analysis of treadmill stepping during the first year. *Monographs of the Society for Research in Child Development, 56*, 30–35.

Todd, R., Hollenstein, T., & Lewis, M. D. (April, 2009). *Pulling it together: Cortical activity associated with cognition–emotion interactions in young children.* Paper presented at the biennial meeting of the Society for Research on Child Development, Denver, CO.

Van Geert, P., & van Dijk, M. (2002). Focus on variability: New tools to study intra-individual variability in developmental data. *Infant Behavior and Development, 25*, 340–374.

Part II

Exploring development: The assessment of mechanisms

7 Toy models and the search for mechanisms

Saskia Kunnen

In the first part of this book we described techniques that allow us to detect patterns and characteristics that are typical of dynamic systems behavior. In this second part we will describe modeling techniques. As mentioned before, building a mathematical dynamic systems model is not strictly required when one studies development from a dynamic systems approach, but is an important tool and it offers ways to acquire knowledge that cannot be acquired in another way.

Models in the dynamic systems approach have other goals and characteristics than the models that are usually developed in the social sciences. Traditional statistical models in the social sciences (e.g. non-linear regression models) are developed to describe the characteristics (the distribution) of a set of data. Often, the model describes the relationships between different variables in a sample. Typically, those relations are formulated as independent variables that may affect dependent variables. An important aim in building such a data-focused model is to keep the model as simple as possible. The best model is one that shows the best representation of the distribution of the data in the simplest way.

Model building in the dynamic systems approach has a completely different aim. The goal in this type of model building is to model the theoretically assumed mechanisms of the phenomena under study. In fact, guided by theory it models the developmental processes. The best model is one that optimally represents the relevant theoretically assumed mechanisms, generates outcomes that fit with empirically found data and is as simple as possible. It is theory driven instead of data driven.

In the social sciences this is an uncommon way of using models. Contrary to the social sciences, in most beta sciences the development of theory-driven models and the study of their behavior is an important source of scientific knowledge (Dyson, 2004; Hawking and Penrose, 1996). For example, Hawking and Penrose (1996) describe a debate between two world famous theoretical physicists about a Theory of Everything, black holes, etc. It is interesting that nobody has ever seen a black hole and there is no empirical finding whatsoever about black holes. The assumption that they exist is based on the behavior of theory-driven models. Much of the scientific debate and the knowledge in this field is based on models, and black holes play an important role in the frontiers of physics.

Of course, models in the social sciences cannot be as elaborate as those in the physical sciences. The processes and concepts studied in social sciences are typically fuzzy, vague and ambiguous. Moreover, the number of data points that are gathered cannot be compared to the thousands or millions of data points that are typical in the physical sciences. Nevertheless, mathematical models offer possibilities to test our theoretical models and gain knowledge on the validity of our theories that cannot be reached any other way. As van Geert and Steenbeek (2005, p. 436) state:

> The function of a mathematical model, whatever its nature, is to express the sometimes complex relationships in a concise way and to provide a means for inferring predictions or any other type of conceptual consequence in a more rigorous way. Even simple equations may thus contribute to a further understanding of a particular process. One of their important functions is that they oblige the researcher to be as explicit as possible about the theoretical assumptions needed to construct a usable model.

The primary aim of a dynamic systems model is to clarify the mechanisms and factors involved in the developmental process. To do this it is necessary to have a theoretical conceptual model of the developmental process under study. This conceptual model describes which factors play a role and how the different variables in the developmental process are related to and affect each other. However, descriptive models are difficult to validate. They often assume the existence of mutual relations and complex interactions between the relevant variables. A descriptive theoretical model only allows for very general statements about the developmental process, and offers little possibility of clarifying, for example, which factor, in what way and at what time, might affect development. Predicting the development of a system consisting of mutually and non-linearly-related components is virtually impossible. Because of the non-linear character of the relations, linear extrapolations do not make sense. The same change in one component may, depending on the value of the other components, result in quite different changes in the whole system. It is thus very hard to imagine and foresee the exact behavior of the system once it has undergone more than two or three changes.

This problem can be solved by using a quantitative dynamic systems model. In fact, such a model consists of a quantitative translation of the descriptive theoretical model. This quantitative model can be used for computer simulations (van Geert, 1994). For example, the effect of a specific variable on the development of commitment development can be translated into an equation that describes the change in commitments as a result of the variable of interest and other characteristics, represented as parameter values in the mathematical model. By repeatedly running such an equation, the development of commitments can be simulated under different conditions. In Chapter 8 we will describe such a model in detail.

In such a way, one can see whether the computer simulations fit with longer term expectations based on the theory and also with empirical data. When there is a lack of fit, then the theory, the mathematical model or the adequacy of the empirical data might be reconsidered. The mathematical models or so-called "toy models" help us to sharpen our thinking about development and our insight into non-linearity and its implications for development, and to explore and test whether conceptual and theoretical models and their assumed relations between variables result in plausible trajectories of development. Outcomes of simulations help to elaborate and fine-tune theoretical models.

From theory to model

A major challenge in making mathematical models, running computer simulations and analyzing the simulated developmental trajectories is that this work requires clear-cut and unequivocal statements about the relationships between the variables and factors involved in the developmental process. The conceptual model that we need to build a mathematical model needs to be more specific than the models we often see in social sciences. Most conceptual models consist of variables with arrows that indicate the direction of the effects. In order to be the basis of a quantitative dynamic systems model, the conceptual model should specify the type of relationship between two variables. For example, we assume that parental support positively affects an adolescent's autonomy. In order to build a model, we need to know how this relation works in different situations. Is there a linear relation, meaning that an increase in support is related to a comparable increase in autonomy? Or is there a kind of "good enough" level of support, meaning that autonomy can grow if the support is above this level? Can there be too much support for the development of autonomy? What is the role of time? Does a specific level of support today affect the autonomy immediately or tomorrow? Or is there a longer period of support needed for autonomy to start to grow?

Since developmental theories are often not detailed or sufficiently elaborate enough to answer such questions, the researcher who wants to apply a dynamic systems approach is forced to pose and answer new, more detailed and often quite fundamental questions about the theory under consideration. Answers to these questions form the basis of the mathematical model. Because these answers are often hypothetical, the resulting model can best be seen as a kind of "Gedankenexperiment". By exploring how the model behaves one can see if the answers to these questions – the assumptions about the variables and factors involved in the developmental process – are valid. The fact that we need to formulate such specific questions for which there are often no answers available is not looked at as a disadvantage and the act of building itself provides new insights. Each researcher who really tries to build a dynamic system of the topic in which she is an expert will find that new and important questions arise that she had never thought about before. It helps to learn what we do not know yet, and that knowledge can be an important input for further research.

The role of chance and error in dynamic systems models

In the popular literature, a famous example of a dynamic system is the British butterfly that caused, by a flap of the wing, a hurricane in China. The example was based on the findings of Lorenz that very small changes in parameters resulted in completely different outcomes of his weather-predicting models (Gleick, 1987). The core message of this example is that any very small event can have huge consequences, and we cannot know which event that will be (there are far fewer hurricanes than butterflies, so not all butterflies cause hurricanes). For social scientists building dynamic systems models this is a somewhat discouraging idea. We generally work with fuzzy concepts and study processes that take place in a non-controlled environment. Thus, in the social sciences it is much more difficult to estimate the parameter values than in the weather models. Based on the example of Lorenz's butterfly, social scientists may assume that model building is not possible in their field. However, the weather-predicting models of Lorentz are just one specific type of model, a type that is extremely sensitive to initial conditions. Models that are applicable for social sciences in general are less sensitive, although the sensitivity to initial conditions is an important characteristic as well (we come back to that later).

Models in social sciences should be fit to describe fuzzy, ambiguous concepts that develop in an unpredictable environment. Most relations in social sciences are chance relationships, meaning that a specific event becomes more or less likely to happen given the change of another condition. This is not typical for the social sciences only, with economic and biological models also having that characteristic (Peters, 1991; Prigogine and Stengers, 1985). Fuzziness, chance and unpredictable influences are important characteristics of all biological, economic and psychological models.

In the social sciences, fuzziness, chance and unpredictability are often seen as noise, as error and often as something that can and should be averaged out by using bigger samples. Mathematical dynamic systems models show that on the level of individual development this is not true. By means of model simulations it can be demonstrated that, even in models that consist of strong clear relations, fuzziness and chance may determine the course of development. To give an example, let us imagine a model that simulates the daily school performance during the first months in secondary school, based on intelligence, motivation and family support. Depending on the values of these variables, the model can simulate different types of trajectory that represent positive, moderate or negative development of performance. When we enter in this model the values describing a child of above average intelligence with moderate motivation from a supportive family, there is a fairly good chance that the model will generate a positive developmental trajectory. However, unexpected things may happen. The child may fall ill and miss the first weeks in secondary school. This may set her back so far that she does not understand the lessons once she is recovered; her performance and motivation decrease and she ends up with a negative trajectory. Or she may have a long-lasting fight with her best friend that causes her to be less attentive in class. It is simply not possible to include illnesses and fights and thousands of other factors in the model. What we can do is include chance factors. The above-mentioned child has a good chance to have good performance in the first weeks and to build on this performance to develop a positive performance trajectory.

However, we can build the model so that the performance outcome is randomly generated in such a way that it is positive 95% of the time (in 95 of 100 simulations) and negative 5% of the time. Given that the model is iterative, and that bad performance increases the chance that subsequent performance will also be less good, the further consequences of the illness will be covered by the mechanisms in the model. This means that the model does predict the individual trajectory of child X, but it generates different types of trajectories and results in a distribution of different trajectories that have different chances to become true. Note that this distribution for the child in our example is not necessarily a distribution with 5% negative and 95% positive outcomes. A specific characteristic of random influences in a dynamic systems model is that the effect of these influences is conditional rather than additional: The state of the system determines to what extent a random influence has any effect. In our example, it is most probable that a negative random influence in the first weeks in school has more effect than the same influence later in the school year. Later in the school year the child has already acquired the most basic skills and background information, and probably has developed more general skills to cope with missed classes.

We have already mentioned the sensitivity to initial conditions. Although it is not a general rule, very often systems are most sensitive to small disturbances and chance influences at the beginning of a new development. A system that is very stable and settled in an attractor will not easily be pushed out of the attractor by a disturbance. However, a developmental process that is just beginning may be very vulnerable and be affected strongly by a disturbance. It has no attractor and can be pushed in other directions easily. Thus, both initial conditions and early disturbances may cause the development to go one way or the other. Later in the development a similar or much bigger disturbance may have less effect.

This mechanism is directly relevant in psychological theory and practice, which means that the timing of support or intervention on developmental processes is very important. By means of simulations, we can find out at which periods in the development the system is vulnerable for disturbances. This can be used in different ways. On the one hand, such a vulnerable period is a period in which support and guidance is needed. On the other hand, we may also detect vulnerable periods in development that is going awry. In that case a period in which the system is sensitive for disturbance may be a good period to start an intervention. In general, mathematical simulations of developmental processes may help here to determine the best time to start an intervention. This is just one example of knowledge that can be gained only by actual model building and simulating development. In the following chapters in Part II of this book other advantages will be illustrated.

The importance of playing with toy models

We borrowed the term "toy model" from a reviewer, about 10 years ago, who apparently did not take our model too seriously. However, we adopted the nickname because it describes our models well. We admit that compared to the physical models our models are simple and small, but most importantly, one of the best things we can do with a model is to play with it. Developmental psychologists know that playing is an important way to learn about almost everything, and this is definitely true for learning about models. By playing, we mean that it is important to try out the different possibilities of a model. Most models include parameters that represent relevant concepts in reality. Once a model has been built, the working of the simulated mechanisms can be tested by running the model. To learn whether the model does include the relevant mechanisms in the right way, we have to try out different possibilities by simulating different combinations of parameter values. Often, this first testing of the model reveals serious flaws in the conceptual model.

In my experience as a model builder, it happened several times that my new model generated only growth of the phenomena I studied. Theoretically and empirically this was not realistic. Apparently no negative influences on the developing phenomena were included in the model. Then the theoretical question arises: What kind of mechanisms may affect the development of this phenomenon in a negative way? How can I include that in the model? In psychological processes, it is not uncommon that just the passage of time results in the diminishing strength of a previously strong phenomenon. Take anger. If one is angry and nothing happens, then over time the anger will – for most people – become less strong. The basic mechanism here is that most strong factors in human life, such as feelings or skills, need time and energy to stay strong. If nothing happens, then their strength decreases (van Geert, 1994). This notion is only seldom included in psychological theories. Only when confronted with a model that only simulates increases in whatever variable is one forced to specify how the phenomena under study may decrease. In this way, the dynamic interchange between theoretical assumptions, characteristics of the model and practical knowledge about possible developmental trajectories results in improvement of the model and at the same time in development of theoretical ideas and hypotheses about how the developmental process under study actually takes place. In the following three chapters of Part II three different types of models are described that may provide you with such new theoretical insights.

References

Dyson, F. (2004). Turning points. A meeting with Enrico Fermi. *Nature, 427*, 297.

Gleick, J. (1987). *Chaos: Making a new science*. New York: Viking.

Hawking, S., & Penrose, R. (1996). *The nature of space and time*. Princeton: University Press.

Peters, E. E. (1991). *Chaos and order in the capital markets*. New York: John Wiley & Sons.

Prigogine, I., & Stengers, I. (1985). *Orde uit chaos (Order out of chaos)*. Amsterdam: Bert Bakker

Van Geert, P. L. C. (1994). *Dynamic systems of development. Change between order and chaos*. New York: Harvester Wheatsheaf.

Van Geert, P. L. C., & Steenbeek, H.W. (2005). Explaining after by before: Basic aspects of a dynamic systems approach to the study of development. *Developmental Review, 25*, 408–442.

8 The art of building dynamic systems models[1]

Saskia Kunnen

In this chapter (and its two appendices) we aim to provide the reader with guidelines to build one's own quantitative dynamic systems model. To be able to build such a model, two types of knowledge are important. The first type concerns the knowledge of how to translate theoretical notions into a conceptual dynamic systems model, and how to translate that conceptual model into quantitative expressions. The present chapter will focus on this first type of knowledge. The second type of knowledge concerns the technical part – knowledge about which software to use, the type of equations that represent different types of development, etc. In addition, knowledge is needed about how to enter quantitative mathematical expressions in a spreadsheet, how to generate simulations and how to make graphs. We provide this type of knowledge in Appendix 8(1) on the website[1]. In our examples and explanations we use spreadsheets, because our aim is to make the art of model building available for all colleagues, not only for those highly skilled in computer programs and mathematics. Spreadsheet programs have proved to be very useful for building dynamic systems, and most people have these programs. In Appendix 8(1)[1] we describe, step by step, how different types of models can be built.

So, in this chapter we will describe the process from general theories to a quantitative dynamic systems model. We will do that by means of an example: the building of a model of commitment development. This chapter will describe the modeling process in different steps.

The first step in building a quantitative dynamic systems model is to develop a conceptual model. In other words, we have to explicate our ideas about which variables affect commitment development and how they affect them. In general, these ideas are based on a mixture of empirical knowledge, theories and common sense. As we will see, the common sense is especially needed when it comes to the question of how other factors affect the development of the target grower. The next step is the actual building of the model. The conceptual model is the basis for the quantitative model. In fact, the quantitative model is a translation of the conceptual descriptions in formulas and equations. As we will see, in that translation a lot of choices have to be made. Especially for the value of the parameters in the model these choices are seemingly arbitrary. As a third step it is therefore necessary to explore with different sets of parameters to find out which value sets "work". We call this the calibration. The final step is to evaluate and validate the model, which can be done in different ways. The most straightforward way is to gather data that closely resemble the simulated process of commitment development and compare the simulated trajectories with the empirically found trajectories, but this is practically and theoretically difficult. Often the first steps in validation are more indirect, caused by lack of longitudinal data.

In the final section we will discuss both the possibilities and the limitations of this technique, illustrated by the model that has been developed in this chapter.

Developing a conceptual model of identity development

In this first step we have to define the core characteristics of the model, starting with defining the target variables and the time span. To do that, we start with a short description of the theory that is directly relevant for the model. Theories on identity development consider the development of commitments in different domains of life as one of the core characteristics of identity development. A commitment can be described as identity choices that give the individual clarity about who he is and what he wants to be and help to define his place in society both for himself and for others. Marcia (1980) distinguishes two core processes in identity development: commitment formation and exploration. Strong commitments give one a strong sense of knowing who one is. Exploration means the process of considering alternatives, of exploring different possible commitments. The development of a mature identity concerns the development of strong and flexible commitments following a period of exploration (Marcia, 1980). The element of actively making identity choices is central in Marcia's identity status model, which is the empirical approach to identity in adolescence and adulthood that is most often used (Marcia, Waterman, Matteson, Archer and Orlafsky, 1993). Identity statuses are "modes of dealing with the identity issue characteristic of late adolescents" (Marcia, 1980, p. 161), and they form an extension of Erikson's bipolar description of the outcome of the identity crisis in adolescence (identity versus identity diffusion). According to the identity status model, by the end of adolescence, adolescents have either actively made identity choices and in this way solved the normative identity crisis (Achievement), or have not made such choices (and end up in a state of Identity Diffusion), or are still actively exploring identity choices (Moratorium), or have never experienced an exploratory period (Foreclosure).

The change of commitment strength and level of exploration over time will be our target. In dynamic systems language, commitment strength and exploration are the main growers in our model. Depending on the conceptual model, there may be other growers. Commitment change and development is not restricted to adolescence, but most identity work does take place in late adolescence and early adulthood. With our model we aim to describe the development of commitments in a specific domain in the period between about age 16 and age 24.

A conceptual model of the development of commitments means that we make a scheme or a flow chart that shows which variables affect commitment strength, and how they do so. It should also include how commitment strength affects the other variables in the model. To develop such a model we start with an exploration of existing research and theories.

Theoretical background

In the last decades the development of commitments has received increasing attention in research. However, actual data in the mechanisms and processes of commitment development are still scarce. Moreover, not all findings concerning the relation between commitment development and other variables are useful: we need information concerning the actual mechanisms, and the usefulness of, for example, correlational data is limited. A major limitation of the usefulness of existing empirical findings is the problem of ergodicity (see Chapter 1). Most data on identity development concern group data. These data may be useful in a later stage, in the evaluation of the model, but they are not helpful in the model building itself. We need insight into the question of what exactly happens during the development of commitments. Which variables interact with commitment development? What makes the strength of commitments stronger or weaker? As a basis for our model we will use the conceptual model discussed in a paper by Bosma and Kunnen (2001, p. 63):

> Let us resume the model described above: the development of identity could be seen as an iterative process. Each iteration concerns a transaction between person and context. In these transactions, a conflict may occur. Initially, people will try to resolve this conflict by means of assimilation, by adjusting their interpretation of the situation in such a way that it can be assimilated into their existing identity. If this fails, the conflict will remain and weaken the existing commitments, until accommodation, or change of identity occurs. Development results from such accommodational changes. People differ as to how long they stick to assimilation and how easily they change their commitments. Personal and contextual determinants determine the ratio between assimilation and accommodation, and the optimal balance. As discussed, we cannot separate the effects of different determinants. Their effects can be seen only in relation to each other.
>
> Although rooted in theory, the model described above remains to be proven. A first step could be an intensive and longitudinal study of commitments. Regular assessments of commitments and of conflicts people encounter, will give some insight into the validity of the process described in the model.

Since the publication of that paper in 2001, at least two longitudinal studies have appeared on the development of commitments: one by Luyckx, Goossens and Soenen (2006) and our own research (Kunnen, 2009). In both studies university students were followed for a period of at least 4 years, with identity assessments every 6 months. The findings in these studies largely confirm and elaborate the model presented in 2001. We demonstrated that conflict is an important factor in the development of commitments (Kunnen, 2006). We have found some evidence for the assumption that in conflicts the strength of commitments decreases. A factor that is closely related to the development of commitments is exploration. Exploration means the active exploring of different commitments by gathering information, talking with people, behavior, etc. Kunnen, Sappa, van Geert and Bonica (2008) state that crises can be described by both an increase in exploration and a decrease in commitment strength. Luyckx, Goossens and Soenen (2006) differentiate between exploration in depth, which means that the commitment that has been chosen is explored, and exploration in breadth, which means that a whole range of potential commitments is explored. They found that:

> Commitment making and exploration in breadth were negatively interrelated, indicating that both are at odds with each other, at least concurrently. Identification with commitment and exploration in depth were positively interrelated at each measurement time.
>
> Commitment making was positively related to both identification with commitment and exploration in depth. Finally, exploration in breadth and exploration in depth were positively interrelated, as an indication of their common focus on gathering identity-relevant information.
>
> (p. 372)

Luyckx, Goossens, Soenen and Beyer (2006) differentiate between two cycles: commitment-formation and commitment-evaluation. The commitment-formation cycle consists of exploration in breadth, which is related negatively to commitment making and unrelated to identification with commitment. This exploration dimension seems to be associated with a period of crisis and existential doubt about important life-choices that precedes the actual formation of commitments. The commitment-evaluation cycle consists of exploration in depth, which is related positively to both commitment making and identification with commitment, emphasizing that it serves the strengthening and evaluation of commitments. During crises, a strong negative intra-individual relation between commitment strength and level of exploration was found (Bosman, 2009).

The conceptual model

Now, based on the theory and findings described above, we see some contours of our model. Our model will describe the sequence of interactions between person and context. The development of commitments can be assumed to be driven by events. These events consist of examples, experiences, pieces of information, and they affect the strength of a commitment in either a negative or a positive way. Basically, this interaction can have two outcomes: a fit or confirmation of the commitment, or a conflict or crisis. A conflict that concerns a commitment or a domain that is important for the person will trigger strong negative emotions and a sense of urgency: something should be done (Frijda, 1986). Thus, a conflict triggers exploration. However, we do not know yet whether exploration has a negative effect on the growth of commitment, or whether the conflict, or the negative emotions accompanying conflict, has a negative effect on commitment growth/making. Based on common sense, we assume that level of exploration and commitment strength directly mutually affect each other. It seems plausible that an active exploring of different possibilities undermines the existing commitment, and that the loss of a strong commitment makes exploration urgent.

The choices that we make here clearly demonstrate the lags in our knowledge concerning mechanisms and processes. There is – as far as we know – no empirical knowledge concerning the mechanisms in the relation between exploration and strength of commitment in the case of crisis.

The shape of commitment development is different in different people (Kunnen et al., 2008). Bosma and Kunnen (2001) suggest that stable differences exist between people in how they cope with identity conflicts: in how long they stick to assimilation and how easily they change their commitments. Personal and contextual determinants determine the ratio between assimilation and accommodation, and the optimal balance. This means that the model also needs some parameter that represents this stable inter-individually different preference. Research shows, for example, relations between the development of an achieved identity (which implies that commitments have been developed) and personality factors such as openness to experience (Marcia, 1993) and identity styles (Berzonsky, 1990).

Each iteration starts with the outcome of an interaction. This outcome can be a conflict or a fit. However, the outcome is not a simple dichotomy. Conflicts can be small or big, and positive outcomes can be very confirmative for a commitment or more or less neutral. Therefore, we will express the outcome of each interaction by a number in the range between –1 and +1. Numbers below zero express a negative outcome, thus a conflict, and numbers above zero express a positive outcome, thus a fit. The other variables in the model are the commitment strength, the exploration in breadth and the exploration in depth. We assume that commitment making and identification of commitment can both be expressed in one variable: the strength of commitment. The making of commitment is a process that is related to the growing of the commitment. The identification of commitment refers to the process of evaluation. It is the process that keeps the commitment strong. With regard to both types of exploration this is less clear. They may have different roles, and we will start by including them as two different growers.

Based on the theory and research described above we can formulate relations that should be included in the model:

1 The commitment strength.

   i Affected by outcome: a positive outcome increases the strength; a negative outcome decreases the strength.
   ii Negatively affected by exploration in breadth.

2 The exploration in breadth.

   i Affected by outcome: a negative outcome triggers exploration.

ii Affected by changes in levels of commitment strength: increase in strength reduces the exploration in breadth.

3 The exploration in depth.

i Active only in the case of high levels of commitment.
ii Affected by a stable personal characteristic (openness to experience)

4 The outcome.

i Determined by chance and normative environmental events.
ii Affected by stable personal characteristics such as openness to experience. This can be seen as a tendency to assimilate or accommodate: higher tendency to assimilate means lower openness, which reduces the chance of conflict.
iii Influenced by the importance of the domain: a relatively irrelevant domain will contain smaller conflicts and successes.
iv Negatively affected by the commitment strength: strong commitments reduce the openness to conflicting information.

Figure 8.1 shows a schematic representation of the conceptual model.

Now that we have sketched the contours of the model, the next step is to specify the type of relations in a quantitative way. For readers who are not interested in the technical description but who like to see the model, we refer to the demonstration model on the website.

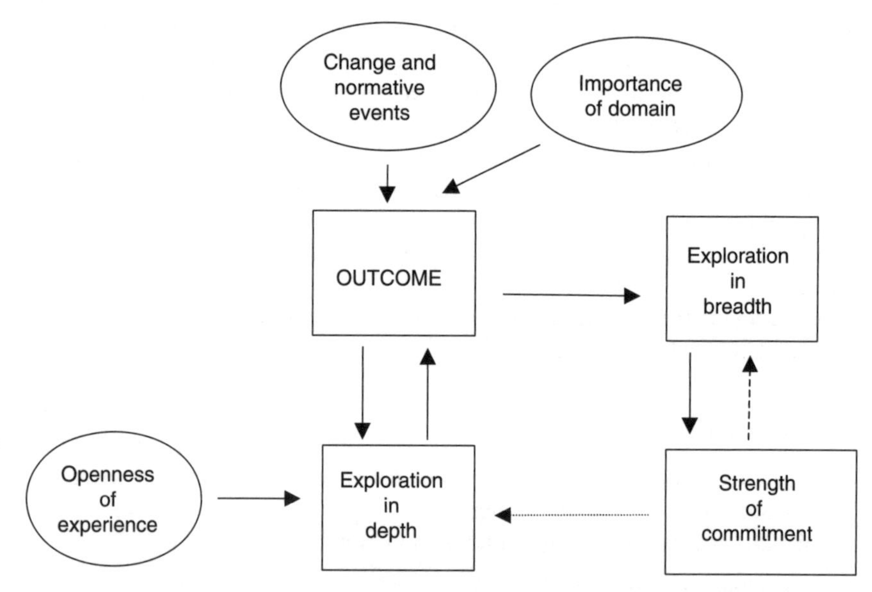

Figure 8.1 A schematic drawing of the conceptual model. Dotted arrows indicate a conditional relation, the broken arrow indicates an effect of the change of the grower.

Developing a quantitative model of commitment development

As the next step, we have to choose the type of equation that describes the change of the variables and the relations between them. Let us start with the equation for the growth of commitment strength. The simplest form is the linear one. However, as argued in the first chapter in this book, linear relations in psychology are almost non-existent. With regard to commitment growth, it is evident that it cannot be described in a linear way. There is a limit to the strength of a commitment; it cannot grow endlessly. The same holds for the decrease of commitment strength. The most plausible shape of the growth of a commitment is the S-shaped curve: a slow start, growth and then slowing down at the end. However, fluctuating change also is possible (Kunnen, 2009; Kunnen et al., 2008). Starting from the principle that we choose the most simple equation that works, we select the logistic growth equation. This equation allows for different shapes of development, and it meets the demands concerning the limitations in growth and decay. In Appendix 8.1 we describe different types of equations with their characteristics. The basic form of the logistic growth equation is given below:

$$C_{t+1} = C_t + a * C_t - a * C_t^2/C_{max} \tag{8.1a}$$

where C_t is the commitment strength at time t and a is the growth rate. In normal language, Equation 8.1a says that the value of the commitment strength C at some time t+1 is the result of the value of C at the previous time (C_t) plus a growth rate times the actual level of C. The part after the minus sign includes C_{max}, which represents an upper limit for the value of the commitment strength. The part of the equation that follows the minus sign has the characteristic that it increases as the level of C approaches this upper level.

The behavior over time of this equation depends on the value of the growth rate a. For values of a below around 1 the equation generates a smooth S-shaped curve. For values above 1 the curve fluctuates once the value of C approaches C_{max}. A value of a above 2.7 results in chaotic behavior (Figure 8.2).

Commitment strength

Equation 8.1a is the basis of the equation for commitment growth in our model. The next step is to integrate the two factors assumed to affect commitment growth into the equation. The outcome of an experience is expected to have a positive effect and the level of exploration in breadth is expected to have a negative effect. These variables have been included in the equation by integrating them in the growth rate. The new equation then becomes:

$$C_{t+1} = C_t + (\mathrm{OUT}_t - \mathrm{EB}_t) * C_t - (\mathrm{OUT}_t - \mathrm{EB}_t) * C_t^2/C_{max} \tag{8.1b}$$

where C_t is the commitment strength, OUT_t is the outcome and EB_t is the exploration in breadth, all at time t.

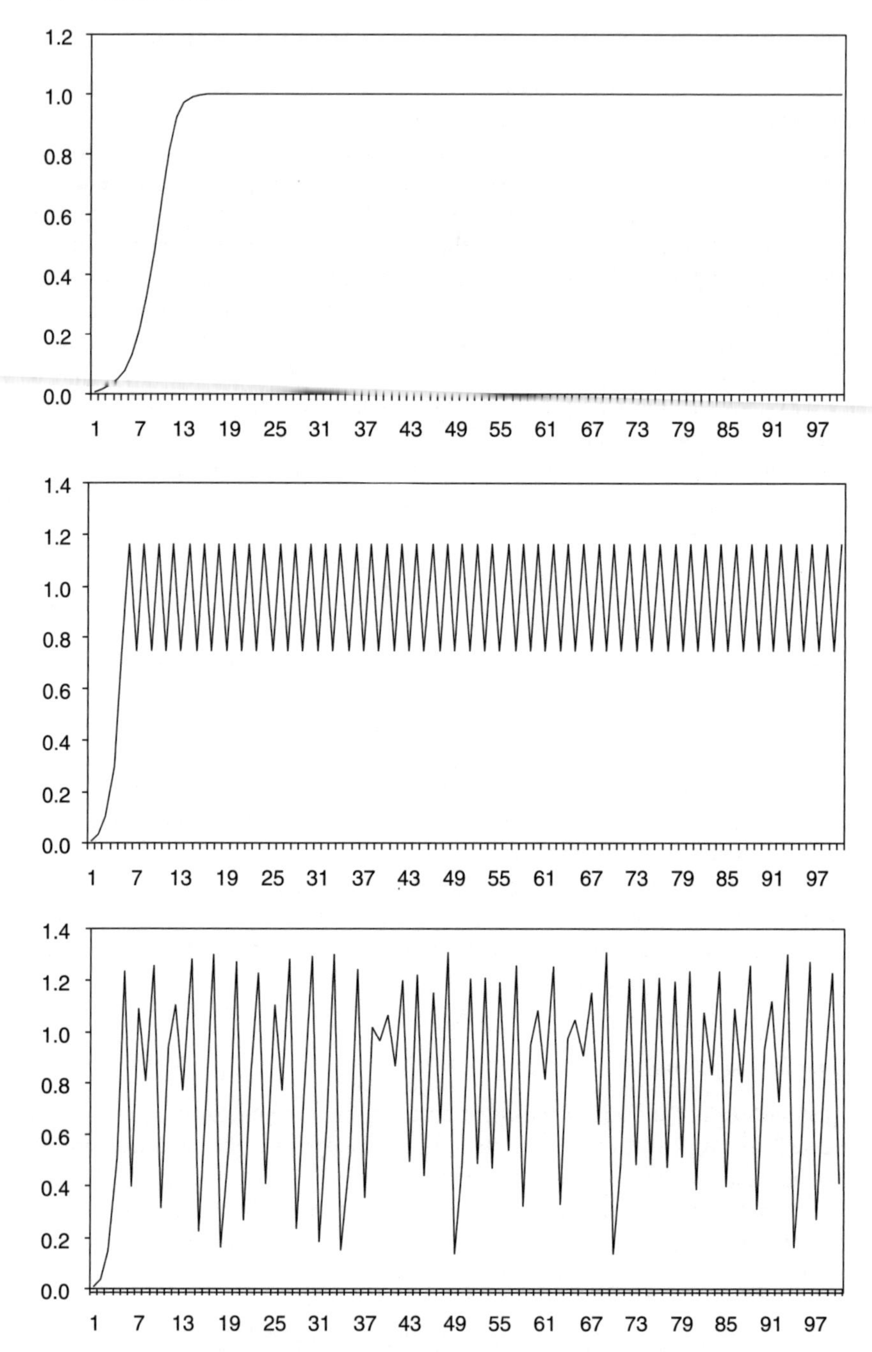

Figure 8.2 Trajectory generated by a basic logistic growth equation with growth parameter values of 0.7, 2.2 and 2.9, respectively.

As a final step we add, for technical reasons, parameters that we can use to regulate the relative impact of each of the components of the equation:

$$C_{t+1} = C_t + (h * \mathrm{OUT}_t - k * \mathrm{EB}_t) * C_t - (h * \mathrm{OUT}_t - k * \mathrm{EB}_t) * C_t^2/C_{max} \quad (8.1c)$$

where h regulates the impact of OUT and k regulates the impact of EB.[2]

In the same way, we choose equations for the change of exploration in depth (ED) and exploration in breadth (EB). These growers also have an upper limit and can be expected to show S-shaped changes or fluctuations, therefore the logistic growth equation seems a good choice for these growers as well.

Exploration in depth

The basis for the equation describing the levels of exploration in depth over time becomes:

$$\mathrm{ED}_{t+1} = \mathrm{ED}_t + b * \mathrm{ED}_t - b * \mathrm{ED}_t^2/\mathrm{ED}_{max} \quad (8.2a)$$

where ED is the exploration in depth and b is the growth rate.

We hypothesized that the growth of exploration in depth is affected by one factor: the openness to experience or tendency to accommodate. Because we have conceptualized the tendency to assimilate and the tendency to accommodate as two poles of the same construct, the growth rate should consist of the negative pole of the assimilation tendency s. We include this in the equation as f-s:

$$\mathrm{ED}_{t+1} = \mathrm{ED}_t + (f\text{-}s) * \mathrm{ED}_t - (f\text{-}s) * \mathrm{ED}_t^2/\mathrm{ED}_{max} \quad (8.2b)$$

where f is a parameter that regulates the impact of s and s is the tendency to assimilate. We assume that the growth of exploration in depth is conditional: it can grow only in the case of a high level of commitment strength. We include this condition in the equation by means of an IF statement (IF $C_t < 0.75$, THEN 0, ELSE f), which says that the growth rate is 0 as long as the level of commitment strength is below 0.75.

Compared to commitment growth, exploration is a time- and energy-consuming activity. As a consequence, high levels of exploration cannot continue forever due to exhaustion. This has to be integrated into the equation. We do that by adding a component that consists of the average value of exploration over, say, the previous 100 iterations. A high value of this component should have a negative effect on the level of exploration in breadth. However, we want an effect of exhaustion only if the exploration in breadth has been really high for a long period. We do not want a median effect in the case of a prolonged period of a median level of exploration. This can be achieved by not simply using the average of the level of exploration over the previous 100 iterations, but to raise this average to the second power. In this way, an average exploration level of, for example, 0.4 results in the value 0.026, while an average level of 0.9 results in the value 0.666.

$$ED_{t+1} = ED_t + ((f\text{-}s) - w * EDA_t) * ED_t - ((f\text{-}s) - w * EDA_t) * ED_t^2/ED_{max} \quad (8.2c)$$

where w is a parameter that regulates the impact of ED and EDA is the average of the previous 100 values of ED.

Exploration in breadth

The change of the third grower, exploration in breadth, is represented by the logistic growth equation based on the same arguments as the two other growers:

$$EB_{t+1} = EB_t + g * EB_t - g * EB_t^2/EB_{max} \quad (8.3a)$$

where EB is the exploration in breadth and g is the growth rate.

We assumed that two factors influence the change of commitment in breadth: a negative outcome triggers exploration and an increase in commitment strength reduces the exploration in breadth. These two factors are integrated in the growth rate g:

$$g = (m + (C_t - C_{t+1}) * n) - (p * OUT_t) \quad (8.3b)$$

where m is a constant, n regulates the impact of the change in C and p regulates the impact of OUT.

The first part of Equation 8.3b describes the effect of the change in commitment strength ($C_t - C_{t+1}$), and the second part describes the effect of outcome (OUT_t). The parameters p, m and n have been included in order to be able to regulate the relative influence of both factors. We find the complete equation for the growth of exploration in breadth when we combine Equations 8.3a and 8.3b:

$$EB_{t+1} = EB_t + (m + (C_t - C_{t+1}) * n) - (p * OUT_t) * EB_t - (m + (C_t - C_{t+1}) * n) - (p * OUT_t) * EB_t^2/EB_{max} \quad (8.3c)$$

where $C_t - C_{t+1}$ is the change in commitment strength. Also here we add an exhaustion factor:

$$EB_{t+1} = EB_t + (m + (C_t - C_{t+1}) * n) - (p * OUT_t - EBA_t * z) * EB_t - (m + (C_t - C_{t+1}) * n) - (p * OUT_t - EBA_t * z) * EB_t^2/EB_{max} \quad (8.3d)$$

where EBA_t is the fourth power of the average of the previous 100 values of EB and z regulates the impact of EBA.

Outcome

Finally, we have to define an equation for the outcome. As mentioned, the outcome of identity-relevant events is determined by chance and normative environmental events. In the model each event is generated separately by a random number in each iteration. We assume that most events do not have a strong impact: there are more events with a low impact value than with a high value. Most spreadsheet programs generate random values between 0 and 1. To generate random values that can have a positive and a negative value, and with a distribution that peaks around the middle (i.e. low values around zero), we choose the equation:

$$OUT_t = \text{random number} - \text{random number} \tag{8.4a}$$

We assume that openness to experience, or the tendency to assimilate or accommodate, affects the outcome values. A higher tendency to assimilate (i.e. lower openness) reduces the chance of conflict and thus the chance that high negative outcomes occur. Furthermore, the outcome is influenced by the importance of the domain: a relatively irrelevant domain will contain smaller conflicts and successes. Finally, the outcome will be negatively affected by the commitment strength: strong commitments reduce the openness to conflicting information. Thus, the equation becomes:

$$OUT_t = r * (\text{RANDOM} - \text{RANDOM}) + s + t * C_t \tag{8.4b}$$

where OUT_t is the value of the outcome at time t; r determines the possible range of the outcome values, and thus represents the importance of the domain; RANDOM is a random number between 0 and 1; s represents the tendency to assimilate; C_t is the level of commitment strength at time t; and t regulates the relative impact of the value of the commitment strength.

All four equations described above (Equations 8.1–8.4) together form the model. The next step is to enter these equations in a spreadsheet file in such a way that we can simulate the behavior of the model – that is, we can generate sequences of values over a period of time for each of the growers in the model.

In this phase we have to decide on the time period we want to simulate and the number of iterations the model should include. In our model, each iteration represents an identity-relevant event. These events may be small. Let us assume that there will be such an event about once in every 3 days, say 100 in a year. We want to simulate the development of commitment and exploration over a period of 5 years, ranging from age 17 until age 22. This means that our model should contain 500 iterations. The trajectory of each variable thus consists of a sequence of 500 values. For readers who want to build the model themselves we refer to Appendix 8(2) on the website.[1] The website also contains an Excel file with the complete model.

Calibration of the model

Until now, the choice of equations was mainly theory driven. In the next step we have to choose values for the different parameters, and this step is purely technical. The values of the parameters have no theoretical meaning. We cannot say that a value of 100 for parameter t is a high value because it depends on the scale we use. Later on we will show that the differences between values of the parameters do have a theoretical meaning. The goal of this calibration is to find values for the parameters in the model for which the model behaves more or less in the expected way. This means that the simulations should not explode into infinity or get stuck at zero, but result in trajectories for the parameters that are theoretically possible. The upper graph in Figure 8.3 shows an example of an exploding model. The values of commitment strength and exploration in breadth fluctuate between extremely high and extremely low and then collapse. Exploration in depth remains low. The second graph in Figure 8.3 shows an example of a simulation that is theoretically possible. This simulation shows a period of fluctuation of commitment strength, followed by an increase in value. Exploration in breadth is high in the period when the commitment strength fluctuates, but decreases after the growth of commitment strength. At that time, exploration in depth starts to grow.

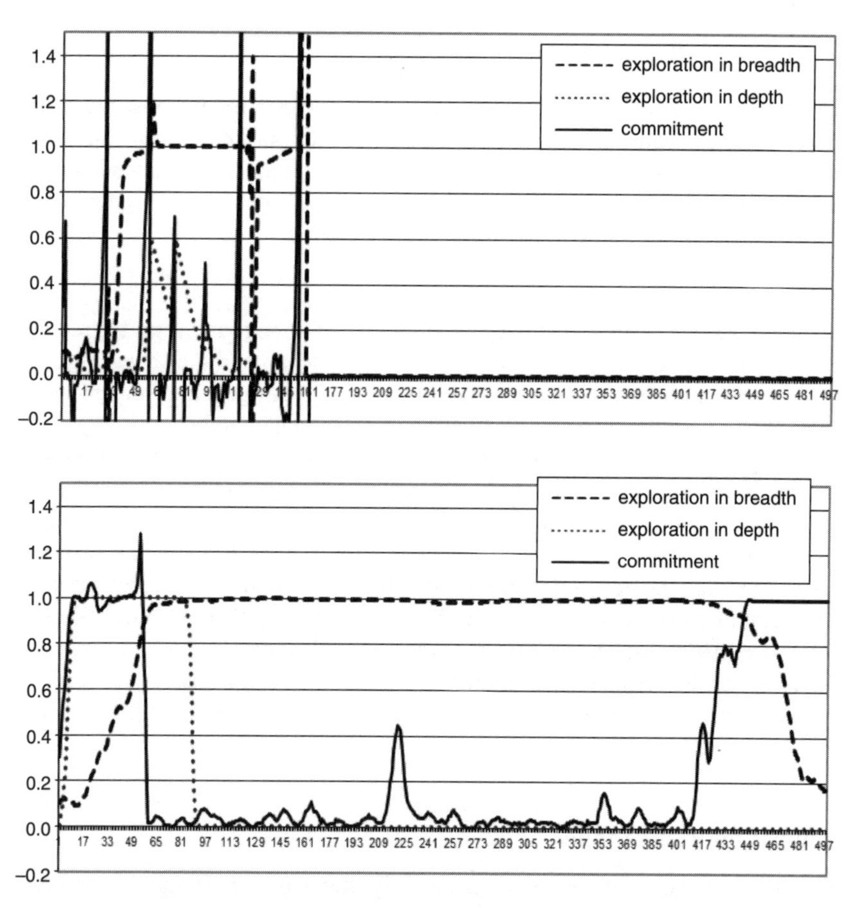

Figure 8.3 Examples of an exploding model (upper graph) and a theoretically plausible simulation (lower graph).

Basically, finding a plausible parameter set is a matter of trying different values and analyzing the sequences of values to get an idea of how the simulated trajectory evolves over time. For example, if a simulated trajectory explodes, one should look at the iterations preceding the explosion and analyze which grower starts, for example, to grow very fast or to fluctuate between high positive and negative values, and which influence causes this. It is best to start with low values for the parameters (close to 1 if they are multiplied with a grower, and zero or close to zero if they are added). For the model described here we chose the set of parameters presented in Table 8.1. For some parameters we mention a range instead of a fixed value. These are the parameters that represent factors that we can manipulate in simulations in order to represent different individual and contextual characteristics.

Once a set of values is found for which the model shows simulations that are theoretically possible, we can start to fine-tune the model. In this step, the theoretical meaning of the growers and the parameters becomes important again. We have to make assumptions about the effects of slight differences in the parameters. For example, what do we expect to happen when we slightly increase the value of parameter s in Equation 8.4b? Parameter s represents the tendency to assimilate. Its theoretical meaning is that it represents stable differences between people with regard to their preference to assimilate or to accommodate. We assume that these differences in preference manifest themselves in types of identity development. A high tendency to assimilate means a high chance that the person develops foreclosed commitments: commitments that become strong and remain strong without much exploration. A low preference for assimilation and thus a high preference for accommodation means that there is a high chance that the person will develop commitments only after periods of exploration, and will show fluctuations in commitment strength. An extremely high tendency to accommodate may result in a prolonged period of exploration without the development of strong commitments. The mathematical effect of parameter s is that the outcomes of commitment-relevant events become a little biased towards the positive side. This means that relatively more events stimulate the formation of a commitment,

Table 8.1 Chosen parameter values in the model

Parameter	*Description*	*Value*
m	Growth rate of EB	0.015
h	Effect of OUT on C	0.6–1
k	Effect of EB on C	0.1
n	Effect of C on ED	5
s	Assimilation tendency	0–0.06
p	Effect of OUT on EB	0.3
t	Effect of C on OUT	0.05
f	Regulates impact of s on ED	0.06
r	Range of OUT	1.5–2.5
z	Effect of previous levels of EB	0.3
w	Regulates impact of time lag on ED	1

whereas there are less negative experiences related to the commitment. We thus expect an accelerated growth of the commitment strength. Figure 8.4 shows two simulations as typical examples. In the upper graph the value of s is less than in the lower graph. The graphs show what was theoretically expected. Due to the random values in the model, no two simulations are the same.

In the process described above, we looked for a set of parameter values that result in plausible simulated trajectories. What "plausible" is depends on general theoretical notions and expectations. For example, we expect the model to generate trajectories with rapidly growing levels of commitment strength more often if the assimilation level is high, but we also expect the same parameter set to generate different trajectories due to the random influence of the outcomes, (i.e. the unpredictable influence of the context). In some simulations high levels of commitment strength should decrease again, representing a period of crisis, when

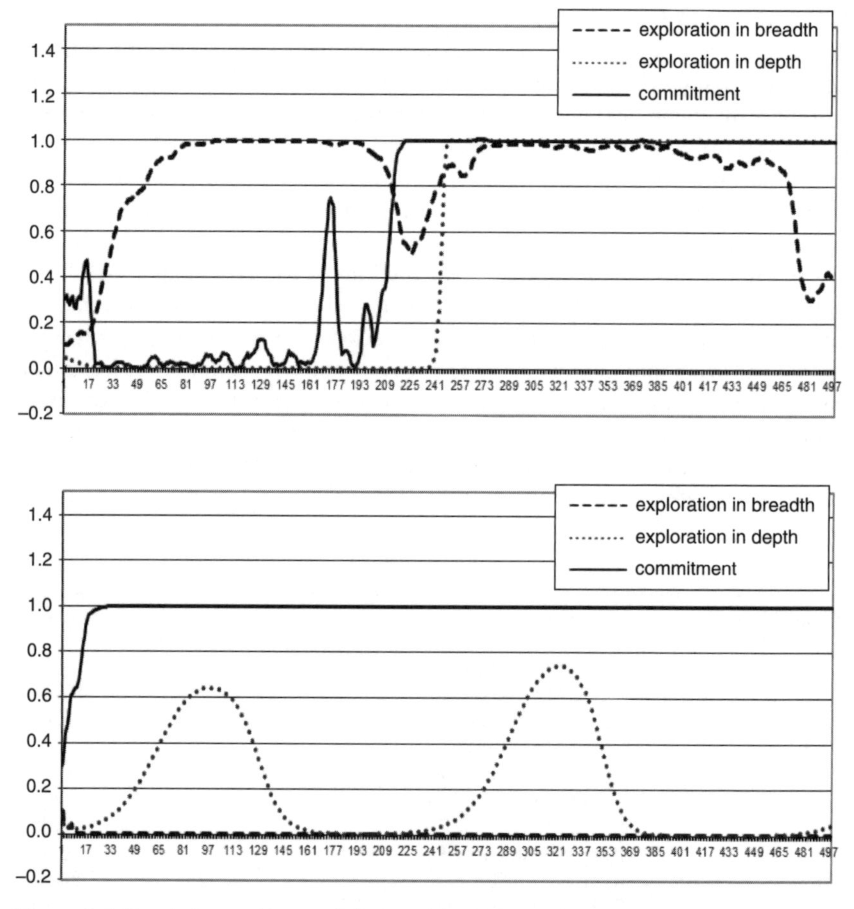

Figure 8.4 Simulations with two different values of s. In the upper graph $s = 0.01$; in the lower graph $s = 0.1$.

existing commitments have to be reconsidered. In some simulations no commitments should develop, especially if the ratio of assimilation to accommodation is low. This phase in model development is basically the playing phase. One has to imagine the real-life meaning of differences in parameter values, and to make assumptions about what that could mean for the generated trajectories. Now that we have found such a set of parameters, we are ready for the next step.

Evaluation and validation of the model

Now our model behaves more or less in the way that we expect on the basis of our common sense and theoretical expectations. This is already a first and important step in the validation of the model. Some critics argue that this is a trivial step, because the equations and parameter values have been manipulated and changed until it behaves in the desired way. However, this argument is valid only in linear models, such as those in regression analysis. Our model building is different in two ways. Technically, it is not possible to manipulate the model into desired behavior by just selecting the right parameter values. Because of the non-linear iterative character, it is not possible to determine the generated trajectories in any desired way: the model is underdetermined by the parameters. Second, and still more importantly, as discussed in Chapter 7 our aim is not to fit an existing set of empirical data. Our aim is to make a model that represents theoretically plausible variables and relations, and that generates trajectories that fit with empirical data. With regard to the manipulation of the equations, our main restriction is the theoretical assumptions underlying it. All our equations are chosen in such a way that they represent theoretically postulated mechanisms of commitment development. The adjustments we made to correct undesired outcomes were done in such a way that they represent the theory. This means that every adjustment of the equations is an adjustment of the theoretical assumptions that we want to test. Our initial model was based on a theoretical model that was too simple, because we did not take into account the relevance of factors that result in reduction of the level of exploration. Thus, the components we added in Equation 8.3d are the result of a refinement of our theoretical assumptions.

As a next step, the model has to be validated in a more stringent way. But how? We may gather longitudinal data on the development of commitment strength and levels of exploration that can be compared with simulated trajectories, but that is not so easy. Practically, we have no methods to assess commitment strength and explorations in breadth and depth in a direct, unobtrusive and easy way. We cannot think of methods to gather 500 data points over a period of 5 years without driving the subjects crazy and disturbing the development we want to observe. Theoretically, also, this way of validation is problematic because of the role of chance and unpredictable events. When we run the model 10 times with the same parameter values it generates 10 different trajectories, and most probably none of these trajectories is based on a patterning of events that is the same as the life events encountered by the real subject. Thus we need to develop more indirect methods to validate the model.

One way to do so is to use the model to simulate groups of people and compare simulated outcomes with existing data from group studies. For example, we may simulate a group of say 1000 young adults at age 20. Let us assume that the value of the assimilation tendency is more or less evenly distributed in the range between 0 and 0.06. Let us also assume that the level of challenges in the adolescents' environment is normally distributed. This means that we run 1000 simulations with different values for the parameters representing the assimilation tendency and the level of challenges. For each simulation we register the level of commitment strength and exploration at the data point that represents age 20. (Remember that our model represents a period of 5 years and starts at age 17, so data point 300 represents age 20.). As a next step, we may assess the commitment strength and exploration levels in 1000 20-year-olds and compare the distribution of values. A more detailed example of this way of validating a quantitative model can be found in Kunnen and Bosma (2000).[3]

There are still other ways to validate the model. For example, even though it is not possible to fit empirical and simulated trajectories in a one-by-one way, it is possible to compare the types of trajectory generated by the model with those found in empirical research. We can compare distributions of simulated trajectories with trajectories found in a population. We can assess differences in the ratio of assimilation to accommodation in that population, and compare the trajectories of different empirical subgroups with simulations of the same subgroups. We can simulate and thereby predict the effects of sudden life events, such as a sequence of events that challenge one's commitments. In the context of a university, such predictions could be tested by investigating study commitment trajectories in students who repeatedly fail their exams.

The ultimate model of identity development?

Given that we succeed in all validations of the model, does that mean that our model is the model of commitment development? We do not think so. Reality is too complex to achieve that, and the development of commitments concerns many different aspects. This means that other models, based on (slightly) other assumptions, are also possible and may be equally valid. A model represents only a few growers and parameters. Which growers are included in the model depends, among others, on the research questions one wants to address. For example, in 2001 we published a model that describes commitment development from a slightly different perspective: as a development of competing commitments (Kunnen, Bosma and van Geert, 2001). Of course, the basic notions concerning the effect of positive and negative events on the growth and decrease of commitment strength are the same in both models. These are the basic assumptions about the underlying mechanisms of commitment development, and of course different models that simulate the same time span of the same grower should generate comparable trajectories. The proof of all models lies in the validation of simulated trajectories with empirical data.

The gain in knowledge offered by this technique

Translating theoretical assumptions into a mathematical model allows us to generate detailed and testable hypotheses and it necessitates and allows for far more specific questions and assumptions than a theory or a conceptual model can ever do (Nowak and Vallacher, 1998). Playing with the model – exploring different plausible sets of parameters – generates trajectories that can be the basis of new hypotheses. The simulations help to specify and evaluate the plausibility of theoretical ideas and thus restrict the number of alternative hypotheses that have to be put to the empirical test. The confirmation of hypotheses by the simulations with the mathematical model will provide us with evidence for the plausibility of the model and its underlying theoretical assumptions. We should realize that verbal models alone do not allow us to arrive at predictions beyond a few steps in the developmental process. The point is that the wealth of – often mutual – relationships discerned by those models prevents us from verbally anticipating the intended effect of those relationships beyond a very short time window. We need a "mechanical" device in order to infer the results of the developmental mechanisms. Such a device takes the form of a simple computer program – a spreadsheet model – that allows us to run numerical experiments with various types of – psychologically plausible – conditions. For instance, our very simple model has shown under which circumstances (the type of sequence of events) an individual tendency to assimilate may result in a foreclosed, diffused or achieved identity trajectory.

One major advance in building mathematical models is, thus, that it forces researchers to be very explicit about their assumptions concerning the developmental mechanisms and processes. Although these assumptions underlie the theories, they often remain hidden. By exposing them, and comparing the simulations with the expected trajectories, these assumptions can be tested and challenged. As for the development of commitments, a well-accepted and explicit assumption is that differences in the tendency to assimilate are important. In our model, we represented the strength of this tendency as a bias in the interpretation of events. The stronger the bias, the more events were seen as supporting one's existing preferred commitment. In our simulations, the effects of differences in the tendency to assimilate accorded with theoretical expectations and empirical findings: higher assimilation results in more foreclosed trajectories. However, alternative representations of the assimilation tendency are possible. The simulations of models including these alternative representations could be compared with those presented here. Moreover, further research could be carried out to test different representations of the tendency to assimilate more directly.

Notes

1 Two demonstration files and two appendices for this chapter can be found at www.psypress.com/dynamic-systems-approach/appendices.

2 In this equation, the model remains stuck once the value of C reaches below zero. This is a kind of mathematical artifact. It can be prevented by adding an IF-THEN statement

to the equation, which resets the value of the grower just above zero. In the actual model Equation 8.1c is preceded by the statement. IF $C_t < 0$ THEN $C_{t+1} = 0.05$ ELSE, where ELSE is folllowed by the actual equation. This type of IF-THEN statement is added to the equations of all growers, but for the sake of simplicity we do not include it in every equation.

3 An argument we sometimes hear is that this is a very complex way to model the outcome of an empirical study. Standard statistical techniques offer simpler ways to model data sets. However, as discussed before, we cannot compare those statistical models with our theoretically based model. When we succeed in this validation process, we have validated a highly elaborate theoretical model of the processes underlying commitment development.

References

Berzonsky, M. D. (1990). Self-construction over the life span: A process perspective on identity formation. In G. J. Neimeyer & R. A. Neimeyer (Eds.), *Advances in personal construct psychology* (Vol. 1, pp. 155–186). Greenwich, CT: JAI Press.

Bosma, H. A., & Kunnen, E. S. (2001). Determinants and mechanisms in identity development: A review and synthesis. *Developmental Review, 21*, 39–66.

Bosman, K. R. (2009). *The role of exploration and emotions in commitment development.* Master's thesis, Department of Developmental Psychology, University of Groningen, The Netherlands.

Frijda, N. H. (1986). *The emotions*. Cambridge, UK: Cambridge University Press.

Kunnen, E. S. (2006). Are conflicts the motor in identity change? *Identity, 6,* 169–186.

Kunnen, E. S. (2009). Qualitative and quantitative aspects of commitment development in psychology students. *Journal of Adolescence, 32,* 567–584

Kunnen, E. S., & Bosma, H. A. (2000). Development of meaning making. A dynamic systems conceptualization. *New Ideas in Psychology, 18,* 57–82.

Kunnen, E. S., Bosma, H. A., & van Geert, P. L. C. (2001). A dynamic systems approach to identity formation: Theoretical background and methodological possibilities In: J.-E. Nurmi (Ed.), *Navigating through adolescence: European perspectives* (pp. 247–274). New York: Garland Publishing.

Kunnen, E. S., Sappa, V., van Geert, P. L. C., & Bonica, L. (2008). The shapes of commitment development in emerging adulthood. *Journal of Adult Development, 15,* 113–131.

Luyckx, K., Goossens, L., & Soenen, B. (2006). A developmental–contextual perspective on identity construction in emerging adulthood: Change dynamics in commitment formation and commitment evaluation. *Developmental Psychology, 42,* 366–380.

Luyckx, K., Goossens, L., Soenen, B., & Beyer W. (2006). Unpacking commitment and exploration: Preliminary validation of an integrative model of late adolescent identity formation, *Journal of Adolescence, 29*, 361–378

Marcia, J. E. (1980). Identity in adolescence. In J. Adelson (Ed.), *Handbook of adolescent psychology* (pp. 159–187). New York: John Wiley & Sons.

Marcia, J. E. (1993). The status of the statuses: Research review. In J. E. Marcia, A. S. Waterman, D. R. Matteson, S. L. Archer, & J. L. Orlofsky (Eds.), *Ego identity. A handbook for psychosocial research* (pp. 22–41). New York: Springer Verlag.

Marcia, J. E., Waterman, A. S., Matteson, D. R., Archer, S. L., & Orlofsky, J. L. (1993). *Ego identity. A handbook for psychosocial research.* New York: Springer Verlag.

Nowak, A., & Vallacher, R. R. (1998). *Dynamical social psychology*. New York: Guilford Press.

9 A logistic growth model

Stage-wise development of meaning making[1]

Saskia Kunnen and Harke Bosma

One possible form of non-linear development is stage-wise development. Several leading theories in developmental psychology (e.g. those of Piaget) are based on the notion that development proceeds by means of discrete stages. Also, in the domain of self and identity several theories (e.g. those of Erikson, Kohlberg, Kegan, Loevinger, Blos; see Kroger, 2004) conceptualize development in terms of a progression through a hierarchically ordered set of stages. The notion of development proceeding by means of discrete stages with stable periods in-between raises process-related questions into the mechanisms and causes of the "jump" from one stage to the next. These questions have drawn attention in the field of non-linear dynamic systems for several decades (van der Maas and Molenaar, 1992; van Geert, 1991, 2000; van Geert and Fischer, 2009).

In this chapter we will describe a stage model for the development of meaning making in adolescence and adulthood. Although the model is basically built by the same dynamic systems approach and the same techniques as the model discussed in the previous chapter, we decided to include this model as well because the stage assumptions have specific implications for the theoretical model and the model demonstrates how these assumptions can be translated into a quantitative model. The model discussed in this chapter concerns the process of development of meaning making in adolescence and adulthood. The description is based on a paper in *New Ideas in Psychology* (Kunnen and Bosma, 2000).

Based on the theory of Kegan (1994) we developed a model that describes the development of meaning making through the different stages. First we describe the conceptual model of the mechanisms and processes of the development of meaning making. As a next step, we discuss the translation into a mathematical, dynamic systems model. Then we explore the behavior of this model, and compare its behavior with theoretical expectations and available empirical knowledge. Finally, we show how the model can generate new ideas about the developmental process, which can be translated into testable hypotheses.

A conceptual model of the development of meaning making

The structure of the conceptual model comprises seven basic questions concerning the triggers, determinants, mechanisms and influencing factors in the development of meaning making. The general developmental principles of assimilation and accommodation, and the driving force of disequilibria or conflicts, form the core of our reasoning.

We base our model on Kegan's conceptualization of meaning making. Meaning making refers to the way in which people actively organize their own experience. Each individual experiences his or her world in a unique way; the same situation can have wholly different meanings for different individuals, or for the same individual at different times. People organize their experience according to certain principles, which have been extensively described by Kegan (1982, 1994). Kegan's notion that the development of meaning making shows a stage-like pattern consisting of five increasingly complex levels forms the basis of our model. Young adolescents function mainly at level two. Most young adults have reached level three. However, this development shows huge inter-individual differences and end-levels. Our conceptual model describes how the process of development from one stage to the next might proceed.

Conflict is conceptualized as the central force in the development of meaning making. Conflicts concern discrepancies between societal demands and the level of a person's meaning, demands that are patterned in age-related expectations. Thus, one can describe a life-span trajectory of meaning making as a sequence of confrontations between one's actual way of making meaning and societal demands: as a sequence of conflicts, solutions for these conflicts and new conflicts.

The impact of a conflict depends on different factors. A conflict occurs if an individual cannot give meaning in a stable and satisfactory way to a relevant demand, whether in daily hassles or in major life events. These conflicts occur in an unpredictable, non-systematic way. However, the higher the discrepancy between the demands and one's level of meaning making, the greater the chance of conflict. Also the number of conflicts at the same time plays a role: if one is already dealing with several conflicts, the new conflict is more serious than if one had no other worries. Third, the seriousness of a conflict will depend on general cultural demands and expectations: there will be more pressure and the conflict will be greater if one's actual level of meaning making is below the modal level in one's culture. This modal level could be seen as a kind of magnet: as a pressure to conform to the majority. The exact value of the magnet may vary slightly between individuals, depending on one's specific environment.

The outcome of the conflict is described in terms of assimilation and accommodation – that is, one adjusts one's perception of the situation to one's actual way of meaning making (assimilation), or one adjusts one's level of meaning making (accommodation). However, still another way to solve the conflict is hypothesized. In contrast to children, adults have considerable freedom to escape from the demands made of them. To solve the problem, either the level of meaning making should increase or the level of demands should be reduced, which means distancing oneself from the demanding environment.

In general, people tend to try assimilation first and persist in this attempt for some time. However, although an assimilative response – a solution in terms of the actual order of meaning making – may resolve the conflict temporarily, it does not reduce the discrepancy between meaning making and curriculum. Solving conflicts in an imperfect or partial way by means of assimilation will, in the long run, lead to an accumulation of inadequately resolved problems. This cumulation will only exacerbate new conflicts, until finally assimilation is no longer possible. Consequently, the conflict is not solved at all and remains. This situation results in a rapid rise of unresolved conflicts, which in the end create more and more tension, and the need to resolve these in a different manner will become increasingly urgent. So, finally, people have to abandon their old meaning-making structure for a new, higher order way of meaning making. That is, they either accommodate – they change how they think, feel and behave with regard to the accumulated conflicts – or they escape from the tension by withdrawing from the situation. Whether accommodation or withdrawal is chosen depends on non-systematic situational circumstances, on individual characteristics (discussed below) and on the personal history of the person.

Each outcome has a different effect. In the case of a discrepancy, assimilation is an imperfect solution and does not reduce the discrepancy. It will result in an accumulation of only partially resolved conflicts and increase the likelihood of new conflicts arising. Not resolving the conflict at all amplifies this effect. Withdrawal reduces the level of the demands and thus the discrepancy. Whether this reduction lasts depends on the level of demands compared with the modal level of demands in society. Although it may be possible to escape from above-modal demands, everybody has to meet minimal demands in order to survive in society. Accommodation means an increase of the level of meaning making, which reduces the discrepancy between meaning making and demands. Both accommodation and withdrawal also result in a resolution of the conflicts that were not previously solved.

Conflicts are caused by a discrepancy between demands and the level of meaning making. Development of meaning making resolves this discrepancy. However, almost all developmental theories assume that such a new equilibrium is temporary, such that over time new demands and new conflicts will arise. According to Kegan, the increase in the level of the demands is mainly determined by age-related, normative, societal expectations. Consequently, over time, a subject will be confronted with more and more demands of a higher curriculum level. A higher level of meaning making will temporarily reduce the discrepancy between demands and meaning making but, in the long run, the new level of meaning making will make individuals sensitive to and allow them to meet new, higher level demands.

Inter-individual differences in the development of meaning making are caused firstly by differences in the kind and seriousness of life events and conflicts between people, and second by differences in the way people cope with situations – in the tendency to stick to assimilation, to stay with their current way of meaning making, to withdraw or to persist in trying to resolve the problem. These individual differences are probably caused by a set of influences and factors that have developed from an early age and consist of stable individual characteristics and environmental support. Although there may be reasons to differentiate between different factors affecting the tendency to assimilate or accommodate, for the time being we assume that these factors can be integrated into one general

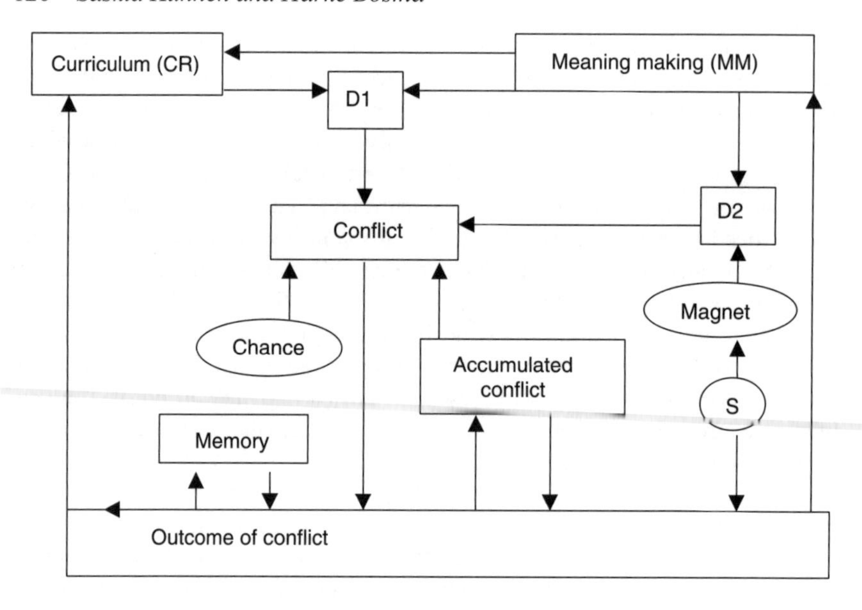

D1= discrepancy between MM and CR
D2 = discrepancy between modal MM and own MM
S = supportive factors (social support, assim./accomm. ratio)
Magnet = modal level of MM
Chance = chance factors

Figure 9.1 A flow chart representation of the theoretical assumptions concerning the development of meaning making.

factor representing all the positive and negative influences on the tendency to accommodate or assimilate in concrete situations.

Life-span trajectories of meaning making can take different shapes. People may, once or more often in their adult life, face conflicts that result in a development of meaning making to higher levels. Where people find a niche in which they can function reasonably well on a rather low level of meaning making, one sees a lack of development. On the other hand, people may face conflicts, withdraw and repeat this pattern, in which case one can well imagine a life-span trajectory characterized by broken relationships, jobs held for brief periods and withdrawal from a romantic involvement, from friends, from college, etc.

Figure 9.1 shows a flow chart representation of the theoretical assumptions discussed in this section.

A quantitative model of the development of meaning making

Building a quantitative model based on the flow chart model (Figure 9.1) means that the arrows representing the relations between the components have to be translated into mathematical equations. Together, these equations form the mathematical model in which stable factors are represented as parameters. The variables that change or may change over time are the so-called "growers". The equations describe the developmental mechanisms (our assumptions about the specific ways in which factors and growers affect each other). The whole set of parameters, growers and equations represents the developmental process.

In order to make such a model, all variables have to be quantified. The variables "meaning making" and "curriculum", for example, will be expressed by the numbers 1 to 5, analogous to Kegan's five orders of meaning making. This quantification is an abstraction, and does not imply any assumption that the differences between the orders of meaning making themselves are in fact merely quantitative.

The flow chart model is basically an IF-THEN model. Whether and how the growers change depends on the outcome of the conflict. This outcome can be any of four nominal categories. We have translated our theoretical assumptions concerning the emergence of conflicts (CF) and the factors that determine which solution is chosen (OUTCOME) into two simple equations. The rest of the model consists of an equation for each of the three growers in the flow chart model: meaning making (MM), the curriculum (CR) and the cumulation of unsolved conflicts (CC). Each growth equation specifies how (depending on the outcome) the grower changes after one iteration, as a function of the actual value of the grower itself, of some parameters and of the value of the other growers in the system that are theoretically assumed to affect the grower. Because the values of the growers are included in the equations describing the emergence and solution of a conflict, the iterative circle is closed. Thus, with each iteration a new outcome is computed for each equation, and that outcome serves as input in the next iteration.

Also in this model, the logistic growth equation forms the basis. The three growers of the model – the level of meaning making (MM), the level of the curriculum (CR) and the cumulation of unsolved conflicts (CC) – are represented by a logistic growth equation. As discussed above, individual differences are related to a cluster of factors. In the model this cluster is subsumed in one parameter, called the support parameter, which gives a one-dimensional representation of the net result of individual differences in conditions enhancing or impeding the development of meaning making.

In each iteration, a conflict (CF) can occur. A conflict only occurs if the value of the "event" exceeds a specified threshold. This event is determined by the discrepancy between the curriculum (CR) and meaning making (MM), and by a random number representing the non-systematic influences from the context.

Random numbers are an important part of the model because chance and unpredictable influences are important characteristics of all biological and psychological models. A specific characteristic of random influences in a dynamic systems model is that the effect of these influences is conditional rather than additional: the state of the system determines to what extent a random influence has any effect.

The equation that defines the value of the event is stochastic: the higher the discrepancy, the higher the chance that a conflict will occur. The numerical value of the conflict (how serious the conflict is) is higher if there are already several unsolved conflicts (if the accumulated conflict CC is higher) and if there is a discrepancy between the person's actual level of MM and the median level of MM in the person's environment (the magnet). This median level in turn is a function of general societal factors (parameter a) and specific individual factors (the support parameter). Here also, a random number gives the equation a stochastic character. A conflict occurs if the discrepancy between demands and level of meaning making plus some chance factor (random1) is higher than a predefined threshold. In an equation the conflict is defined by:

$$\text{IF } CR_t - MM_t + \text{random1} < \text{threshold THEN } CF_{t+1} = 0 \tag{9.1}$$

where CR_t is the curriculum at time t, MM_t is the meaning making at time t and CF_{t+1} is the conflict at time $t + 1$.

If the outcome of Equation 9.1 is not zero, then the size of the conflict is determined by:

$$CF_{t+1} = \text{random2} * (CC_t + p * (\text{magnet} - MM_t + z * (\text{support}))) \tag{9.2}$$

where CC_t is the cumulated conflict at time t, random1 is a random number, random2 is a random number, magnet is the modal value of MM in society, p regulates the effect of magnet–MM and z (support) is the level of support.

According to our theoretical model, a conflict may have four qualitatively different outcomes: assimilation, no solution, accommodation and withdrawal. If Equation 9.1 results in a value below zero, there is no conflict. In other cases, if the value of conflict in Equation 9.2 is higher than zero but below a specified threshold (h), the outcome is assimilation. This threshold h is different for each individual: if the support level is lower, the threshold is higher. If the value of conflict is above threshold h, it will not be resolved and the conflict will thus persist (and contribute to CC; see Equation 9.6). If this number of accumulated conflicts exceeds a critical value (j), then "not resolving" is no longer possible. In that case, only the withdrawal and accommodation options are left. Which of these is chosen depends on chance factors (a random factor), on the level of support s (more support means a higher chance that accommodation will be chosen) and on the past choices (ME): there is an increased chance that a choice made once will be made again. The equation showing the different outcomes is:

$$\begin{aligned}\text{Outcome}_{t+1} = {} & \text{IF } CF_{t+1} <= 0 \text{ THEN no conflict,} \\ & \text{ELSE IF } CF_{t+1} < h \text{ THEN assimilation,} \\ & \text{ELSE IF } CC_{t+1} < j \text{ THEN no solution,} \\ & \text{ELSE IF random} + \text{support} + ME_t < -0.2 \text{ THEN withdrawal,} \\ & \text{ELSE accommodation}\end{aligned} \tag{9.3}$$

where random = a random number, h = threshold for assimilation and j = threshold for no solution. Factor ME is a non-linear counter based on the choices that were made in the past. The equation is chosen in such a way that one choice does not yet have much impact, but if the same choice has been made four or five times in a row then ME strongly increases the chance that the same choice will be made again:

$$ME_{t+1} = ME_t + \text{IF Outcome}_t = \text{accommodation THEN } 0.2/(2+|ME_t|) \text{ ELSE IF Outcome}_t = \text{withdrawal THEN } -0.2/(2+|ME_t|) \text{ ELSE } 0 \quad (9.4)$$

Meaning making (MM) only develops when a conflict is resolved by means of accommodation. It does not change when a conflict is resolved by assimilation or withdrawal, or is not resolved at all. The development following accommodation is described by *a logistic equation*:

$$MM_{t+1} = MM_t * (1 + r) - r * MM_t^2/CR_t \quad (9.5)$$

where r is a growth parameter.

The cumulated conflict (CC) is also described by a logistic growth equation: its growth depends on its own previous value, on the growth capacity (see Equation 9.1) and on a discrete parameter (the outcome of the conflict). If there is no resolution, CC increases; following assimilation there is a slight increase and following accommodation or withdrawal it decreases. The equation is:

$$CC_{t+1} = CC_t * (1 + W) - W * CC_t^2 + \text{random} \quad (9.6)$$

where random = a very small random number, the function of which is to prevent the grower from getting stuck at 1; W is a weight factor that has a low positive value if the outcome is assimilation, a higher value if the outcome is "no resolution" and a negative value if the outcome is accommodation or withdrawal.

The curriculum (CR) starts to grow if the discrepancy between CR and MM has been very small for some time (the period of 3 years is an arbitrary choice). When that is the case, the carrying capacity increases and CR grows very slowly to the new carrying capacity. The new carrying capacity is the next order – that is, one order beyond the actual order of meaning making. Withdrawal, however, means a decrease of the carrying capacity to the actual order of meaning making. Because order 3 is assumed to be the minimum level that adults need in our society, the carrying capacity consists of a stable parameter 3 and an additional parameter KC that may be zero or higher, depending on the developmental history of meaning making. The equations are:

$$CR_{t+1} = \text{IF Outcome}_t = \text{withdrawal; THEN MM ELSE } CR_t * (1 + e) - e * CR_t^2/(3+KC_t) \quad (9.7)$$

$$KC_{t=1} = \text{IF } CR_{t\,delay} - MM_{t\,delay} - \text{random} > \text{f; THEN } KC_t \text{ ELSE } q * (MM_{t\,delay} - 2) \quad (9.8)$$

where random = a random number, f = threshold of the discrepancy between and CR MM, q regulates the impact of MM on KC, e = growth parameter of CR and $MM_{t\,delay}$ is the value of MM at some time in the past.

The behavior of the system over time is simulated by computing the complete set of equations again and again (here with the spreadsheet program Excel). The three growers (MM, CR and CC) and the equations for conflict and outcome (CF, OUTCOME) together represent the development of meaning making of an individual person. A demonstration and detailed description of the model is given on the website.

Calibration of the model

The next step is the parameter calibration: choosing parameter values for which the model generates trajectories that have an empirical and/or theoretical validity. Differences in parameters representing well-defined individual and contextual variations should result in theoretically interpretable differences in simulated trajectories.

Each simulated curve can be seen as a set of simulated data, with information about characteristics such as the duration of transitions and stable periods, the age of onset of transitions, the size of the substeps in these transitions and the speed of development during transitions. Running a large number of simulations provides a large sample of simulated individual trajectories, which allows for the comparison of these characteristics with those of an empirical sample, or the prediction of such characteristics in the population. But, in order to be able to do this, the abstract notion of 1000 iterations has to be mapped onto age, and the values of the support parameter have to be translated into meaningful definitions of more or less optimal conditions.

For mapping the simulations onto age, the levels of meaning making and curriculum have to be translated into initial values of the growers, and the iterations have to be translated into time periods. This translation must be based on theory and the available empirical findings. We wanted the model to represent the development of meaning making from the beginning of adolescence, around the age of 12, to old age, say around the age of 70. The simulated trajectories consist of 1000 iterations. Each year then covers 17.5 iterations with 1.5 potential conflicts per month. Furthermore, the value of the grower "curriculum" was set at 2.5 at the age of 12 and it should reach 3 around the age of 16, after 70 iterations (4×17.5). The initial value of the order of meaning making was set at 2.

The support parameter represents differences between people. In order to be able to relate the simulated trajectories to empirical data, it is necessary to know which value represents a normal condition and which values represent optimal or non-optimal conditions. A normal value of the support parameter should result in a normal developmental trajectory. Higher values should show – on average – more optimal development but within realistic ranges. Lower values should show less optimal development. Based on this simple reasoning and 240 simulated trajectories, values ranging from –0.3 through to 0.4 were chosen for the support parameter.

As an illustration, some trajectories will be presented that result from simulations with different values of the support parameter. Figures 9.2 and 9.3 show the graphical representation of the trajectories of meaning making, curriculum level

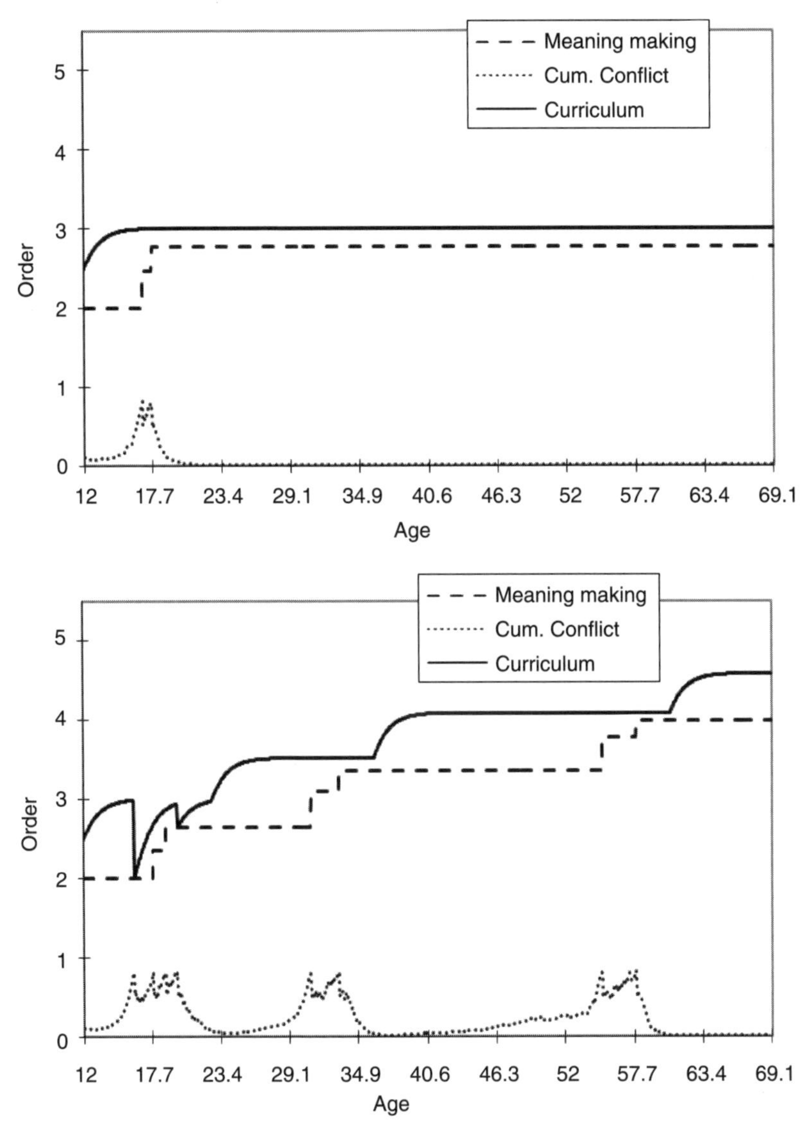

Figure 9.2 Two simulated trajectories with a low value for the support parameter (0.1). The frequency of occurence of these types is 48% (top) and 14% (bottom).

and accumulated conflict over 1000 iterations. In both figures the most frequently occurring types of trajectories are presented. These types have been defined by the number of jumps and withdrawals. The differences between the types within each figure are wholly due to the role of chance factors in the simulations. Figure 9.2 shows typical outcomes of 50 simulations with a low value for the support parameter whereas Figure 9.3 shows typical outcomes of 50 simulations with a high value for the support parameter.

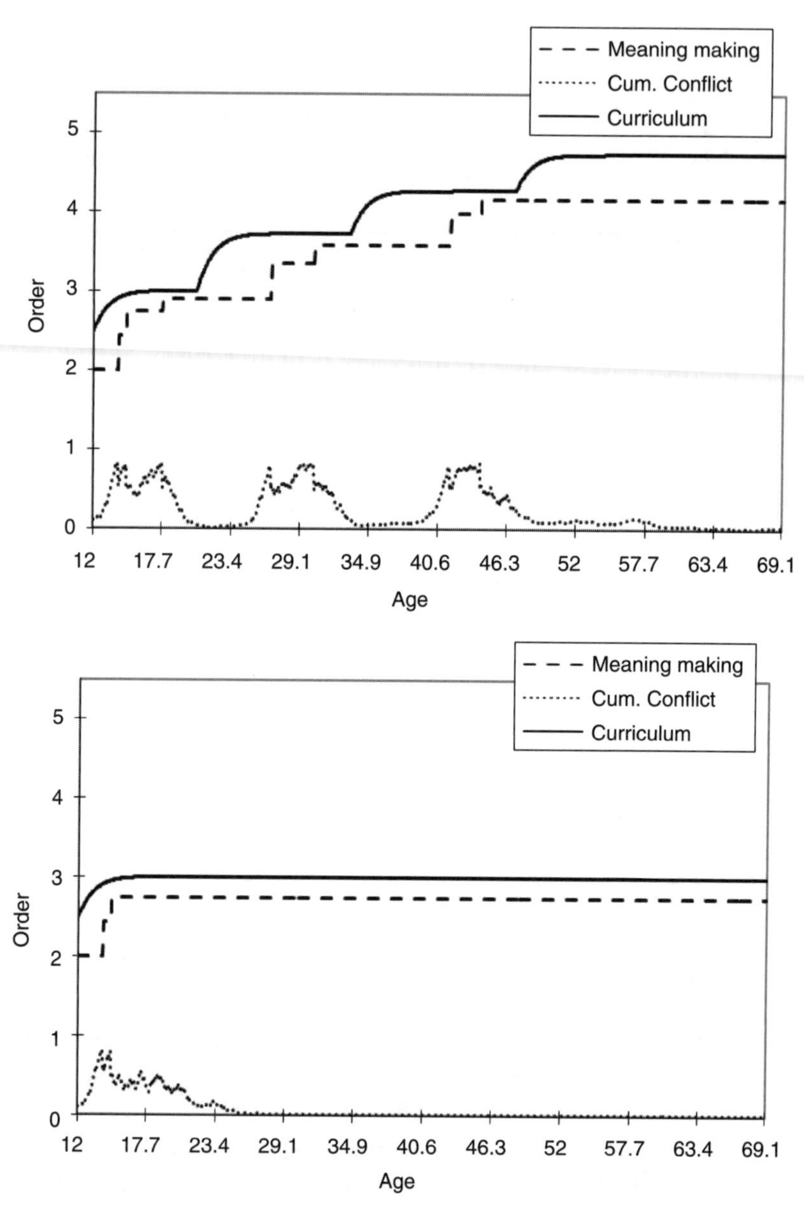

Figure 9.3 Two simulated trajectories with a high value for the support parameter (0.2). The frequencey of occurrence of these types of trajectories is 50% (top) and 6% (bottom).

The implication of calibration is that the parameter values cannot be changed further, except for the support parameter within the defined range. Now the model can be put to a much harder test: The simulations with the model should lead to well-specified outcomes that can be predicted on the basis of the theory and the available data.

However, in the field of adult development of meaning making, longitudinal data that are necessary for a thorough test of the model (and for investigating developmental processes in general) are lacking. At present, the only test is to verify that the behavior of the model is not at odds with the basic theoretical assumptions and does not generate data that are incompatible with what little data are available. In comparing simulations with empirical data we do not try to fit the data set, but we just look to see whether the data set could be a subsample of a population that has been generated by the model. The theory and empirical data used here are all presented in Kegan (1994). The data in Kegan (1994) are presented in a general fashion: as orders 2, 3, 4 and 5 and transitional positions 2-3, 3-4 and 4-5. The mathematical model generates continuous scores. Scores 2.85 to 3.15 were rounded off to 3, and scores >3.15 but <3.85 were coded as transitional position 3-4, etc.

On the basis of general theoretical propositions we expected that the simulations should show the following: in adolescence, scores of levels 2 to 3 only; at the end of adolescence (age 20) most people should approach or have reached level 3; in young adulthood (age 30) a low frequency of level 2 scores, a high frequency of scores around level 3 and few level 4 scores; by the age of 40, a minority of the simulations should progress to level 4 and at age 50, a very small minority should show further development.

In order to compare a simulated distribution of orders to these theoretical predictions, a set of 175 simulated trajectories was created that was meant to represent the population in general. A normal distribution of support parameter values was used. The frequencies of the levels of meaning making in this series of simulations at the ages of 16, 20, 30, 40, 50 and 70 are shown in Table 9.1. Although the theory says nothing about the development of meaning making in

Table 9.1 Percentage distribution of orders at different ages in a simulated population ($n = 175$)

	Age					
Order	16	20	30	40	50	70
2	28	8	5	5	5	5
2–3	67	44	27	26	26	26
3	5	48	19	3	2	2
3–4	0	1	40	39	26	9
4	0	0	9	22	23	27
4–5	0	0	0	5	17	30
5	0	0	0	0	1	1

Table 9.2 Distribution of orders in the empirical and the simulated samples

Order	*Empirical data* (n = *75)*	*Simulations* (n = *250)*
2	13%	5%
2–3	23%	30%
3	12%	16%
3–4	31%	29%
4	18%	16%
4–5	3%	5%
5	0%	0%

old age, the oldest age group (70) was included in order to check whether the developmental trajectories remain at least plausible. The development of meaning making in these later years of life should not go beyond the 5th order.

Table 9.1 shows that the simulations confirm the theoretical, developmental assumptions.

A second comparison involved simulations and a combined empirical sample of three studies (Kegan, 1994, pp. 192-196, samples 1, 5 and 11) that are assumed to be fairly representative of the population. In order to do this, a group of simulated trajectories was generated that resembled Kegan's sample as closely as possible with regard to age and level of the support parameter. However, for the simulations it is assumed that the most disadvantaged people, such as drug addicts or inhabitants of slums, were absent from the empirical samples. Therefore, a slightly skewed distribution of the support parameter was used here, in which the least optimal values are less frequent. In addition, an age distribution in the simulated sample was chosen that resembled the estimated age distribution in the empirical samples. The simulations (*n*=250) should result in a distribution of levels comparable to the distribution in the combined empirical samples (Table 9.2).

A chi-squared analysis yielded a non-significant difference between both frequency distributions ($chi^2 = 8.5$, df = 5, $p > .10$). Thus, the simulated data are not at odds with the empirical data and they could well belong to the same population. The biggest difference between both samples concerns the higher frequency of subjects of the empirical sample in the 2nd order, and their lower frequency in order 2-3. However, the percentages of subjects in orders 2 and 2-3 together are almost the same for both samples. The same holds for the orders 3, 3-4 and 4, and 4 and 4-5. The discrepancies between the simulations and the data, therefore derive from adjacent categories.

The gain in knowledge offered by this technique

We have shown that the model behaves according to theoretical assumptions and is not at odds with empirical data. This finding validates the model in the same way that confirmation of hypotheses that are based on a theory validates the theory. This means that our assumptions about the factors and mechanisms in the process of meaning making development, which forms the core of the model, have some validity. However, as discussed in the previous chapter, quantitative dynamic systems models offer further possibilities. Based on simulated trajectories, hypotheses can be formulated concerning phenomena wherein different theories contradict each other or a theory says nothing or no data are available. In this way a theory can be challenged to become more refined and more explicit, and empirical research can be initiated to explore new kinds of empirical data. In the original paper (Kunnen and Bosma, 1999) examples have been given of this way of using this mathematical dynamic systems model for expanding our knowledge of the process of the development of meaning making. As an illustration, we mention one of them. It concerns the effect of different patterns and frequencies of conflicts on developmental differences in meaning making. Some theoretical notions exist concerning the relation between the number of problems adolescents or young adults encounter and their developmental trajectories. The model in this chapter is based on the theoretical assumption that conflicts are the motor of development. However, based on Coleman's focal theory (Coleman and Hendry, 1990), problematic or stagnated development would be expected to go together with a very high frequency of all types of problems. According to Kegan (1994) a higher frequency of relatively small conflicts may be expected in more optimal developmental trajectories. By means of a quantitative model such hypotheses can be explored. We analyzed the number of conflicts in each of the three types of developmental trajectories. The mean scores are given in Table 9.3 and *t*-tests were used to compare these means.

Stagnated development, compared with average development, is related to a higher frequency of problems in all categories. The least problems occur in average development. Optimal development is characterized by a significantly higher rate of intermediate conflicts (between .2 and .5) compared with average development. This confirms Kegan's assumptions. The finding that stagnated development involves a higher frequency of conflicts in all categories, compared with average and optimal development, is consistent with Coleman's focal theory. The simulations, though, show an even more detailed picture, which suggests that there might be an optimal number for certain types of conflict. A low number of conflicts of moderate seriousness might retard development, while too many lead to stagnation.

Of course, such a finding requires a more thorough theoretical elaboration and empirical exploration. However, it demonstrates just one of the many possible applications of simulations generated by a dynamic systems model. These run

Table 9.3 Frequency of conflicts in three types of developmental patterns between ages 12 and 20

	Seriousness of conflicts					
Development	0 – .1	.1 – .2	.2 – .3	.3 – .4	.4 – .5	> .5
Stagnated	52[a]	33	24[b]	17[d]	9[e]	6[a]
Average	66[b]	33	19[a]	12[e]	7[d]	4[b]
Optimal	57[c]	32	24[b]	14[e]	9[e]	4[b]

Note: Different letters indicate significant differences: [a, b, c] $p < .005$; [d, e] $p < .05$.

from testing existing hypotheses or theoretical assumptions to the generation of new hypotheses. To give some more examples, in our original paper we demonstrated how the model can generate hypotheses concerning the distribution of different stages at different age levels (Kunnen and Bosma, 2000). Building dynamic systems models can also generate hypotheses concerning the types and timing of interventions that may be useful in the case of stagnating development. Based on the assumption that support stimulates development, one could, in the model, increase the level of support during specific periods and test the changes in trajectories that result from these changes. In addition, one can manipulate the timing of the simulated intervention and test, for example, the assumption that intervention is most effective in transition periods. In this way, many more examples could be generated, but the main point is that this type of theoretical experimental psychology generates interesting suggestions and empirical questions and in this way offers possibilities that are not available without a quantitative dynamic systems model.

Note

1 A demonstration model and an appendix for this chapter can be found at www.psypress.com/dynamic-systems-approach/appedices.

References

Coleman, J. C., & Hendry, L. (1990). *The nature of adolescence.* London: Routledge.

Kegan, R. (1982). *The evolving self: Problem and process in human development.* Cambridge, MA: Harward University Press.

Kegan, R. (1994). *In over our heads.* Cambridge, MA: Harward University Press.

Kroger, J. (2004). Identity in adolescence. *The balance between self and other.* London: Routledge.

Kunnen, E. S., & Bosma, H. A. (2000). Development of meaning making. A dynamic systems conceptualization. *New Ideas in Psychology, 18,* 57–82.

Van der Maas, H. L. J., & Molenaar, P. C. M. (1992). Stagewise cognitive development: An application of catastrophe theory. *Psychological Review, 99*, 395–417.

Van Geert, P. L. C. (1991). A dynamic systems model of cognitive and language growth. *Psychological Review, 98*, 3–53 .

Van Geert, P. L. C. (2000). The dynamics of general developmental mechanisms: From Piaget and Vygotsky to dynamic systems models. *Current Directions in Psychological Science, 9*, 64–68.

Van Geert, P. L. C., & Fischer, K. W. (2009). Dynamic systems and the quest for individual-based models of change and development. In J. P. Spencer, M. S. C. Thomas, & J. McClelland (Eds.), *Toward a new grand theory of development? Connectionism and dynamic systems theory reconsidered* (pp. 313–336). Oxford, UK: Oxford University Press.

10 Agent-based modeling in developmental psychology[1]

Paul van Geert, Henderien Steenbeek and Saskia Kunnen

So far, the book has described typical dynamic systems as variables that are changing over time. A dynamic systems model, in that case, is some sort of mathematical function that describes this change over time – describes how the next level of the variable, the next state of the dynamic system, results from the current level of the variable or current state of the dynamic system. We have also seen that more complex dynamic systems consist of coupled variables, in which the state of one variable depends on its preceding state and on the preceding states of a number of other variables to which it is coupled. Couplings are often reciprocal, where one variable depends on another, and the other depends on the first. The coupling, however, need not be symmetrical: one variable can exert a positive influence on the other, while the other has a negative or competitive influence on the first. These reciprocal, symmetrical or asymmetrical relationships can create interesting non-linear trajectories over time, as demonstrated in various chapters of this book.

In the social sciences, roughly three types of simulation models can be distinguished: system models, connectionist models and agent models. System models describe a process in the form of a set of coupled equations, similar to the format described in Chapter 8. Connectionist models specify relations between an input (e.g. an adolescent's request for autonomy) and an output (e.g. the reaction of the mother). The input–output relation is modeled by means of layers or nodes. Agent or multi-agent models consist of components or models that model real agents (i.e. persons that act on other persons and on their environment). Each agent contains a model description that can either be a system or a connectionist model. These types of models have in common that they deal with dynamic systems in which variables mutually interact, influence each other and change over time. Thus, basically all the models can be described as dynamic systems models that only differ in the way they realize the dynamic system character (see Thelen and Bates, 2003; Spencer, Thomas and McClelland, 2009).

An example of a comparison between different types of models is the simulation research of mother–child interaction by Olthof, Kunnen and Boom (2000), who compared a connectionist and a system model. In the system model, three variables were distinguished that acted as determinants of the interaction process, namely the irritability of the child, the sensitivity of the mother and the intensity of an external stressor. The results of both types of simulation differed considerably. However, in both types of simulation small changes in the intensity of the stressor cause abrupt changes in the type of interaction, for example changing an effective interaction into an ineffective one.

The current chapter deals with the third type of model, namely the agent model, agent-based model or adaptive agent model (Axelrod, 2005; Elliott and Kiel, 2004; Frantz and Carley, 2009; Gilbert, 2007; Grimm et al., 2005; Schlesinger, 2001; Smith and Conrey, 2007). The central building block of this model is the agent, or actor, which is a collection of dynamic variables. Agent models are typical dynamic systems models of the life sciences (biology, sociology, economics, psychology, etc.). The life sciences typically deal with agents such as animals, people, firms or organizations. In this book, we have seen that properties of what we now call agents – children, adults, adolescents – can be treated as variables in the classical sense (e.g. the lexicon of the child can be treated as a simple numerical variable that changes as a consequence of the child's interactions with a linguistic environment). Hence, such classical variable-based models can be very fruitfully applied in the life sciences, psychology in particular. However, the reason why we also need agent-based models in the life sciences is that agents are the natural units in the realm of the living. A developing child or a developing adolescent is a living unit, and variables such as the adolescent's need for autonomy and the amount of oppositional behavior are properties of the adolescent qua agent acting in a particular meaningful environment (Schlesinger and Parisi, 2001). An agent is a dynamic system in and by itself, because the agent has a number of properties that change over time, as a consequence of the agent's interaction with other agents, who also have a number of properties that define the nature of the interactions that the adolescent can have. So the first question we must ask ourselves is: What is an agent?

What kind of dynamic system is an agent?

Remember that an agent can take a wide variety of forms: flies, pigeons, adolescent boys, firms producing candy bars, etc. These agents have a number of general properties in common (for an overview of agent properties, see Steenbeek and van Geert, 2007). First of all they are autonomous, but to maintain their existence they depend on the environment, an environment that could be as simple as another agent or that consists of other agents and physical resources, and so forth. Second, agents can act, they can do something, and what they do is in principle something that affects not only themselves but also other agents or the environment. Third, agents act because they have some sort of goal, interest or concern, and their actions are aimed towards realizing these goals, interests or concerns. In order to reach these goals, they need other agents and the environment (in some cases they do not need other agents to achieve their goals but they always need to take other agents into account). Fourth, agents are subject to entropy, which means that as time flies their state of goal satisfaction, if any, will decrease and thus they will be forced to act in order to reach their goal. The entropy sometimes means that agents can actually disappear from a system if their basic goals are not sufficiently maintained.

Take for instance a very simple unicellular organism, such as an amoeba swimming in a drop of water. The amoeba must maintain its internal metabolism within certain limits, and if these limits are exceeded the amoeba will die. Even if it does nothing, its internal metabolic resources will nevertheless be consumed and then it will reach a critical state – death. In order to avoid this, it must do something, which in the case of the amoeba is to swim around and catch food. The amount of food it can catch depends on the amount of food available in its drop of water and on how active it is in searching for food (i.e. how much and how fast it swims around). Now let us take a different example, which is that of an adolescent living with his family, going to school, having friends, etc. The adolescent has a myriad of goals, concerns or interests but we can simplify the adolescent qua agent by treating him or her as having two goals: autonomy and "all other goals". In principle, adolescents begin as children, and as a child the adolescent has relatively little autonomy. In fact, as the adolescent grows older he will find his autonomy not to be sufficient and will strive towards greater autonomy (e.g. the adolescent wants to determine himself how late he shall come back from a party and he does not want his parents to do that for him). The adolescent will have to do something to increase his autonomy towards a level that he finds satisfactory. For instance, he will have to enter into discussions with his parents, he will have to disobey rules, he will have to stand sanctions, and so forth. Whether or not the adolescent achieves a satisfactory level of autonomy depends not only on his own actions but also on the actions of the environment. For instance, if his parents grant him all the autonomy he can take as soon as he asks for it, he will have very little to do. However, if his parents are very authoritarian and strict, he will have to work hard in order to obtain even a little bit of autonomy and freedom, which will most likely be well below what he would like to have.

Given all this information, is it possible to construct a mathematical model of autonomy building in the adolescent? One answer to this question would be no, that is impossible: An adolescent is a hugely complicated system, and there are so many variables that affect the adolescent's wish for autonomy, or the parent's reaction, that we cannot hope for a more or less realistic model at the moment. Such a model is simply beyond our powers and means. From a dynamic systems point of view, however, the answer is a simple yes: What is at stake here is to provide a mathematical formulation of the agent model as it was conceptually described above, and from a mathematical point of view this agent model is relatively simple.

Modeling the flow of events

Let us now ask ourselves how we can model these agents as dynamic systems. A characteristic property of dynamic systems modeling is that it tries to capture the most essential aspects of the system and based on these aspects, which are also often simplified as much as possible, tries to reconstruct the dynamics as something that emerges out of the basic dynamic principles. Thus, a dynamic systems model simplifies to the most fundamental aspects of the dynamics, and by doing so implies a bottom-up strategy towards explaining the phenomena in which it is interested. For instance, earlier in this book we have seen examples of S-shaped developments in various psychological variables. That is to say, the pattern of change (i.e. the process that occurs from moment to moment) follows an S-shaped trajectory if it is plotted across a long enough period of time. The more classical, macroscopic mathematical model of this S-shaped trajectory would be to apply an equation that describes the overall form of the trajectory at once (and, in fact, there are many mathematical equations that describe this form). A dynamic systems explanation of this S-shaped trajectory, on the other hand, asks itself: What are the principles that determine how the next state of the variable results from its preceding state? These stepwise changes (which might also be continuous changes) are like the elementary temporal building blocks of the process. By applying these stepwise changes in an iterative fashion (step one leads to step 2, step 2 leads to step 3, 3 to 4, and so on) the model hopes to construct or build an S-shaped trajectory – the model generates a flow (i.e. a continuous or eventually stepwise change over time) that hopefully has the long-term properties that we wish to explain.

The same principle of bottom-up explanation applies to agent models. Take the example of the adolescent. When observed over a sufficiently long duration, we see that the adolescent begins to defy his parents' authority, runs into conflicts or not, increases attempts to gain more autonomy or not, achieves a sufficient level of autonomy or not, is more or less happy with the situation, and so on (Lichtwarck-Aschoff,van Geert, Bosma and Kunnen, 2008). We could approach the explanation of this macroscopic pattern from a more classical point of view by stating that this overall pattern is in some way or another built into the system, for instance in the form of a pattern of genetic instructions or of existing cultural scenarios. Although this is of course a naïve way to express this type of explanation, it nevertheless amounts to the idea that there is some sort of pre-existing map or set of instructions specifying this particular developmental trajectory as some overall pattern. An agent model, on the other hand, will start from the agent's first principles: it will begin with an increase in the desire for autonomy, which leads to an action aimed at increasing this autonomy, which will lead to a particular reaction from the environment (e.g. the parent granting autonomy or not or to a particular extent), leading to an action from the adolescent based on the amount of goal satisfaction that this particular preceding action has brought about, which is followed by another action of the environment, which is based on the effect the preceding action of the environment had on achieving the environment's goal (which, if the environment in this particular case is a parent, consists of maintaining the status quo or granting autonomy to the adolescent with considerably smaller steps than the adolescent finds acceptable). All these interactive steps can lead to a long-term pattern of actions and changes in autonomy and emotions (if emotions are part of the agent model), and if the agent model is a good model it will reconstruct the flow of events that is characteristic of what has been observed in reality.

An example of how to build a simple agent model: The growth of adolescent autonomy

The adolescent goal is to achieve a sufficient level of autonomy, and at the beginning of the process this autonomy is at a minimal level (in reality, the level might already be quite high, but for the adolescent it is not enough and is in fact well below the level he or she would like to achieve). So, for simplicity, let us represent autonomy as a simple variable, the minimal value of which we set to 0 and the maximum value to 1. We need not be concerned with what this 0 or 1 means in reality; for now it will serve the purpose of setting the limits of the autonomy variable. Let us see how far we can get in building an agent model with the instrument that has been used throughout the book, Microsoft Excel.

Let us open a new file, write down "autonomy" in cell K4 and introduce the initial value of the variable of autonomy in cell K5.[2] For reasons that will become clear afterwards, I propose to enter an arbitrarily small number instead of zero, for instance 0.01.

Being an agent, the adolescent has certain means (behaviors or actions) by which he can reach his goal (i.e. increase his level of autonomy). Of course, there are a myriad of different ways in which the adolescent can do this and numerous behaviors that will affect his autonomy negatively or positively, but all these behaviors have one thing in common – they are autonomy-affecting behaviors. In terms of modeling this suffices to bring them all together into one variable that we shall call autonomy-affecting behaviors, or behaviors for simplicity. Hence, in addition to the first building block of the adolescent agent, which was the variable autonomy, we now introduce the second building block of the adolescent agent, which is the action aimed at changing autonomy. If the cells represent steps in some time series, which they usually do, the occurrence of an action at a particular moment of time can be represented by 1 and the absence of such an action by 0. Hence the time series will consist of a series of zeros and ones. These actions are some sort of event generated deliberately by the adolescent agent and have the simple effect of changing the autonomy level either positively or negatively and to various extents. The question is how we can model the adolescent's intentions to perform some sort of action aimed towards increasing his autonomy to the desired level. I shall meet the following theoretical choice. Any act aimed towards increasing one's autonomy is in fact an act of autonomy (it is certainly not an act of dependence on others, for instance). Hence, the probability that at any moment in time the agent will perform an autonomy-increasing act is a function of the level of autonomy already attained by the agent. Since at any moment in time an act either occurs or not, we can model the adolescent's intention to perform an autonomy-affecting act as a random function of the level of autonomy already attained. As already mentioned, cell K5 contains the initial value of autonomy and let us further assume that the autonomy-affecting behaviors appear in the L-column. Hence, in L4 we write "behavior", and then in L5 we can write the following equation:

```
= IF(RAND() < K5,1,0)
```

This simple equation will yield a series of zeros and ones, with, in the long run, a proportion of ones that is equal to the level of autonomy. As the level of autonomy changes, the proportion will also change. However, we shall also assume that the tendency to perform an autonomy-affecting act depends on the adolescent's drive to become autonomous. For simplicity, we assume that this drive is proportional to the distance between the current level of autonomy, the level of autonomy that the adolescent wishes to attain in the long run (represented by the numerical value 1) and some personal drive that we call p_autonomy.

The value of p_autonomy is written in cell D2. In cell M4 we write "Drive" and we specify this condition in cell M5 as follows:

= IF(RAND() < (1-K5)*p_autonomy,1,0)

This equation will specify a series of zeros and ones with a probability equal to the difference between 1 and the current level of autonomy. This probability is of course maximal at the beginning (if the initial level of autonomy is very small it approaches 1) and approaches 0 as the level of autonomy approaches the intended level, which is 1. Since the actual occurrence of an autonomy-affecting act at any moment in time depends on both conditions, the system generates such an act if both conditions are fulfilled (i.e. if both values are 1). We write "occurrence" in N4, and specify this in cell N5 as follows:

= IF(SUM(L5:M5) = 2,1,0)

This N-column specifies the occurrence of an autonomy-affecting act in the form of the value 1, and the absence of such an act in the form of the value 0. If we copy these cells a sufficient number of times (e.g. 2000 times, thus from L5:N5 to L2000:N2000) we basically obtain a simulation of the time series of autonomy-affecting acts carried out by our adolescent agent. If each cell represents 1 day in the life of the adolescent agent, the total time series is approximately equal to the period of 3 years, based on the assumption that on average every day provides the adolescent agent with the opportunity to perform an autonomy-enhancing act (of course this is a very simplifying assumption, and it can be replaced by any other one, but for the time being we can use this assumption as an approximation of what could go on in the real system).

Autonomy-affecting acts carried out by our adolescent agent are not very useful unless they have some sort of effect on the adolescent's actual autonomy. The adolescent performs these acts with the intention to increase his or her autonomy, and thus the average effect of such an act should consist of an autonomy increase. Let us begin with the very simplifying assumption that every act is successful and indeed increases the adolescent's autonomy. Remember that the A-column specifies the level of autonomy. Thus, in cell K6 we specify the level of autonomy that follows from the preceding moment in time, which was represented in cell K5. If cell N5 accidentally contained an autonomy-affecting act, the effect of the effect will be that it increases the value of autonomy in the next step, which is in cell K6.

Let us assume, for simplicity, that every increase in autonomy is equal to a step size of 0.01 (which is of course too much of a simplification) and we can write the following equation[2] in cell K6:

= IF(N5 = 1,K5 + 0.01,K5)

This equation says that if an autonomy-enhancing act was performed at the time before the current one the effect of autonomy will be an increase of 0.01, and if no such act occurred there will be no effect on autonomy and it will remain the same as the level during the previous moment in time. If we run the simulation a couple of times, we will see that growth towards the maximum level of autonomy follows a roughly S-shaped curve that reaches its maximum at very different moments in time (on average it takes about 880 "days" to reach the maximum, with a standard deviation of 140 "days").

An important property of an agent model is that acts are not always successful, or more precisely that the success of an act depends on the effect it brings about in the environment (the probability that such an effect occurs depends on the properties of the environment, and of course on the quality or adequacy of the act, but for simplicity we shall assume that all acts are equally adequate or competent, and that the effect of the act solely depends on the reaction of the environment). In this particular agent model, the environment of the adolescent agent that determines the agent's success is the parent (we represent the parents by one parent agent, again for simplicity). The parent can either yield to the adolescent's autonomy-enhancing act, such as the adolescent asking whether he or she can stay out at night until 10 or resist it. If the parent yields to the request, the adolescent's act is successful and this results in an increase in adolescent autonomy, but if the parent resists the request then the adolescent level of autonomy will remain the same. How can we determine whether a parent will yield to the request or resist it? We can do that by treating the parent as the second agent in the agent model, and by giving the parent a particular goal – in this case to keep the adolescent's level of autonomy within certain limits. What these limits are is not very important, but we can assume that the parent associates the level of tolerable autonomy in their adolescent child to the child's age – that is, as the adolescent grows older the parent will grant him more autonomy until he is old enough to take full responsibility for his acts. If the adolescent asks for more autonomy than the parent finds acceptable, then the parent will resist any requests for autonomy that the adolescent makes. A very simple way of specifying the parent goal is to give the parent a certain autonomy norm that is proportional to the adolescent's age. Suppose that the parent is willing to grant the adolescent full autonomy no earlier than 3 years from now (this is of course a ridiculously simplified way of specifying the parent norm, but for the moment it will do).

Let us use column S and those further to the right as columns specifying the parent agent. We use column I to specify time in days, running from 1 to 1100, which is approximately 3 years from now. To do so, write "Time" in I4, =1 in I5 and =I5+1 in I6. In cell S5 we specify the level of autonomy that the parent finds acceptable at this particular moment in time. We write "accepted level" in S4. If maximal autonomy is set to 1 and acceptable autonomy is proportional to age, we can specify the current level of autonomy that the parent accepts as:

= I5/1095

The number 1095 is exactly 3 years from now, and if the time index equals 3 years (i.e. 1095 days) then the acceptable level of autonomy or the autonomy norm will equal 1, which corresponds to full autonomy. In order to keep the autonomy norm to a maximum of 1, we will need to rewrite the equation somewhat by entering in cell S5

= IF(I5/1095 > 1,1,I5/1095)

Instead of entering the value 1095 in the equation, it may be better if you first define a variable name, "parent_norm_moment", and set the value of that variable to 1095 (or any other value you wish). You can specify the equation as follows:

= IF(I5/parent_norm_moment > 1,1,I5/parent_norm_moment)

To do this, write "parent_norm_moment" in cell C6 and give D6 the name "parent_norm_moment". How this is done is explained in Appendix 8(1) (Exceltip: Introduce Named Variables)[1]. In general, working with the specified variable names is considerably more convenient than writing the values in the equations themselves. If the parent's resistance to the adolescent's autonomy request stochastically depends on the parent's norm, we can write an equation for the parent's resistance in column T in the following way (by convention: value 1 means that the parent resists the adolescent's autonomy request; value 0 means that the parent does nothing or, more precisely, yields to the adolescent's autonomy request). Write "parent resistance" in T4 and write in T5:

= IF(AND(N5 = 1,RAND() > S5),1,0)

This equation means that if the adolescent performed an autonomy-affecting act such as making an autonomy request (which we can find in cell N5) and if some random number is greater than the parent's current autonomy norm, the parent will react with resistance to the adolescent's autonomy request and will do nothing or, in practice, yield to the autonomy request in all other cases.

Thus, the parent's act of resistance, or the absence of such an act, is the environmental effect that determines whether the adolescent agent's act will be successful or not (if there is resistance it will not be successful and, in principle, will not lead to increase in autonomy). So we have to go back to the adolescent agent and specify a column in which we define the autonomy increase dependent on the presence or absence of resistance in the parent. We shall use column O to do this.

Let us randomly choose the autonomy increase from a normal distribution. To specify a normal distribution, you must define its average and standard deviation. We use the dNormaldev function[3] to do this. For instance

= dNormaldev(0.5,0.1)

will randomly draw a value from a normal distribution with mean equal to 0.5 and standard deviation equal to 0.1. Before specifying this equation we should set a value for the average autonomy increase (call this variable autonomy_increase and place it in D4) and its standard deviation (call it stdev_divider and place it in D8): 0.025 and 0.0125, for example. We now decide that if the parent resists an autonomy request from the adolescent the change in autonomy is drawn from a random distribution with mean equal to zero and standard deviation equal to the standard deviation variable just defined (i.e. 0.0125). Thus, if the parent resists the autonomy request the change in autonomy can be negative (i.e. autonomy is reduced or eventually positive, but with an average effect of zero). However, if the parent does nothing to resist the adolescent's autonomy request, the gain in autonomy is drawn from a random distribution with a mean equal to the value of the autonomy_increase variable (i.e. 0.025) and a standard deviation equal to the value just determined (i.e. 0.0125). Remember that we find the parent's resistance or absence thereof in the T column. In cell O4 we write "Parental influence" and in O5 we write the following equation

= IF(T5 = 1;dNormalDev(0;autonomy_increase/stdev_divider);dNormal
Dev(autonomy_increase;autonomy_increase/stdev_divider))

If the adolescent has performed an autonomy-affecting act (i.e. has made some sort of autonomy request to the parent) then his autonomy will be changed in accordance with the autonomy increase that has resulted from this act, which depends on the presence or absence of resistance of the parent to this act. In cell K6, which specifies the next level of autonomy based on the level specified in cell K5, we elaborate the equation by replacing the predefined increase of 0.01 by the influence of the parental resistance as given in cell O5. We write in K6 the following equation:

= IF(N5 = 1,K5 + O5,K5)

This equation means that if the adolescent made an autonomy request in the preceding moment (i.e. if the value of N5 was 1) then the level of autonomy specified in cell K5 increases with the value specified in cell O5, whereas if there was no preceding autonomy request the value of autonomy does not change. If we copy all these equations 2000 times, we obtain a simulated time series of approximately $5\frac{1}{2}$ years (if one cell represents a single day).

By changing the values of the parent's norm (the average autonomy increase and standard deviation) we can experiment with various scenarios in this very simple two-agent model. One interesting finding of this model is that the average age at which the adolescent agent achieves maximal autonomy is significantly below the level at which the parent has set his norm of full autonomy. For instance, if the starting age of the model is 15 years and the parent has a norm of full autonomy set to the age of 18 years (value 1095 if one row equals one day), the average age at which the adolescent agent reaches full autonomy is 17 years and 5 months. Of course, these agents as such have no real psychological meaning; they just serve the purpose of illustration, and what they illustrate in this particular case of the current model makes a prediction about the age of autonomy that we most likely could not have foreseen if we had based our prediction on some sort of linear simplification of the model. For example, if we had reckoned with the fact that the parent's resistance is a simple linear function of the parent's norm age for adolescent autonomy, and also with the fact that if the parent resists the adolescent's autonomy request the average gain in autonomy is zero (which are indeed simple rules according to which this agent model operates), we would probably have predicted that the average age at which the adolescent reaches autonomy is around the age of the parent's norm. However, this is not what the model produces; it predicts that, on average, the adolescent is able to lower the age of full autonomy. Another result of this particular agent model is that in the majority of cases the growth of autonomy has an introductory period in which virtually nothing happens, which is then followed by a period of rapid growth. We mention these results not because of their direct empirical implications, but because they illustrate the fact that agent models such as this one display properties that are not particularly expected on the basis of linear extrapolations from the basic principles of the agent model. This observation illustrates that such models show emergent properties (the emergent properties in this particular case are very simple, but nevertheless unexpected).

From dyadic to multi-agent systems

Agent systems are typically used to model emergent phenomena that arise from the interaction of many agents: economic phenomena, traffic and traffic jams, demographic phenomena, interactions between individuals in biological populations, and so forth. "Many" in this case really means "a lot". Such models are simplified versions of collective actions in populations (i.e. actions that result from the interactions between a multitude of individual agents) and thus are not particularly suited for the purposes of the developmental psychologist. Developmental psychology primarily focuses on patterns of change in individuals as they interact with their environment or with the significant persons in their environment. In that sense, the multi-agent system that a developmental psychologist will primarily focus on consists of two or a few agents, rather than the hundreds or thousands that occur in real multi-agent systems in sociology or economics. In developmental psychology there is of course room for multi-agent systems, for instance when modeling the interactions in a classroom. In one research project we have tried to build multi-agent systems to model the formation of friendships in adolescent groups that were about the size of a regular class, with regard to the question of how friendship relates to similarity in person-properties between agents that are likely to become friends, and how friendships eventually relate to increasing or decreasing similarity between friends (Ballato, in press). In another project we have tried to understand the emergence and maintenance of high levels of aggressive interaction in groups of children from special education (Visser, 2011). Again the size of the group was that of a class, which in the case of special education consists of no more than 10–15 individual children. In yet another project, which we will discuss in this chapter, we focused on the agent dynamics in the microgroup, namely the dynamics in a dyad consisting of children playing together (Steenbeek, 2006; Steenbeek and van Geert, 2007, 2008).

Before discussing these micro-group agent dynamics we shall refer to another distinction, in addition to the distinction between micro- and macro-group agent models that we have just discussed. This particular distinction refers to the different time scales that developmental psychologists are interested in. Developmental psychologists primarily focus on the long-term process of development, which takes place over the course of years or even decades (i.e. a long-term time scale). This long-term process comes about as a result of processes that occur on the short-term time scale of experiences, actions, interactions with others, and so forth. For instance, the sociometric status of an adolescent in a class results from and is maintained by the many interactions that the adolescent has with the peers in the class, and the change and stability of sociometric status is a matter of at least months to years. The social interactions that are the expression and eventually the cause of the particular sociometric status consist of the events that take place on the time scale of minutes, or at most hours. During such a social interaction, one adolescent may take an initiative towards a classmate, who might reciprocate or not, to which the first adolescent might reply in a consistent or inconsistent way; both youngsters might perform some kind of solitary action for a couple of minutes or a shorter time span, and then interact again, before actually separating in order to introduce another activity or interaction with somebody else. Viewed from the long-term time scale of sociometric status formation or friendship formation, the actual micro events of the interaction are not particularly important. What is more important is whether the interactions with a particular classmate in the long run are on average rewarding or not, pleasurable or not, whether there is resistance from one person to contact with another, and so forth. These macroscopic properties of the interaction clearly result from the microscopic, short-term interactions between the participants. Thus, in order to understand where these macroscopic properties come from – properties that are basically taken for granted if one focuses on the level of the long-term process – one has to construct a model that focuses on the agent dynamics of real-time interactions. This was the growth the present authors focused on by studying the agent dynamics of dyadic play between children of different sociometric statuses. The study features much younger children, but the mechanisms and underlying assumptions are not qualitatively different from the social processes in adolescence. We shall present the study as an example of the non-technical aspects of the building of an agent model: the technical aspects, (how to actually construct an agent model, for instance in the form of a simple Excel spreadsheet) were the topic of the preceding section. In the next section we will focus on the conceptual aspect of the building of the major model: What kind of conceptual decisions and building blocks are required before the actual technical construction of an agent model can take place? Note that this particular agent model considers the real-time (i.e. the short-term) interactions in a micro-agent system consisting of only two agents.

Conceptual steps towards building an agent model: The example of dyadic play

The aim of the research project on modeling dyadic play was far more pretentious than just modeling dyadic play. In fact, we used dyadic play in the data that we have collected from various videotaped dyadic play sessions in young children, as a concrete example of human action in general and dyadic interaction in particular. What we wanted to arrive at was a general and generalizable dynamic model of an agent that can be used in simulations of real-time agent interaction.

In line with the requirement that a dynamic model should capture only the most essential aspects of the phenomenon it models, we asked ourselves if there is any existing theory that provides a comprehensive description of the essential aspects of human (inter-)action. We found such a theory in Frijda's emotion theory (1986). Although Frijda's theory focuses on emotions, it encompasses a general theory of action – that emotions are changes in action readiness, emerging as reactions to events that are crucial for the concerns of the individual. An emotion is a tool for realizing concerns, finding its expression in the behavior of the individual. A concern is "the concept used for an individual's motives, major goals, interests, attachments, values, ideals, sensitivities, and aversions and likings" (Frijda, 2001, p. 54; see also Hermans and Hermans-Jansen, 2001). Concerns can be defined at various time scales and levels of generality. For instance, the concern "love for a person" is reflected both in the concern to strive for nearness and in the concern to maintain the relationship. An example of a short-term concern is a child's current, context-dependent preference for a certain balance between playing together with another child and playing alone. Depending on what level of generality a concern is describing, concerns can refer to something that is largely person-dependent, context-dependent or something that emerges in the interplay of a specific context and a specific person. Thus, the notion of "concern" has a broad range of meanings, which all refer to an essential feature of intentional – as opposed to purely reactive – systems, namely the system's or organism's current intention that it tries to achieve through its actions. In our dynamic model, we define "concern" in a way consistent with Thelen and Smith's (1994) notion of "soft-assembled" properties, namely as the temporal and local set of factors that cause a person to strive for a certain balance of actions with which that person is optimally satisfied.

The level to which concerns are realized or satisfied in the present situation is constantly evaluated and this evaluation is expressed in the form of a direct emotional appraisal (Frijda, 1993). Emotional appraisals are linked to drives (see also Damasio, 2003). The notion of "drive" is of comparable generality to the notion of "concern" and refers to the intensity of the action by means of which the organism tries to achieve its concerns. Realization of a concern (or bringing it closer to realization) has a positive influence on the emotional appraisal of this moment. If the concern is not (sufficiently) realized, the emotional appraisal of this moment is negatively influenced. With a negative emotion, a drive will emerge that leads to behavior aimed at undoing this negative emotion. Emotions can be distinguished both on qualitative (different emotions) and quantitative (intensity) grounds (Oatley and Johnson-Laird, 1996; Sonnemans and Frijda, 1994). In our model, we simplify emotions by reducing them to a single quantitative dimension that specifies the intensity of the emotional expression regardless of the accompanying emotional quality (for similar approaches, see Cacioppo and Gardner, 1999; Russell, 1980; Watson and Tellegen, 1985). On the other hand, our model represents the qualitative distinction between emotions in the form of different effects that positive, neutral or negative emotions have on the preference for concerns. So, the emotion theory of Frijda forms the basis for our model. As a next step, we distinguish different groups of parameters that are theoretically expected to play a significant role in the interactional processes.

Input parameters

Our dynamic model specifies the realization of one important concern dimension – namely, the specific balance between the concern "autonomy" and the concern "involvement". Autonomy is the tendency to be or to act on one's own, and involvement is the tendency to direct one's behavior towards another person. Consistent with our earlier claim that a concern can be defined on different time scales and levels of generality, we justify the choice for these two concerns in the following way. First, autonomy versus involvement can be conceived of as referring to a general, long-term aspect of a person's identity or personality. Finding a good balance between autonomy and involvement can be seen as one of the greatest challenges of development over the course of a lifetime (Grotevant and Cooper, 1998; Guisinger and Blatt, 1993). At a similar level of generality, autonomy and involvement can be conceived of as important factors in social competence. Popular children have obtained a good balance between autonomy and involvement (De Koeijer, 2001). On the other side of the spectrum, we find children with a completely different balance between autonomy and involvement, namely autistic children and children with related problems.

On the time scale of real action that our model intends to describe, involvement and autonomy are specified as strictly context-dependent temporal properties, deriving from the general properties described above and from the context in which they occur. They refer to the child's and peer's temporal, context-specific value of self-directed and other-directed play behaviors. In the dyadic play situation that forms the topic of our study, the play behavior of the children can vary from strictly solitary play with toys to highly interactive constructive play. At any moment in the play situation they can choose a form of play behavior that is either autonomy-oriented or involvement-oriented, depending on what the most obvious or pleasurable choice is at that particular moment. This temporal preference is determined by child-specific aspects (a child's general tendencies towards autonomy versus involvement) and by context-specific aspects (a host of properties relating to the attractiveness of the play partner). In the model, the values of involvement (play actions directed towards or together with the other child) and autonomy (play actions directed towards the child him- or herself) are represented by two parameters, which together form the first group of parameters.

The second group of parameters refers to the influence of behavior on the realization of concerns. As described above, at each point in time, evaluation of the concerns in the form of an emotional appraisal leads to a drive, which in turn leads to specific behavior. The group of behaviors referred to by the collective term "Playing together" is connected with the current, context-dependent concern: involvement. The group of behaviours "Playing alone" is coupled to the current, context-dependent concern: autonomy. The basic idea is that by expressing a certain behavior (e.g. responding to the play partner in cooperative playing action) the child aims at increasing his or her appraisal (e.g. increasing pleasure), which in model terms is formally equivalent to bringing the corresponding concern (involvement in this example) closer to its realization. As appraisal increases, the effect of a particular action (e.g. playing together) on the further increase of appraisal diminishes. This means that, at some time in the process, the effect of a more preferred action (e.g. playing together) on the increase in appraisal will be smaller than that of a less preferred action (e.g. playing alone). At that time, the child will switch to the other type of action (the switch being co-dependent on a host of additional, contextual factors). The relation between evaluations (e.g. the amount of "reward" expected from an activity), preferences and proportions of activities over time is a well-documented principle from learning theory, known as the Matching Law (Hetherington, 1992).

An obvious property of involvement is that it can only be well satisfied if there is real joint action or communication (i.e. if the play partner responds coherently). If the response of the play partner is enjoyable and fun, it will contribute more to increasing appraisal than if it is unpleasant or annoying. Put differently, the appraisal effect of an action diminishes less rapidly if the action has more pleasurable consequences. This principle is expressed in our model by means of the second group of input parameters, namely the magnitude of the effect of the behavior on the realization of concerns.

The third group of parameters concerns the strength of the relation between emotional appraisal and emotional expression. The model makes the simplifying assumption that a drive is linearly dependent on the level of emotional appraisal of this situation. This appraisal can be translated into a positive, neutral or negative emotional expression of the child. The limits of the appraisal (i.e. the level at which a neutral expression is likely to turn into a positive or a negative expression) can vary per child, and eventually also per situation (Oatley and Jenkins, 1996). The ease with which a child translates an emotional appraisal into a specific expression can be tuned by means of the third input parameter group.

The fourth group of parameters concerns the influence of emotional expression on the preference of concerns. A central feature of a functionalist theory of behavior, or of emotions for that matter, is that the effects of behavior regulate the way the behavior will be displayed in the future. In our model we assume that an emotional expression is such an effect. For instance, a positive emotional expression following or accompanying a particular behavior will tend to increase the future frequency of that behavior, which, in our model, is similar to saying that it will increase the strength of the concern that corresponds to this behavior. In social organisms, such as human beings, emotional expression regulates not only one's own behavior but also the behavior of conspecifics, assuming of course that the latter perceive this emotional expression. According to Preston and de Waal's perception–action model of empathy (Preston and de Waal, 2002), perception of emotional expression in another subject automatically invokes the associated behavioral response. We assume that emotional expression has an effect on the preference of a child's concern, irrespective of whether it is the child's own or that observed in the play partner.

The preceding four groups of parameters govern the intentional aspect of action, linking concerns to appraisals, appraisals to drives, actions and emotions, and emotions back to concerns. In addition to these intentional aspects, we believe that actions are also driven by automatic, non-intentional processes. In a social organism, humans in particular, the perceived behavior of conspecifics has a direct influence on the organism's own behavior, which is most directly seen in the act of imitation. Comparable forms of direct effects on other persons' behavior are behavior, social and mood contagion (for a more detailed description see Steenbeek, 2006; Steenbeek and van Geert, 2007, 2008). Thus, there exists a certain non-intentional tendency to mirror what another person is doing, and this tendency may not always be consistent with the action related to the person's immediate concern. In the model we introduce this tendency in the form of a symmetry parameter, which is a non-intentional action parameter (i.e. it is not related to the immediate concern, such as playing together). A second non-intentional action parameter refers to the fact that in a dynamic systems model the next step in an action sequence is a function of the preceding step. The recursive nature of action thus corresponds with a certain, automatic tendency to remain in one's action mode, until this tendency is overruled by an intentional drive towards a different action. The action mode is an attractor. Attractors differ in terms of stability, that is, in the strength of the influence needed to move the system towards another attractor state. These additional influences are implemented in the form of an adjustable random factor that is added during each step in the model. Dependent on person- and context-characteristics, a child shows more or less continuity and symmetry.

The output variables of social behavior and expression

The model distinguishes two kinds of observable (i.e. overt) output variables that have already been introduced in the preceding sections, namely behavior and emotional expression. The behavior output variable consists of either behavior directed towards the other person (all behaviors falling under the denominator "Playing together") or behavior aimed at oneself (behaviors falling under "Playing alone"). All actions that are aimed at interaction – ranging from actual playing together to attempts to engage the other child in doing things together – fall under the denominator "Playing together". Emotional expression is every form of utterance that accompanies and expresses an experienced emotion (Oatley and Jenkins, 1996; Russell, Bachorowski and Fernández-Dols, 2003) and is related to a specific context (Camras, 1992). As stated earlier, our model specifies only the intensity of the emotional expression, varying from negative to positive on a nine-point scale.

Time course of the model

Temporal resolution

As explained earlier, dynamic models have a characteristic temporal resolution – that is, they have a characteristic number of steps, ranging from continuous time to steps covering successive generations (e.g. in biological population models). Since the scoring of behaviors and emotional expressions of the observed play sessions occurred with a 1-second resolution, the dynamic model consists of discrete steps corresponding to 1 second. Thus, a 7-minute observation is modeled by 420 steps.

The process at one moment (one step in the model, for instance a second)

Figure 10.1 shows a schematic representation of the model. The upper part shows that at time *t* the child has a particular value for the preferred level of a concern and a particular value for the realized level of a concern (what is shown for one child applies also to the other). At time *t* (and every point in time) the difference between the preferred and realized value of a concern results in a specific drive, which, in the model, is nothing but the absolute numerical difference between the two proportions. Since there are two concerns (autonomy and involvement), the total drive is the sum of the two differences. An ideal situation has a drive with value 0, which means that the preferred and realized levels of both concerns are the same. It is a situation in which the concerns are optimally satisfied.

First, the total drive is linearly transformed into a particular emotional appraisal. This emotional appraisal is transformed into a positive, neutral or negative expression by means of an S-shaped (sigmoid) function that determines the probability of a particular expression (e.g. a mild positive expression such as a smile). Second, the drive generates a specific behavior, which in the model is limited to either "Playing together" or "Playing alone". Since there are two drives, one drive for each of the two behavioral categories (the playing together or playing alone), the drive with the highest current value determines which of the two behaviors will actually be displayed. The levels of drives – concern realization, play behavior and

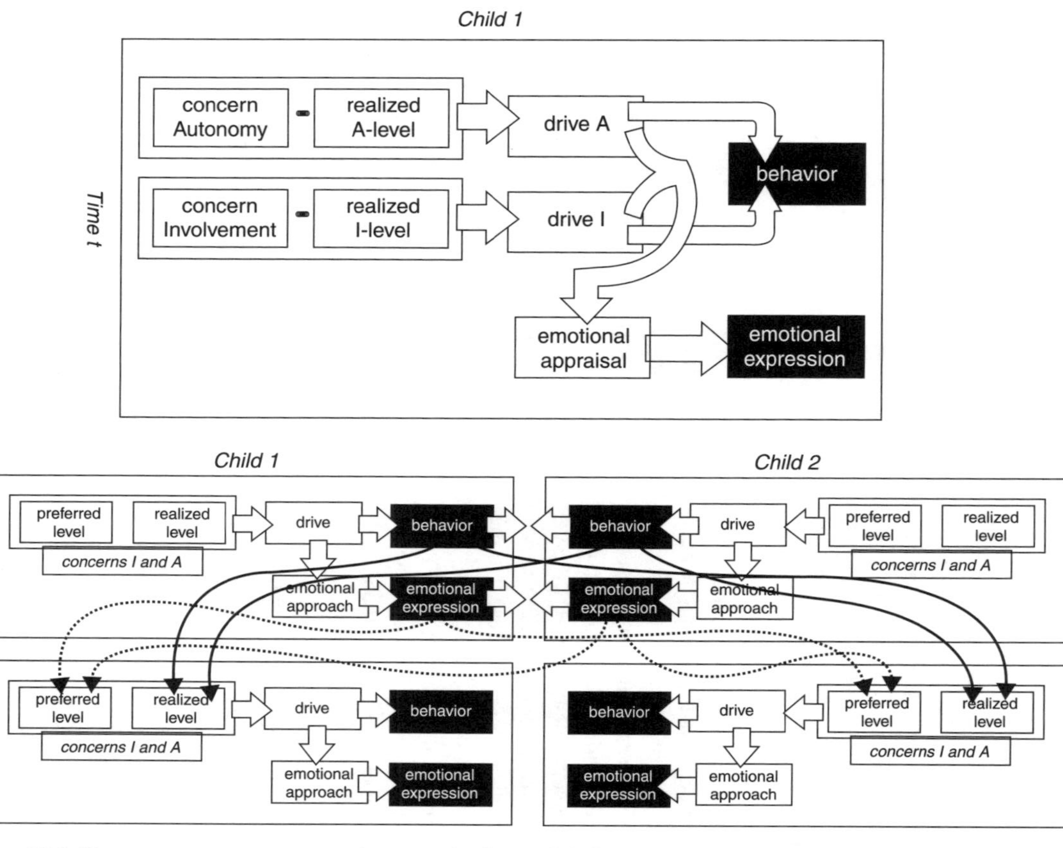

Figure 10.1 The process at one moment (one step in the model, for instance a second) and the process at two consecutive moments in both children (see text for explanation).

emotional expression of Child 1 and Child 2 – that result from the model calculation at time t will now form the input of the calculation at time $t + 1$.

The process at two consecutive moments

The lower part of Figure 10.1 shows the processes occurring between two children over two consecutive time steps. Suppose that at time t Muriel and Rosa are playing together (i.e. both display the behavioral category "Playing together"). Also at time t Muriel begins to laugh, thus at time t a positive expression accompanies the playing-together behavior. First, the occurrence of playing together in both children at time t will result in an increased level for the realized value of the involvement for both children at time $t + 1$ (see the section on the second input parameter group). If only Rosa had displayed behavior from the Playing-together category, for instance by trying to capture Muriel's attention for what she is doing, the realization of the involvement would not have changed because realization of that concern requires both children to show Playing-together behavior. For playing alone, concern satisfaction is updated if only the child herself displays Playing-alone behavior. Second, the co-occurrence of the positive expression of Muriel with both children displaying Playing-together behavior at time t will result in an increased level for the preferred value of the involvement for both children at time $t + 1$ (see the section on the fourth input parameter group). This means that at time $t + 1$ the values of involvement are increased, whereas the values for autonomy are the same as at time t. On the basis of these new concern and realized level values, it is now calculated which behavior and emotional expressions both children will show at time $t + 1$, in accordance with the rules specified in the preceding section.

The description above is a general description aimed at demonstrating how the different components in the model are defined on the basis of theoretical notions, and how their interactions are conceptualized. For a more detailed technical description, see the appendix on the website. (For a manual of the model, see Steenbeek & van Geert, 2002.) A copy of the model can be found in appendix-model chapter 10 adolescent autonomy.xls on the website www.psypress.com/dynamic-systems-approach/appendices.

A short note on the technical construction of the present agent model

A model of this sort of complexity cannot be constructed in the form of a relatively simple Excel model, which is limited to equations and functions that can be written down as parts of a spreadsheet. Almost all the agent models discussed in the literature either take the form of specific code in some general programming language, such as C++ or Visual Basic, or they take the form of an application written in the language of software specially dedicated to the construction of agent models. In the final section of this chapter we shall review some of this dedicated software. Technically, the model simulating dyadic interaction, based on our general theory of agents, was written as a kind of compromise between spreadsheet functions and possibilities in Excel on the one hand, and a program in a general programming language on the other hand. Microsoft Excel, like many other software programs nowadays, offers the possibility to write programs in Visual Basic, more precisely Visual Basic for applications, which is integrated into the Excel environment. Visual Basic for applications offers all the functions available in Excel, it offers a language to use Excel for the purposes of visual representation, data storage, and so forth and of course it offers all the programming possibilities present in Visual Basic.

The process describing the real-time interaction between the two playing children was represented as a series of columns in Excel. The Visual Basic routine consisted of an iterative process, taking the values of all the variables associated with each of the agents determined during the preceding step in the interaction in order to calculate or update the values of all the variables for the next step in the interaction. A step in the interaction was arbitrarily associated with the duration of 1 second, which is on average enough for the real children to show some sort of observable reaction, such as changing the visual focus, starting to smile, starting to say something, and so forth. As we have seen in the description of the agent model, the actual output was extremely simple, and every possible action of the real children was reduced to an action dimension to distinguish acts aimed towards the other person (other-directed acts) from acts not aimed towards the other person (solitary acts or parts of solitary acts). Real interaction was determined as the co-occurrence of an other-directed act in the two agents. In addition to the dimension of other- versus self-directed acts or action fragments, the program also produced output referring to the emotional expression accompanying other- or self-directed acts. Emotional expression was simplified to one intensity dimension ranging from very negative to very positive. Patterns or combinations of such acts and emotional expressions correspond with chunks of playing together or playing alone, with pleasurable or less pleasurable feelings. It goes without saying that the simulation program does not produce realistic descriptions of action and only produces sequences of signs corresponding to particular properties of acts as defined above. It is the task of the researcher to systematically associate patterns of such sequences with observable behavior, and to theoretically justify why such associations are valid.

A short overview of agent modeling software

In this chapter, we have demonstrated that it is possible to build agent models with the aid of general-purpose calculation software such as Excel. The model was limited to the interaction between two agents only, and there was also no reference to the actions that agents perform in order to get in touch with each other or to find each other in order to have some sort of communication. In the model demonstrated in this chapter, we simply assumed that on average (i.e. during each tick of our modeling clock) the agents found some opportunity for having a discussion with each other that could result in an autonomy issue or not. Many agent models, however, require the ability to actually describe actions in space and time that lead to interactions or exchanges – that is, the events described by the model take place in a simulated space–time environment. In principle, one could use the cellular structure of a spreadsheet program such as Excel to simulate such a spatial environment (on the internet, for instance, one can find Excel-based simulations of the game of life, which uses the cells of the Excel spreadsheet to simulate the life space). On the website accompanying this book, the reader can also find an Excel-based model that simulates interactions between students in a classroom that lead to the formation of friendship patterns, rejection and popularity. The model simulates this process without any explicit reference to the spatial layout of a classroom and successfully models interactions between a considerable number of agents (e.g. 20 or more). However, anyone thinking of modeling agent interactions taking place in a specific space–time environment, the properties of which constrain the co-determining actions of the agents, will soon be confronted with the limitations of spreadsheet programs such as Excel, however functional they have turned out to be for the modeling of dynamic systems relationships between variables. In this chapter, for instance, we have described our own work on the interactions in a dyad of children playing together, and we explained that we needed to write Visual Basic for applications programs under Excel in order to be able to model the kind of agent interactions that we intended.

As agent-based modeling is becoming increasingly more popular and important in many different fields, a considerable number of modelers and research groups have begun to build general-purpose software for agent-based modeling, much of which is made freely available on the internet, or is available at very low cost. A good starting point for obtaining an overview of what is available and which purposes are served by the available software is the Wikipedia article "Comparison of agent-based modeling software" (http://en.wikipedia.org/wiki/Comparison_of_agent-based_modeling_software), which provides an overview of about 70 agent-based modeling programs, the great majority of which are available at no or very little cost. Examples of popular freeware are Starlogo and Netlogo, which, like many other agent-based modeling software tools, can be applied for a large variety of purposes ranging from very serious scientific model building to making educational demonstrations for (or by) young students (see also Robertson, 2005). It is recommended that researchers seriously considering using agent-based modeling as a research tool should try several of the available programs first, and then decide which software tool to focus on. Many of these software tools are not very difficult to learn, but they nevertheless require effort and time, especially if they are going to be used to support serious empirical research. The aforementioned Wikipedia article also provides a list of references to articles giving an overview of the available software.

Notes

1 A demonstration model and an appendix for this chapter can be found at www.psypress.com/dynamic-systems-approach/appendices. Note that the model in this file refers to parameter names instead of cell addresses. Appendix 8(1) explains how this can be done.

2 In the equation in the model an additional condition is added. The only function of this condition is to prevent the value of autonomy from becoming negative.
3 The function dNormalDev is part of Poptools.

References

Axelrod, R. (2005). Agent-based modeling as a bridge between disciplines. In K. L. Judd & L. Tesfatsion (Eds.), *Handbook of computational economics, Vol. 2: Agent-based computational economics*. Amsterdam: North-Holland.

Ballato, L. (in press). *A dynamic model of friendship interaction and risk behaviour*. Doctoral dissertation, University of Groningen, The Netherlands..

Cacioppo, J. T., & Gardner, W. L. (1999). Emotion. *Annual Review of Psychology, 50*, 199–214.

Camras, L. A. (1992). Expressive development and basic emotions. *Cognition and Emotion, 6*, 269–283.

Damasio, A. R. (2003). *Looking for Spinoza: Joy, sorrow, and the feeling brain*. Orlando, FL: Harcourt.

De Koeyer, I. (2001). *Peer acceptance, parent–child fantasy play interactions, and subjective experience of the self-in-relation: A study of 4- to 5-year-old children*. Unpublished doctoral dissertation, University of Utrecht, The Netherlands.

Elliott, E., & Kiel, L. D. (2004). Agent-based modeling in the social and behavioral sciences. *Nonlinear Dynamics, Psychology, and Life Sciences*, *8*, 121–130.

Frantz, T. L., & Carley, K. M. (2009). Agent-based modeling within a dynamic network. In S. Guastello, M. Koopmans, & D. Pincus (Eds.), *Chaos and complexity in psychology: The theory of nonlinear dynamical systems* (pp. 475–505). New York: Cambridge University Press.

Frijda, N. H. (1986). *The emotions*. Cambridge, UK: Cambridge University Press.

Frijda, N. H. (1993). The place of appraisal in emotion. *Cognition and Emotion, 7:* 357–387.

Frijda, N. H. (2001). The self and emotions. In H.A. Bosma & E. S. Kunnen (Eds.), *Identity and emotion: Development through self-organization* (pp. 39–57). Cambridge, UK: Cambridge University Press.

Gilbert, N. (2007). *Agent-based models*. Los Angeles, CA: Sage.

Grimm, V., Revilla, E., Berger, U., Jeltsch, F., Mooij, W. M., Railsback, S. F., et al. (2005). Pattern-oriented modeling of agent-based complex systems: Lessons from ecology. *Science*, *310*, 987–991.

Grotevant, H. D., & Cooper, C. R. (1998). Individuality and connectedness in adolescent development: Review and prospects for research on identity, relationships, and context. In E. E. A. Skoe & A. L. van der Lippe (Eds.), *Personality development in adolescence: A cross national and life span perspective. Adolescent and society* (pp. 3–37). London: Routledge.

Guisinger, S., & Blatt, S. J. (1993). Individuality and relatedness: Evolution of a fundamental dialectic. *American Psychologist, 49*, 104–111.

Hermans, J. M., & Hermans-Jansen, E. (2001). Affective processes in a multivoiced self. In H. Bosma & S. Kunnen (Eds.), *Identity and emotion: Development through self-organization* (pp. 120–140). Cambridge, UK: Cambridge University Press.

Hetheringtin, C. D. (1992). Levels of aggregation and the Generalized Matching Law. *Psychological Review, 99*, 306–321.

Lichtwarck-Aschoff, A., van Geert, P., Bosma, H., & Kunnen, S. (2008). Time and identity: A framework for research and theory formation. *Developmental Review*, *28*, 370–400.

Oatley, K., & Jenkins, J. M. (1996). *Understanding emotions*. Cambridge, MA: Blackwell.

Oatley, K., & Johnson-Laird, P. N. (1996). The communicative theory of emotions: empirical tests, mental models, and implications for social interaction. In L. L. Martin & A. Tesser (Eds.), *Striving and feeling: Interactions among goals, affect, and self-regulation* (pp. 363–393). Hillsdale, NJ: Lawrence Erlbaum Associates.

Olthof, T., Kunnen, S., & Boom, J. (2000). Simulating mother–child interaction: exploring two varieties of a non-linear dynamic systems approach. *Infant and Child Development, 9,* 33–60.

Preston, S. D., & de Waal, F. B. M. (2002). Empathy: Its ultimate and proximate bases. *Behavioral and Brain Sciences, 25,* 1–72.

Robertson, D. A. (2005). Agent-based modeling toolkits NetLogo, RePast, and Swarm. *Academy of Management Learning and Education, 4,* 524–527.

Russell, J. A. (1980). A circumplex model of affect. *Journal of Personality and Social Psychology, 39*, 1161–1178.

Russell, J. A., Bachorowski, J. A., & Fernández-Dols, J. M. (2003). Facial and vocal expressions of emotion. *Annual Review of Psychology, 54*, 329–349.

Schlesinger, M., & Parisi, D. (2001). The agent-based approach: A new direction for computational models of development. *Developmental Review*, *21*, 121–146.

Smith, E. R., & Conrey, F. R. (2007). Agent-based modeling: A new approach for theory building in social psychology. *Personality and Social Psychology Review, 11*, 87–104.

Sonnemans, J. & Frijda, N. H. (1994). The structure of subjective emotional intensity. *Cognition and Emotion, 8*, 329–350.

Spencer, J. P., Thomas, M. S. C., & McClelland, J. (2009). *Toward a new grand theory of development? Connectionism and dynamic systems theory reconsidered.* Oxford, UK: Oxford University Press.

Steenbeek, H. W. (2006). *Modeling dyadic child–peer interactions: Sociometric status, emotional expressions and instrumental actions during play.* Unpublished doctoral dissertation, University of Groningen, The Netherlands.

Steenbeek, H. W., & van Geert, P. L.C. (2002). Variations on dynamic variations: A commentary on Yan and Fischer. *Human Development*, *45*, 167–173.

Steenbeek, H., & van Geert, P. (2007). A dynamic systems approach to dyadic interaction in children: Emotional expression, action, dyadic play, and sociometric status. *Developmental Review, 27,* 1–40.

Steenbeek, H., & van Geert, P. (2008). The empirical validation of a dynamic systems model of interation: Do children of different sociometric statuses differ in their dyadic play interactions? *Developmental Science, 11,* 253–281.

Thelen, E., & Bates, E. (2003). Connectionism and dynamic systems: Are they really different? *Developmental Science, 6,* 378–391.

Thelen, E., & Smith, L. B. (1994). *A dynamic systems approach to the development of cognition and action*. Cambridge, MA: MIT Press.

Visser, M. (in press). *The tip of the iceberg and beyond.* Doctoral dissertation, University of Groningen, The Netherlands.

Watson, D., & Tellegen, A. (1985). Towards a consensual structure of mood. *Psychological Bulletin, 98,* 219–235.

11 The search for relations between micro and macro development[1]

Saskia Kunnen, Anna Lichtwarck-Aschoff and Paul van Geert

One of the advantages of a dynamic systems approach is that it offers conceptualizations and research tools for exploring the question of how long-term psychological development emerges from real-time day-to-day events and interactions. This is a question that is especially important in adolescent development because studies into adolescent development often focus on broad general concepts and on generalized behavioral tendencies, such as autonomy, identity, substance use, depression, aggression, etc. If we want to understand adolescent development in terms of these concepts from a dynamic systems perspective, it is important to understand how, on the one hand, change and stability in terms of these concepts emerge in the day-to-day events and, on the other hand, how these concepts themselves affect the daily events. Thus, to understand adolescent development, it is very important to focus on the connections between processes on different time scales. In this chapter we will elaborate how these mutual connections can be explored by means of a dynamic systems approach.

In Chapter 2 we described how we can conceptualize dynamic systems on different levels of aggregation, running from emotions and perceptions, via events, to abstract constructs such as identity and self-esteem. These various levels are related to different time scales: lowest level components self-organize in events, that is, momentary emotional experiences on a microscopic time scale; events and experiences organize on a medium time scale; and identity finally emerges on a scale of months or years. It is essential, therefore, to be clear on which time scale the phenomenon of interest is developing. It is also important to be aware of the connections that exist between the different time scales. In this chapter we will elaborate how these different time scales and aggregation levels and the connections between them can be given shape in research designs. The different levels of organization affect each other in two different ways: bottom-up and top-down.

Bottom-up processes are processes in which lower level elements give rise to the emergence of higher order phenomena. As described in Chapter 2, elements self-organize, interact and couple, and this coupling results in the emergence of higher order forms. When, over time, certain emotions and appraisals are being activated in concert, they become coupled and form a stable pattern on a higher level. In that way, an adolescent's real-time experiences of feeling, appraising and acting give rise to a more general sense of being autonomous. For example, if an adolescent who repeatedly fights her parent's refusal to stay out late wins, and has a nice evening out, she may feel confident about her ability to handle threats to her autonomy and develop an active coping style in such situations.

Top-down processes refer to the influence of higher level phenomena on lower level systems. For instance, an adolescent girl with a high level of autonomy, a perception of herself as an autonomous agent, might make it more likely that she experiences any arbitrary conflict with her parents as a "threat" to her autonomy (see Smetana, 1989, 1995; Smetana, Crean and Campione-Barr, 2005), which will influence her emotions, thoughts and behaviors within the conflict interaction. Higher order properties thus constrain the degrees of freedom of the lower order elements. In this sense, they determine how those elements interact and become coupled over time. In several of the methods discussed in Chapters 8, 9 and 10, top-down connections between systems at different levels were included. These connections are found in the parameters that are included in the model. Take for example the assimilation/accommodation parameter that is part of the model in Chapter 10. This parameter refers to a stable characteristic. The formation and change of this characteristic can probably be described by a dynamic systems model on a higher level of aggregation and on a higher time scale. For now, however, the parameter represents the effect of this higher order characteristic on lower order processes.

It is important to note that both levels are recursively influencing each other over time, and thus that bottom-up and top-down processes exist continuously next to each other. There is no simple cause and effect relationship between the short-term level of daily interactions and the developmental time scale of, for example, autonomy or identity, but it is a two-way process consisting of bottom-up and top-down influences (see also the principle of circular causality in Haken and Knyazeva, 2000). Identity on a developmental time scale emerges out of real-time and day-to-day experiences, interactions and processes – that is, how one defines oneself is the product of many cumulative real-time interactions with the environment. At the same time, behaviors, thoughts and emotions are constrained by the way a person defines herself. One's identity, self-definition, commitments and values will determine why, when and how one reacts to a potential threat to one's identity – the identity sets the conditions and defines the parameters of the immediate goals and concerns.

In our view, the perspectives that are offered by modeling bottom-up processes are especially promising in the study of relatively stable concepts that develop on a time scale of months or years. From a dynamic systems perspective, developmental outcomes of such long-term constructs as identity, self-esteem or autonomy "grow" and emerge through day-to-day or real-time experiences, transactions and processes (Lichtwarck-Aschoff, Van Geert, Bosma and Kunnen, 2008; Thelen and Smith, 1994; Van Geert and Steenbeek, 2005), or, as Granic (2005) stated, "Real-time behaviors are the raw material of development" (p. 391). Lichtwarck-Aschoff et al. (2008) described the achievement of autonomy on a developmental time scale as an iterative process in which concrete moment-to-moment and day-to-day experiences and interactions with the environment feed back on the existing level of autonomy. As an example, we will discuss this model in more detail.

A model of connected growers for the development of autonomy and connectedness

We will elaborate on the modeling of connections between different time scales by means of a model we described in Lichtwarck-Aschoff et al. (2008). This model describes the development of autonomy and connectedness during adolescence. Autonomy is assumed to start to develop in this period, due to a number of child-related, parental and contextual changes and transformations. Connectedness is assumed to exist already on a medium level, but a qualitative change of the connectedness is expected. A growing autonomy affects connectedness in a qualitative way: it gets richer, deeper, more mature and realistic. A basic assumption in the model is that the autonomy is mainly attained through conflict events, quarrels and fights over autonomy issues, which have a temporary negative effect on the level of the perceived connectedness. They lead to temporary separation or, more precisely, feelings of separation, difference and opposition.

The mathematical model for the long-term development of autonomy and connectedness is based on these theoretical assumptions. Note that autonomy and connectedness as used in the model refer to perceived properties, in the sense that they are experienced and apprehended by the person himself. Besides this short-term mechanism, the model also contains a long-term influence between autonomy and connectedness.

The relationship between autonomy and connectedness is described by a logistic model of connected growers (Fischer, 1980; Van Geert, 1994). Both growers (i.e. the variables that undergo a process of change) depend on the existence of a set of resources in the environment of the adolescent (e.g. peer relationships that allow adolescents to experiment with autonomous behavior or encourage autonomy strivings). The existence of resources influences the individual change rate of each grower and the maximum attainable level, which is called the carrying capacity (see also Chapters 8 and 9). In the present model this is described by a term in the equation that subtracts the current level of a grower from its maximum, which is a simple linear function of all the resources available. For simplicity, the carrying capacity (i.e. a grower's maximum level) is normalized to 1. Autonomy and connectedness are influencing each other's change over time – that is, one grower depends on an influence parameter of the other grower, and vice versa. Thus, in an optimal situation autonomy and connectedness profit from each other in the long run because they have a mutual positive relationship, leading to an equilibrium between autonomy and a mature form of connectedness. In the model the long-term change in autonomy (ΔA) over a given period of time (Δt) is described by the following equation:

$$\Delta A/\Delta t = A * \text{change\_A} * (1 - A) + \text{influence}_{C \text{ on } A} * A * C \qquad (11.1)$$

Thus, the growth of autonomy depends on:

- the autonomy level already attained,
- its individual change rate (change_A),
- the distance between the current growth level and the carrying capacity,
- the level of connectedness (in the second part of the equation).

In the model, a random effect is included. This effect is modeled as a normal distribution of influences, with a mean that can be negative, zero or positive. If it is negative, the level of connectedness has a negative influence on autonomy (i.e. tends to reduce it). If the mean is positive, connectedness – on average – supports autonomy (i.e. leads to a positive increase). At each time point, a random influence factor is drawn from the distribution (i.e. the effects are random within each trajectory). By modeling the relationship by means of a randomized influence, we can model the real situation in which both tendencies exist – support and suppression of autonomy – but with an average that is either positive or negative. Simulations of the model with different parameter values result in different developmental trajectories.

The development of connectedness is also based on a logistic growth function. In contrast to Equation 11.1; this equation contains three components:

$$\Delta C/\Delta t = C * \text{change\_C} * (1-C) + \text{min\_p} * C * \Delta A/\Delta t + \text{A\_on\_C} * C * A \quad (11.2)$$

The first part of the equation is similar to Equation 11.1. The growth of connectedness depends on the previous connecteness level, its individual change rate parameter change_C and the distance between the current growth level and the carrying capacity (set to 1). The second part of the equation represents the short-term component in the model. This mechanism describes the temporary suppression effect of autonomy on connectedness, which is due to the fact that an increase in autonomy is assumed to depend on conflict-laden interactions, which tend to temporarily reduce the perceived connectedness. By setting the standard deviation of the stochastic parameters to zero, the model is changed into a deterministic model, with the mean of the parameter taking the desired value of the parameter at issue. Mathematically speaking, autonomy affects connectedness negatively by change – there is a negative effect of the first derivative of autonomy on connectedness, which is denoted by a negative value of the interaction parameter min_p.

The third part of the equation is similar to Equation 11.1. This describes the long-term influence of autonomy on connectedness. Again, the effect of autonomy on connectedness is modeled as a normal distribution of influences in the current model. This means that the values can be negative, zero or positive, denoting the kind of relationship between autonomy and connectedness (i.e. competitive versus supportive). Again, in each step of the simulation a random influence factor is drawn from the distribution. In the case of an optimal development increasing levels of autonomy of the adolescent will lead to an increase in connectedness, in the sense that the quality or the maturity of the connectedness increases. To translate these equations in the Excel model we take the following steps.

In Excel language, first we define the growers and parameters. For the growers, we enter A (autonomy) in cell D5, growth A in E5, difference At_At-1 in F5, C (connectedness) in G5 and growth C in H5. Next, we define the parameters defining cell B3 as change_A, B4 as C_on_A, B5 as change_C, B6 as min_p, B7 as A_on_C and B8 as rand_neg. To these parameters we assign the values 0.2, 0.1, 0.2, –0.01, 0.1 and 0.03, respectively.

In cell D6 we enter the initial value for autonomy (A) as 0.1. In cell D7 we compute the new value of A as determined by the previous value of A, plus the change of A, plus the random factor:

= C6 + D7 + dNormalDev(0;rand_reg)

where dNormalDev is part of Poptools.

In cell E8 we enter Equation 11.1, describing the change of A:

= D6∗ change_A ∗(1-D6) + C_on_A ∗D6∗G6

The first part of this equation, D6* change_A *(1-D6), decribes the change as determined by the previous value of autonomy multiplied by parameter change_A, multiplied by the distance between the maximum and the actual value of autonomy. The second part of the equation, C_on_A*D6*G6, adds the influence of the actual value of connectedness, multiplied by the actual value of autonomy multiplied by parameter C_on_A .

In cell F7 we calculate the difference between the present and the previous value of A (we will need that later on, in the equation of connectedness):

= E7 – D6

In cell G6 we enter the initial value of connectedness (C). In cell G7 we calculate the new value of C as based on the previous value, the change and a random factor:

= G6 + H7 + dNormalDev(0;rand_reg)

In H7 we enter Equation 11.2, the equation that describes the change in C:

= G6*change_C*(1-G6) + min_p*G6*F7 + A_on_C*G6*D6

The first part of this equation, G6* change_C *(1-G6), decribes the change as determined by the previous value of connectedness multiplied by parameter change_C, multiplied by the distance between the maximum and the actual value of connectedness. The second part, min_p*G6*F7, describes the short-term negative influence of the change in A (F7) multiplied by the actual value of connectedness multiplied by parameter min_p. The third part, A_on_C*G6*D6, describes the influence of the actual level of autonomy multiplied by the level of connectedness multiplied by parameter A_on_C. As a final step, we copy the range D7:H7 to D8:H150, and make a line graph that shows the columns D and G. An Excel file with the actual model can be found on the website.

In summary, this model of connected growers can be used to describe different developmental trajectories, ranging from healthy to more problematic developments. For illustrative purposes we will discuss three different scenarios. It is important to keep in mind that the core of the short-term model of conflict interactions in these scenarios remains the same – that the autonomy striving expressed in the increased levels of conflicts during the period of adolescence leads to a temporary decrease in parental connectedness. Based on this assumption the short-term influence is kept to a negative value (see Equation 11.2) and we only change the other two influence parameters (i.e. $\text{influence}_{C\ on\ A}$ and $\text{influence}_{A\ on\ C}$). The graph (see Figure 11.1) shows a temporary decrease in connectedness around adolescence, followed by a steady increase of both autonomy and connectedness until both stabilize around a certain maximum during adulthood.

Second, the model can simulate trajectories in which the growth of autonomy competes with the growth of connectedness (think about the development of deviant youth where the adolescent disconnects from family relations). Here, the effect of autonomy on connectedness is negative (see Figure 11.2), which bears several risks for the development and adjustment of the adolescent (think about the potential risks of lacking a social network or a supportive relationship with the parents). As one can see in the graph (see Figure 11.2), connectedness disappears during adolescence as a result of the rising autonomy.

The third example models another problematic trajectory, namely a scenario in which connectedness has a repressing effect on the autonomy development (think about enmeshed family relations, authoritarian parenting or the effect of psychologically controlling parents). In these situations the effect of connectedness on

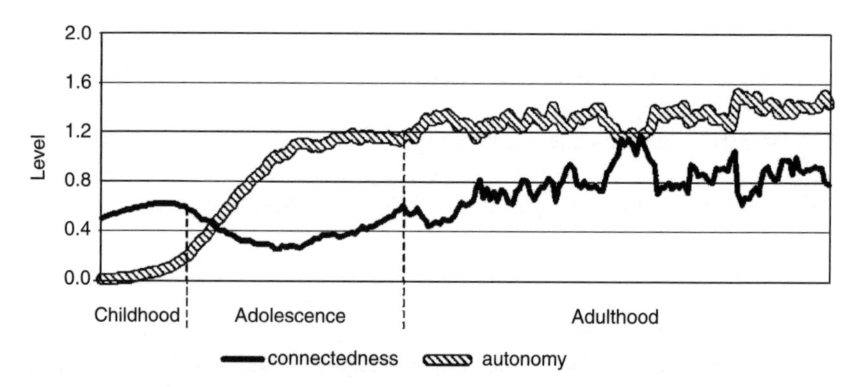

Figure 11.1 Model simulation describing a healthy family relationship in which a supportive interaction between the levels of connectedness and autonomy exists (i.e. both influence parameters are positive).

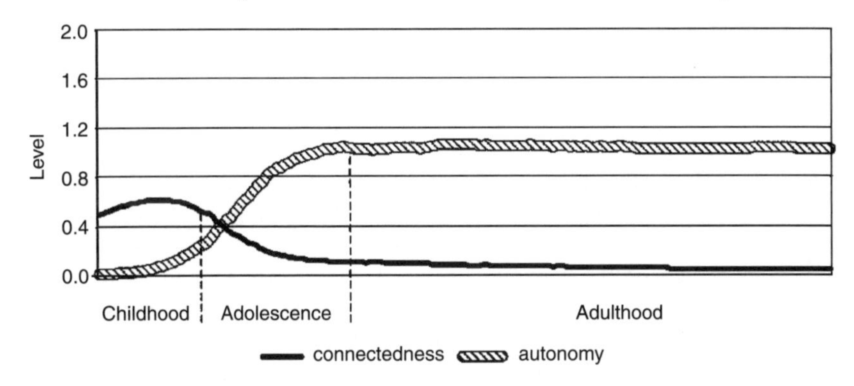

Figure 11.2 The result of the model simulation based on a competitive relationship between autonomy and connectedness. In this case the influence of autonomy on connectedness is negative.

autonomy receives a negative value. Figure 11.3 demonstrates that connectedness shows only a minor dip during adolescence and that autonomy also rises during adolescence and stabilizes afterwards, but on a far lower level than in the other scenarios. This means that autonomy remains under the level that could be achieved if all resource factors could be put to full use.

The parameter values for each of the three scenarios can be found in the model. The differences between the three scenarios demonstrate the two-way process of bottom-up and top-down influences. The differences between the scenarios are caused by different parameter values, that is, by differences in the higher order variables. These higher order differences affect the lower order daily interactions, and at the same time the lower order interactions lead to changes in the higher order properties. Both levels are recursively influencing each other over time. In order to understand the processes and mechanisms that can explain how autonomy emerges from conflict interactions, one has to study the characteristic sequences of events within conflict interactions.

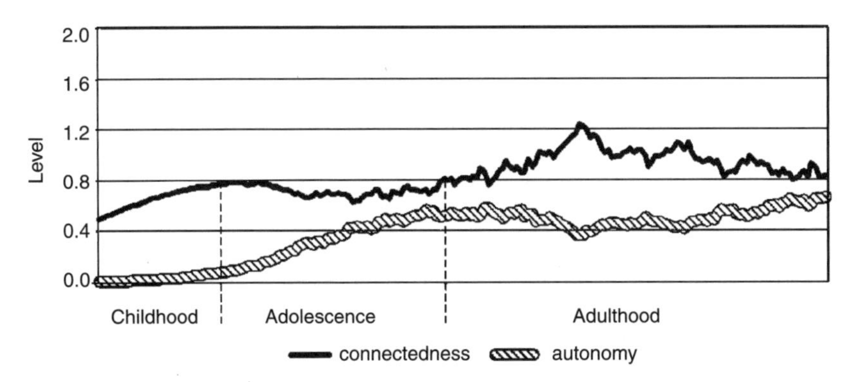

Figure 11.3 The result of the model simulation based on a competitive relationship between autonomy and connectedness. In this case the influence of connectedness on autonomy is negative.

Concluding

Modeling top-down processes and bottom-up processes is extremely promising when one aims to get a better understanding of psychological development in adolescence, and in any other life phase as well. However, this part of the dynamic systems modeling is still in its infancy. Partly, this is caused by the fact that dynamic systems modeling itself is still young, and modeling processes at different aggregation levels can be done only if one has some notion of how to model processes at each of the separate levels. Another, probably more important explanation for this relative absence of models on multiple time levels is that it requires a new way of thinking about the development of higher order concepts. Of course, in an abstract way every psychologist will agree that day-to-day experiences contribute to the development of higher order concepts such as autonomy, identity or self-esteem. However, this notion often remains vague and global. When it comes to an elaboration of how this relation works – which aspects of day-to-day experience contribute to this development – it turns out that there is extremely little theory on this point and even less empirical research. Many of the assumptions we made for the commitment models we developed, both in this book and in other publications (Bosma and Kunnen, 2001; Kunnen, Bosma and van Geert, 2001), were initially based on common sense and sometimes on detailed descriptions of case studies, more often in the romantic literature than in the scientific literature. An example of a model using the non-scientific literature is the model that was developed by Haviland and colleagues, based on the diary of Anne Frank (Haviland, Boulifard and Magai, 2001). The same holds for the question of what mechanisms cause stable properties to remain in place. We have almost no theoretical notions about what keeps stability stable. Stability is often taken for granted. However, to keep higher order properties in place, a lot of work is going on at the micro level. Learning more about these mechanisms is necessary for a better understanding of stability and of change.

Researchers who aim to carry out multi-level modeling have to look beyond the borders of their own research field. We mentioned already the diaries and case studies that exist in the non-scientific literature. Case studies on intervention methods and literature on the effects of specific types of therapies offer suggestions about the kind of influences that are assumed to affect higher order concepts such as self-esteem. Day-to-day data may, for example, consist of observations, diary, beeper studies and simple performances.

Overall, the body of research on micro–macro connections is growing slowly but steadily. One of us (S. K.) performed a study based on diaries where it was demonstrated that conflicts assessed on a real-time level indeed seem to affect identity development in the way that was hypothesized (Kunnen, 2006).

Lewis and colleagues (Lewis 1995, 1997, 2000; Lewis and Ferrari, 2001) developed a model of self-organization in personality development that can be used as a guideline for answering the question of the link between micro-level processes and macro-level structures of identity. In a similar vein, but in a different context, Steenbeek and van Geert built a dynamic systems model of dyadic play interactions (Steenbeek, 2006; Steenbeek and van Geert, 2005, 2007, 2008) that generated testable predictions concerning differences between groups of children of different sociometric statuses. Lichtwarck-Aschoff, Kunnen and van Geert (2010) investigated the development of autonomy by analyzing daily mother–daughter interactions. They succeeded in relating real-time characteristics to abstract (higher levels) levels of autonomy. De Ruiter (2010) developed a coding system with which real-time aspects of parent–adolescent interactions can be coded. She analyzed video-taped interactions of parent–adolescent dyads and coded the emotions and several behavioral aspects of these interactions. She aims to investigate the development of self-esteem in early adolescence on the basis of these day-to-day observations. Preliminary results of the coding system are promising. These two projects demonstrate that this type of research is not easy to carry out. Often, PhD projects will be too short to assess both real-time and developmental processes, and real-time analyses take lots of time. The coding of diaries or video tapes takes a lot of time and a lot of training, which means that studies into the relation between macro and micro development should be planned thoroughly and ideally make use of several PhD projects.

Note

1 A demonstration model for this chapter can be found at www.psypress.com/dynamic-systems-approach/appendices.

References

Bosma, H. A., & Kunnen, E. S. (2001). Determinants and mechanisms in identity development: A review and synthesis. *Developmental Review, 21,* 39–66.

De Ruiter, N. (2010). *Real-time dynamics of global self-esteem in the context of parent–child interactions: A case study.* Master's thesis in Behavioural and Social Sciences, University of Groningen, The Netherlands.

Fischer, K. W. (1980). A theory of cognitive development: The control and construction of hierarchies of skills. *Psychological Review, 87,* 477–531.

Granic, I. (2005). Timing is everything: Developmental psychopathology from a dynamic systems perspective. *Developmental Review, 25,* 386–407.

Haken, H., & Knyazeva, H. (2000). Arbitrariness in nature: Synergetics and evolutionary laws of prohibition. *Journal for General Philosophy of Science, 31,* 57–73.

Haviland-Jones, J. M., Boulifard, D., & Magai, C. (2001). Old–new answers and new–old questions for personality and emotion: A matter of complexity. In H. A. Bosma & E. S. Kunnen (Eds.), *Identity and emotion: A self-organisational process* (pp. 151–171). Cambridge, UK: Cambridge University Press.

Kunnen, E. S. (2006). Are conflicts the motor in identity change? *Identity, 6*, 169–186.

Kunnen, E. S., Bosma, H. A., & van Geert, P. L. C. (2001). A dynamic systems approach to identity formation: Theoretical background and methodological possibilities. In J.-E. Nusmi (Ed.), *Navigating through adolescence: European Perspectives* (pp. 247–274). New York: Garland Publishing.

Lewis, M. D. (1995). Cognition–emotion feedback and the self-organization of developmental paths. *Human Development, 38,* 71–102.

Lewis, M. D. (1997). Personality self-organization: Cascading constraints on cognition–emotion interaction. In A. Fogel, C. D. P. Lyra, & J. Valsiner (Eds.), *Dynamics and inter-determinism in developmental and social processes* (pp. 193–216). Mahwah, NJ: Lawrence Erlbaum Associates.

Lewis, M. D. (2000). The promise of dynamic systems approaches for an integrated account of human development. *Child Development, 71,* 36–43.

Lewis, M. D., & Ferrari, M. (2001). Cognitive-emotional self-organization in personality development and personal identity. In H. A. Bosma & E. S. Kunnen (Eds.), *Identity and emotion: A self-organisational process* (pp. 177–198). Cambridge, UK: Cambridge University Press.

Lichtwarck-Aschoff, A., van Geert, P. L. C., Bosma, H. A., & Kunnen, E. S. (2008). Time and identity. A framework for research and theory formation. *Developmental Review, 28,* 370–400.

Lichtwarck-Aschoff, A., Kunnen, E. S., & van Geert, P. L. C. (2010). Adolescent girls' perceptions of daily conflicts with their mothers: Within conflict sequences and their relationship to autonomy. *Journal of Adolescent Research, 25,* 527–556.

Smetana, J. G. (1989). Adolescents' and parents' reasoning about actual family conflict. *Child Development, 60,* 1052–1067.

Smetana, J. G. (1995). Conflict and coordination in adolescent–parent relationships. In S. Shulman (Ed.), *Close relationships and socioemotional development* (pp. 155–184). Norwood, NJ: Ablex Publishing.

Smetana, J. G., Crean, H. F., & Campione-Barr, N. (2005). Adolescents' and parents' changing conceptions of parental authority. *New Directions for Child and Adolescent Development, 108,* 31–46.

Steenbeek, H. W. (2006). *Modeling dyadic child–peer interactions: Sociometric status, emotional expressions and instrumental actions during play.* Unpublished doctoral dissertation, University of Groningen, The Netherlands.

Steenbeek, H. W., & van Geert, P. (2005). A dynamic systems model of dyadic interaction during play of two children. *European Journal of Developmental Psychology, 2,* 105–145.

Steenbeek, H. W., & van Geert, P. (2007). A dynamic systems approach to dyadic interaction in children: Emotional expression, action, dyadic play, and sociometric status. *Developmental Review, 27,* 1–40.

Steenbeek, H., & van Geert, P. (2008). The empirical validation of a dynamic systems model of interaction: Do children of different sociometric statuses differ in their dyadic play interactions? *Developmental Science, 11,* 253–281.

Thelen, E., & Smith, L. B. (1994). *A dynamic systems approach to the development of cognition and action.* Cambridge, MA: MIT Press.

Van Geert, P. (1994). Vygotskian dynamics of development. *Human Development, 37,* 346–365.

Van Geert, P., & Steenbeek, H. W. (2005). Explaining after by before: Basic aspects of a dynamic systems approach to the study of development. *Developmental Review, 25,* 408–442.

12 Conclusions and future perspectives

Saskia Kunnen

In this book we have presented several techniques for investigating process characteristics and to explore the mechanisms and processes of development. The selection of techniques is to some extent random and by no means exhaustive. We hope we have given an impression of the possible ways to analyze processes, either with simple techniques and data sets that are easy to collect or with more advanced techniques or intensive longitudinal data sets that take more time and effort to collect.

What has become clear in the preceding chapters, I hope, is that you do not need special skills in mathematics and statistics to apply these techniques, but you do need a little bit of time. Some techniques are easy to master; the resampling and state space grid techniques can be mastered relatively easily, in just several afternoons. Learning how to build dynamic systems models takes a bit more time, nevertheless even interested Master's students manage to apply quantitative dynamic systems models in their theses.

In my opinion, the most important skill needed in applying process techniques is the ability to think "out of the box" – the ability to forget for a moment about the techniques one knows, about the common ways of approaching data and just go back to the subject under study and ask oneself: "What is happening here and what exactly do I want to know?" The answers to these questions need to be very specific and concrete. Applying sampling techniques is good training because it forces the researcher to be very specific in what she expects; it does not allow for data mining (i.e. correlating everything with everything) and just looks at what happens. This means that, as has been discussed in several chapters, it is extremely important to start with a good theory because what you expect depends on the theory. Building a dynamic systems model is an even better exercise. The moment one starts to formulate the specific contents of the equation describing the changes on the level of one iteration, questions arise: "What makes a commitment grow on a day-to-day basis?" "What stops this growth?" "What triggers the growth of exploration?" "How long can this go on?" "Does exploration go on forever if there is no satisfying commitment?" A good theory is important here, not in the sense that one needs books in which theoretical answers on all these questions are given, because most probably these books and the answers do not exist, but a consistent, well founded and logical body of reasoning based, where possible, on existing theory is a valuable starting point.

Future developments

We demonstrated that the analysis of processes and the modeling of development generate a completely different type of knowledge than the knowledge gained by the analysis of group data and cross-sectional data sets. By no means do I want to devalue the knowledge that has been gained in the analysis of group data, but it is simply not all there is and it is not enough. For further increase in understanding development, a knowledge of individual processes is necessary and this is widely recognized in the domains of developmental research. The time that developmental psychology mainly focused on comparing age groups is decades behind us. More and more developmental journals demand papers that describe longitudinal data sets. However, using longitudinal data sets does not guarantee that one studies processes.

Comparing group means at different waves or average increases or decreases does not reveal the characteristics of the process, therefore, as mentioned before, the number of publications that really study developmental processes is still small. This book is just one attempt to contribute to that number, by improving the accessibility of techniques for assessing processes and simulating development. The increasing focus on longitudinal studies and the rapidly growing interest in process studies show that this type of research is widely seen as promising for generating new understanding of development. In the first place this concerns the shape of development. Too often we have no idea about whether the development of a specific skill or characteristic develops gradually, in steps or with peaks and regressions. More knowledge about this shape might help teachers, counselors and all those who monitor and guide the development of children and adolescents. A period of stability, despite attempts to stimulate development, may be a cause for worry in the case of a developmental process that should be continuous and ongoing, but for a developmental process that takes place in steps it is just normal. In the latter case, knowledge of the duration of steps and of the conditions that may stimulate the "jump" to the next step would be extremely useful. Another insight that can be gained from model building in particular is the non-linear relation between (change in) influencing factors and the changes in development – for example, time delay is an important concept when one studies the effect of some manipulation, training or whatever. Also, dynamic systems models may show how a specific variable sometimes affects the development while at other times it does not seem to have any effect at all. In the same way, variables sometimes interact and at other times do not, depending on the value of each of the variables involved and of the total network of variables. By means of process analysis and dynamic modeling we may start to unravel such phenomena.

Author index

Subject index

Note: Page numbers in *italic* refer to figures.

0 1341 1431112 6